Christ in a Choppie Box

Sermons from North East England

— MICHAEL SADGROVE —

SELECTED AND INTRODUCED BY
CAROL HARRISON

FOREWORD BY
JUSTIN WELBY

Sacristy
Press

Sacristy Press
PO Box 612, Durham, DH1 9HT

www.sacristy.co.uk

First published in 2015 by Sacristy Press, Durham

Sacristy Limited, registered in England & Wales, number 7565667

British Library Cataloguing-in-Publication Data
A catalogue record for the book is available from the British Library

ISBN 978-1-910519-10-3

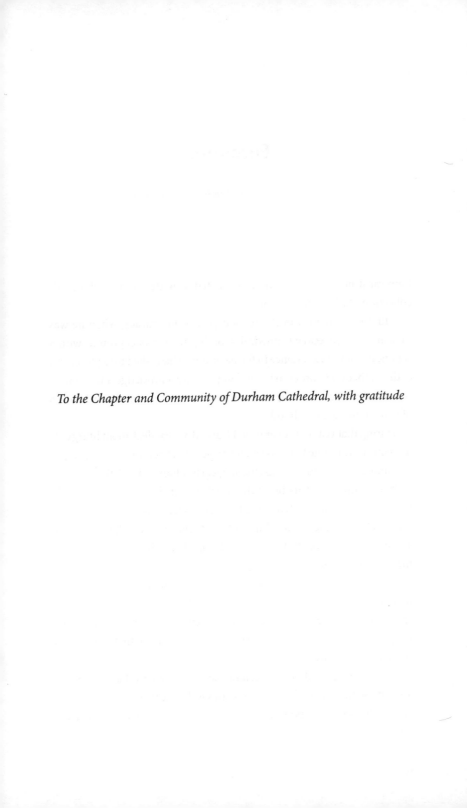

To the Chapter and Community of Durham Cathedral, with gratitude

Foreword

Justin Welby, Archbishop of Canterbury

I am most honoured to have been invited to write a foreword for this collection of Michael's sermons.

I first met Michael in the second year of my curacy, when he was Precentor at Coventry Cathedral. Coming from a background with a significant lack of experience in formal liturgy, I had asked for a placement at the Cathedral in order to try and improve my knowledge. I was sent to serve under Michael in the preparation of the service for the ordination of women to the priesthood.

During that year of preparation I learned a great deal about liturgy. At the same time I came to discover and respect Michael's extraordinary gifts and immense imagination, his theological wisdom and artistic creativity.

The sermons in this book demonstrate all these gifts. Invariably, they are beautifully crafted and admirably concise. The use of English is impeccable and the scholarship profound. The eclectic references to art and literature demonstrate an aesthetic talent and theological versatility that is exceptional.

Yet these sermons are no mere exercise in rhetoric. Underpinning them is a profound devotion to Jesus Christ and to the mission of God in this world. Michael also expresses a deep conviction concerning the purpose of preaching and the particular opportunity that comes with preaching in a cathedral.

In other words, Michael's sermons are both beautiful and inspiring. They draw the reader face to face with God in surprising ways, always feeding the spiritual appetite, yet leaving me thirsty for more of what we have just tasted.

Personally, I owe Michael a huge amount. Not only when I was newly ordained, but much later when appointed Dean of Liverpool, it was Michael who guided me into the role. Then, when I became Bishop of Durham, he was the welcoming figure who installed me and advised me. These sermons come from a deep humanity, a generous humility, a gracious hospitality, and a warm heart. I hope you enjoy them as much as I do.

+Justin Cantuar:
On the commemoration of the Venns—Henry, John
and Henry; Evangelical Divines, 1 July 2015

Preface

Twelve Years in Durham

Twelve years ago, on St Cuthbert's Day 2003, I came to Durham as Dean, arriving in the cab of a Class 91 electric locomotive on the East Coast Main Line. That March was mild and springlike. My wife and I sat every day outside the Deanery, this beautiful and historic home where my predecessors as priors and deans have lived for centuries, thinking that nowhere could be as lovely as this. At the service of installation, a Northumbrian piper played, a symbol of our return to our beloved North East, where my wife's family comes from and where I had been a parish priest in the 1980s.

But a shadow lay across the day. On 20 March 2003, the first missiles were launched against Saddam Hussein's Baghdad. I followed developments by the hour, rewriting drafts of my evening's sermon. I believed it was important not simply to "set out my stall", as new deans do at their welcome services, but to say something that linked Durham, Cuthbert, and our broken world to God and his care for humanity. That sermon appears in this book.

A cathedral is many things. It is a symbolic place of the spirit on to which people's dreams and doubts, helplessness and hope are projected, even if their connection with organised religion is tenuous. To those who love heritage, landscape, and architecture, Durham Cathedral can claim to be among the nation's richest and most beautiful sites. But "heritage", in Durham's case, means much more than this. In a recent book, I described the Cathedral as the "mystic heart of North East England" because of its association with the Saxon saints of the North, its history as a Benedictine priory, and, in later times, its status as a place where Anglican identity was being forged. And to people of faith, not only Christians, it is an emblem of divine presence in the human world, a public symbol of and invitation into God's truth, justice, and love.

This collection of sermons from my twelve years in Durham reflects many different aspects of church and public life. Some were given on "big" ceremonial occasions; others belong to more ordinary times of worship and prayer. The last—and longest—section includes pieces on the people and places of this part of England. Most were preached in the Cathedral, a few in other places. Everywhere, I have felt that I have preached to avid listeners in different communities of friends. Like every preacher, I am grateful for many insights garnered through post-sermon conversations and correspondence, even when, occasionally, dissent has been registered. In a few cases, the original text has been adjusted if the meaning was not altogether clear. Otherwise, these sermons are reproduced as originally given.

The title of this collection was inspired by the sermon "It Seemed We Had Been Sent" (page 159), in which I explored the symbolism of Durham Cathedral's Christmas Crib. This exquisite Nativity was created by an ex-miner who wanted to reference the North East's mining traditions in his work. In the pitmatic dialect of the Durham Coalfield, the "choppie box" is the food trough out of which pit ponies used to feed. So it is a genuine manger in which the Holy Child was laid. This lovely allusion is taken up in one of the poems I quote in that sermon, and I couldn't resist it as a suggestive title.

I am very grateful to my friend Carol Harrison, a former professor in the Department of Theology and Religion at Durham University. As a regular worshipper in the Cathedral, she has heard many of these sermons for herself (I almost said suffered under them), and kindly agreed to my request to make her own selection and write an introduction. All this she did "between times" before taking up her new post as Lady Margaret Professor of Divinity at Oxford. I cannot thank her enough.

I should like to thank Sheila Bryer and Mary Robinson, whose poems inspired a Christmas sermon included in this anthology. Mary's also gave me the title of this collection. My thanks also to the Archbishop of Canterbury, Justin Welby, for writing the foreword. Our paths first crossed in Coventry Cathedral, where he was ordained in the early 1990s. It was a privilege to work with him again when he came to Durham as Bishop—alas, all too briefly.

Michael Sadgrove
Durham Cathedral, April 2015

Contents

Introduction

Carol Harrison

It has been a great delight and a humbling privilege to spend some time in the presence of a master of the art of preaching. While I was selecting and arranging the sermons for this volume, I was also embarking on writing my own first sermons, and was therefore acutely conscious of Michael's generosity and trust in handing them over to a total novice. I hope he doesn't regret it!

Part 1: The Art of Preaching

As I now know from reading hundreds of Michael's sermons, he rarely repeats himself; when he does, however, it is most definitely justified. He refers on a number of occasions to the words which Beethoven wrote on the score of his *Missa Solemnis*: "from the heart, may it go to the heart".

When early Christian theologians reflected on the opening verse of Psalm 45, "my heart overflows with a goodly theme", they interpreted it in two related ways: both as the word of God, eternally brought forth from the Father's innermost being, and as the words which we human beings utter when our hearts overflow with praise of God. Preaching, I think, brings these two words—the divine and the human—together: when someone preaches, what we hear are words which the preacher has first of all received from God, by turning towards him in prayer. What the preacher then says comes not only from their own mouth and heart, but ultimately from the innermost being of God. This may sound odd, but when one listens to Michael's sermons it begins to make perfect sense. This is not to praise Michael (or, at least, not directly) but to acknowledge the gift of God's life-giving, sustaining, inspiring word which the preacher, drawing on the unique gifts God has granted to them, mediates to us.

The first section of this collection contains an address which Michael gave to clergy on the art of preaching, followed by a personal account of his own methods in preparing a sermon and a very revealing list of the "10 deadly sins of preaching". Together, they give us a glimpse of Michael's own approach to preaching as well as a set of rules to measure his sermons against. The reader should discover that Michael does, indeed, practise what he preaches!

Part 2: To Be a Fool for Christ

In one of his addresses, Michael observes that "what is sorely needed today is a presentation of Christian faith that is intelligent, generous, and imaginative, honest, inclusive, passionate, and, not least, attractive." As these comments suggest, the preacher's role as mediator requires some very particular qualities. They might be summed up by borrowing an image which early Christian theologians were fond of using when they reflected on the role of the preacher: they likened him to a bow which, being bent, and then tautened, was made ready to fire the arrows of God's word into the hearts of his hearers. Sometimes, they described the bending of the Old Testament, tautened by the string of the New Testament, so that apostles and preachers could assault their hearers with the word of God from scripture. Either way, I think the image is suggestive.

The preacher does indeed need to do a lot of bending: bending their mind and heart to God in prayer; bending their intellect and imagination to scripture in research and reflection; bending scripture, in turn, to their hearers, by making it accessible, involving, and inspiring for them; bending their will and love to their vocation and ministry, and themselves towards their listeners. This bending is no more and no less than a following of

Christ; a self-emptying and descent; an endless giving of what they have been given.

In Part 2 I have included a selection of Michael's sermons which both demonstrate, and reflect on, these "bendings": sermons on vocation, ordination, and ministry, together with some wonderful examples of the ways in which he bends his own deep scholarship to the pastoral interpretation of scripture.

Part 3: Singing the Lord's Song in a Strange Land

The bent bow must be tautened by stretching out a string as tightly as possible, so that it can shoot arrows effectively. Having bent himself to his task, Michael's sermons make it clear that the preacher cannot afford to flinch from what he calls, quoting Robert Browning, "the dangerous edge of things": natural disasters; untimely death and cruel suffering; the raw, inexplicable realities of human sinfulness, corruption, and greed, which vitiate human relations and which can make the experience of human life one of painful alienation and exile. These are the realities which stretch us almost to breaking point, but they are also those which the preacher must hold taut within his sermons before he can utter words of faith, hope, and love. They make for uncomfortable listening or reading, but sermons such as the ones included in this part of the book, which face the worst of human suffering and evil, while holding steadfastly to the crucified and risen Christ, are, in fact, honest and unflinching statements of hope: songs of charity, unity, and peace, sung with confidence and bravery, in a strange and unsettled land.

Part 4: In Galilee

The same is true of our Christian lives. Michael's sermons are never didactic; they are not primarily intended to inform, explain or to enable us to comprehend anything; they do not aim to give us certainty and clarity, or to provide answers; they aim, rather, at the human heart. To follow through the image of the preacher as a bent and tautened bow, firing the arrows of God's word, these are sermons that pierce the heart of the listener with love. Despite the fact that human life can often feel like a desolate wilderness, or like peering into the empty tomb; despite our failings of trust and lack of confidence; despite our inability to ever understand ourselves or each other fully, they transfix us with a sure faith, hope, love—even passionate longing—for God.

Such was the disconcerting force of the arrows fired from the pulpit when Michael preached that I must admit I sometimes felt like ducking underneath the pew; his sermons always seemed to be aimed directly at where I was—anxious, dithering, confused, depressed, full of self-doubt. They opened up the way ahead, encouraged the next step, offered reassurance, and threw me back upon God and his unfailing presence when I had turned in on myself. At other times, Michael's sermons felt so much like an annunciation that I began to wonder if he might not start to sprout wings as he processed out after a service!

The sermons in this part of the book are among the ones that have pierced my heart with faith, hope, and love. It will become clear on reading them why it is entitled "In Galilee".

Part 5: Common Grace & Part 6: Seasons of Faith

Another image which early Christian theologians often used, as they reflected on the source of their words and the nature of their ministry, was that of the sun. Of course, we cannot look directly at the sun, but we can see it reflected on whatever catches its light. Thus, they likened God's unseeable presence to the radiance of the sun, whose light is first caught by his preachers—the high mountains—so that their congregations—the little hills—might be able to gaze upon him, reflected and refracted in their words.

As you will see, Michael, too, is keen on the image of light, and in particular the low glimmering of the sun, breaking through the shortest days of the deep, dark chill of a northern winter, around the winter solstice; the same sun which magically finds its way into the Cathedral to light up the choir in the early morning. Perhaps this is related to his love of photography. These moments, when the darkest times of the year are illuminated by a light which promises the turning of the seasons: the beginnings of spring, new life—even resurrection—are captured in a number of extraordinary sermons on what might be described as "common grace". In them, Michael demonstrates a great gift for conveying what George Herbert calls "heaven in ordinary": the way in which the routine events of everyday life, the cycles of the seasons, or the pattern of the Church's year (Part 6), capture, contain, and convey divine life and illumination. They become sacramental.

Like the saint and mystic, or the poet, musician, and playwright, the preacher is someone through whom the sacrament of God's presence is conveyed so that we can see, hear, feel, taste, and touch it. Included in Part 5 are a number of sermons which reflect on the ways in which God's grace is tempered through the lives of his human mediators, and especially their works of music, poetry, and drama.

Part 7: Heritage Seeks Holiness: North East People and Places

It is clear that the North East of England has been one of these mediators of grace for Michael: a place where he has found God's glory reflected and refracted in its places, people, history, and saints. His sermons, in turn, allow us to dwell on them, contemplate them, and sense God within them. As he often puts it, they are "thin places", in which the holy lies close to the surface. These sermons read like a lovesong to the North and to the God who reveals himself there: not only to Durham, but to Northumberland, Lindisfarne, the Farne Islands, Bamburgh, Jarrow, Wearmouth—even Sunderland! They chronicle its history, its saints, and its Christian tradition, recollecting and recounting them, making them part of our present and handing them on to the future.

In this sense, Michael's life and work in Durham over the past twelve years have become part of its tradition. He is now written into it and will be remembered as one of the great deans who loved our Cathedral and its people with all his heart and soul; who humbly devoted the gifts of his immense scholarship, profound human understanding, and rich spirituality to mediating to us the word and innermost being of God; who reflected for us God's light so that we might gaze upon and celebrate the gifts of his grace; and who communicated to us, in our darkest moments, faith, hope, and love for God. For all that, we give heartfelt thanks.

Part 1: The Art of Preaching

On Preaching

This introductory essay was first given as a keynote address to the clergy of Wakefield Diocese in 2003, just after I arrived in Durham. I was asked to speak about preaching, and to follow this with a sermon at an act of worship. It may have been a case of "don't do as I do, do as I say"! You can judge from the sermon that follows this essay.

There is a short story by Chekhov called *The Student*. Ivan, a seminarian, is walking home on a cold Good Friday afternoon when he sees a mother and her daughter in their garden by a fire. Both are widows. They talk about the day, and Ivan reminds them how Peter warmed himself by just such a fire on the night of the passion, and denied Jesus there. As he recalls the cock crowing and Peter's tears, the older woman begins to weep and her daughter takes on a look of great pain. Ivan stops talking, and in the silence they are alone with their thoughts. He says goodnight and leaves. Here is how the story ends:

> Now the student was thinking about Vasilisa: since she had shed tears all that had happened to Peter the night before the Crucifixion must have some relation to her . . .
>
> He looked round. The solitary light was still gleaming in the darkness and no figures could be seen near it now. The student thought again that if Vasilisa had shed tears, and her daughter had been troubled, it was evident that what he had just been telling them about, which had happened nineteen centuries ago, had a relation to the present—to both women, to the desolate village, to himself, to all people. The old woman had wept, not because he could tell the story touchingly, but because Peter was near to her, because her whole being was interested in what was passing in Peter's soul.
>
> And joy suddenly stirred in his soul, and he even stopped for a minute to take breath. "The past," he thought, "is linked with

the present by an unbroken chain of events flowing one out of another." And it seemed to him that he had just seen both ends of that chain; that when he touched one end the other quivered.

When he crossed the river by the ferryboat and afterwards, mounting the hill, looked at his village and towards the west where the cold crimson sunset lay a narrow streak of light, he thought that truth and beauty which had guided human life there in the garden and in the yard of the high priest had continued without interruption to this day, and had evidently always been the chief thing in human life and in all earthly life, indeed; and the feeling of youth, health, vigour—he was only twenty-two—and the inexpressible sweet expectation of happiness, of unknown mysterious happiness, took possession of him little by little, and life seemed to him enchanting, marvellous, and full of lofty meaning.

Someone once said that listening to Chekhov was like having an angel sing to you. But I begin with that story because it seems to me to encapsulate beautifully what faith-sharing means. A man speaks naturally about God and uncovers a chain of connection between the gospel and the stories of two women who find that they are not simply *observers* of a drama that happened centuries ago, but participants in an event that is happening now. We never find out what their stories are, only that what Ivan says has this profound effect on them. He stops speaking, for he knows that there is a time for speech and a time for silence. But the inner work goes on, and both he and his audience know that a profound change is taking place, not just in the women but in him as well. Out of his hopelessness springs joy. He glimpses his privileged role in seeing both ends of that chain of connection, touching one end and seeing the other quiver. He knows he has been on both the giving and receiving ends of the gift of transformation we call "grace". This is what it is to preach.

As a church, we don't give nearly enough attention to what, after all, is one of the most public and visible aspects of ministry. And we who preach often easily slip into the assumption that we know what we are doing, and forget that preaching is one of the riskiest aspects of ministry because it exposes very personally both how we have come to speak about God and also with what skill or lack of it we do this. It isn't surprising that some people have lost their nerve when it comes to preaching and question whether, in a post-modern world, with its distrust of grand narratives, it is even possible to speak of God in public any more, at least with the kind of authority the set-piece sermon from the pulpit implies. Yet I want to state, rather than argue, that preaching not only has a place in public ministry but is indeed one of the most important things we can ever do. For me personally, it is one of the most satisfying things I do. And if we are haunted from time to time by that sermon we shall never be great enough to preach, just as clowns long to play *King Lear,* what matters is to want to perfect our craft, work away at it, carry on learning until we preach for the last time.

First, a definition. By preaching I mean publicly communicating the good news of God's justice and mercy, of the kingdom, reconciliation, and hope, and doing this not on our own account but with the authority of the church that is conferred by ordination and affirmed by holding the bishop's licence. Of course, every act of witness or faith-sharing, like Chekhov's student, is preaching or proclamation, as are works of compassion and social justice. St Francis allegedly said: "Preach the gospel. Use words if necessary." But I want in this address to focus on preaching as a public *liturgical* act, preaching in the context of worship. And we must recognise that here again, the sermon is not an isolated activity. It is of a piece with the whole liturgy. St Paul says that the liturgy itself is preaching: "As often as you eat this bread and drink this cup, you show forth the Lord's death until he comes." The word *katangello,* "show forth", is a powerful missionary word used in the New Testament of the proclaiming of the gospel, which is why John Wesley called the eucharist a "converting ordinance". I am sure that our best evangelistic tool, and the one we make least use of, is our liturgy, not only the content of worship, but the quality of life it expresses: the *koinonia* that embraces the love, joy, and peace of Christian faith. The liturgy is holy theatre in which invisible, numinous reality can be felt and touched. This is the setting in which preaching has its natural home.

What I want to do today is to step back from the *practice* of preaching and explore aspects of its inner meaning: *what* is it we do when we preach and *why,* and, above all, *who* we are as preachers. Socrates said the unreflected life is not worth living; certainly, unreflective p runs into the sand. But I hope you will see that to ask these questions doesn't mean retreating into the easy role of theoretician: "Those who can, preach; those who can't, tell others how to preach." I have to put what I say to the test presently and preach a sermon myself. It's good that I am here not just to speak about preaching but also to be a practitioner.

———

"Only connect the prose and the passion, and both will be exalted and human love will be seen at its highest." E. M. Forster was right: making connections is what communication is *for*. We touch one end of Chekhov's chain and the other quivers. But *prose*—is that how we should think of preaching? The director Peter Brook, who coined the phrase "holy theatre" I used just now, speaks of "deadly theatre" in the same pioneering book in which he set out his theory of drama, *The Empty Space*. He means the kind of theatre that never challenges or caresses an audience, neither inspires nor angers them to the point where they begin to be truly *engaged*. There is, if you didn't already know, such a thing as deadly preaching, and it has many of the same qualities. I have a list of the top sins committed by deadly preachers, such as being too long; ignoring the text; playing to the gallery; moralising; lacking shape or direction; falling into cliché. But the biggest sin of all is being boring. Boredom is the kiss of death to preaching. Never mind how worthy you are, or sincere, or well-prepared, or devout, or orthodox, or fluent, or loud. If you are boring, you will not be forgiven.

What is the antidote to boredom? I think it has to do with the *imagination*. When we say that something is "prosaic", we mean that it is run of the mill, ordinary, dull. When we say that it has something of the poetic about it, we mean that our imaginations have been aroused, and we begin to see in new ways. So I want to suggest that preaching is a kind of *art*, like poetry or painting, sculpture or music. The preacher is an artist, and the sermon is an art form. It invites us to see in new ways, re-envision our lives within the bigger frame of God's love, his justice, and the coming of his kingdom. And because preaching deals with depths that language can never fully plumb, a great deal of what we say as preachers stretches language, pulls it around in ways that make it more like poetry than prose. For in religion, words commit us to both less and more than we want to say. We do our best with them, and with ourselves; but when we have finished, we know that Flaubert was right when he said in *Madame Bovary* that "none of us can ever express the exact measure of our needs or thoughts or sorrows; and human speech is like a cracked kettle on which we tap crude rhythms for bears to dance to, while we long to make music that will melt the stars."

True artists are humble before the facts, not least the facts of their own limitations and the limitations of their materials. They know that words and paint and sounds and stone can never fully convey the beauty and splendour and love of God, not even a Dante or a Rembrandt or a Bach or a Rodin. The best they or any of us can do is, to quote *King Lear*, to "see feelingly", and help us to "see feelingly" too. Charles Causley, the Cornish poet who died this summer, spoke of "poetry bursting like a diamond bomb". Art has this kind of sacramental quality: the words, the paint, the sound, the stone bearing meaning beyond themselves, or, if you like, the meaning being "uncovered" by the artist so that the medium becomes transparent with significance. As preachers, our materials are words. So we need to handle them reverently as sacraments of Christ the Word, just as we reverence the bread that will bear the meaning to us of Christ's crucified and risen body.

The Oxford philosopher J. L. Austin wrote a book called *How to Do Things with Words*, published in 1962. It was a highly influential book as well as being both elegant and compact, which is how the best philosophy should be, not to say the best preaching. He examined the various kinds of actions that are performed through the use of words: "speech acts", he called them, words that make a difference to someone or something. Think of the marriage service, where the words "I will" change two lives for ever. Or "I forgive you", "I bet you a thousand pounds", "I confer on you the degree of Bachelor of Arts", and so on. The words, spoken by the authorised or appropriate person in the right context, are *performative*: they bring about new conditions, change situations. Preaching, it seems to me, belongs to this category. It is performative, for we "do things with words" that are transformative: extraordinary things, divine things. So how we preachers practise the art of the wordsmith is pretty important if words are to perform in the way we ask of them.

Rhetoric, one of the seven liberal arts in the medieval curriculum, was classically defined as the art of persuasion. Preachers are practitioners of rhetoric, for a *rhetor* literally was simply a public speaker. Politicians, advertisers, fundraisers invest millions of pounds in effective persuasion every year; communications is a growth industry. Yet preachers are curiously reticent when it comes to learning from practitioners of persuasion: not just about content, but about how this performative power of words can be exploited to maximum effect. Up to a point, we can learn the skills of rhetoric: how to arrange our material and put an argument; how to listen to the sounds of words we use; how to create variety in our sentence patterns and develop a style that flows naturally; how to use figures of speech, repetition, climax, pause; how to begin; and, most important of all, how to end. Some of this we know without thinking about it; but it is good to make it conscious, so that we know that we know it; good to study our own sermons critically or ask for honest feedback, to see how we could sharpen up what we do with words. It may help us to avoid the Bunthorne school of preaching (from Gilbert and Sullivan's *Patience*), according to which "the meaning doesn't matter if it's only idle chatter of a transcendental kind."

So I don't apologise for saying that there is a "virtuoso" element in preaching. The sermon is an interpretation in the same way that a pianist offers an "interpretation" of a Beethoven sonata. Technique is part of this, and rhetoric is about acquiring skill with words just as scales and arpeggios and knowledge of musical form are a necessary part of the pianist's daily routine. But the pianist's interpretation is far more. She has to immerse herself in the score of the sonata, know it intimately, inhabit its world. This is the only way she will bring the dead notes on the printed page to life for an audience.

In the same way, preaching is a "performance" of God's word, to draw on Frances Young's creative phrase. Interpretation and performance are inseparable. But they depend on more than simply the preacher and the text. Interpretation and performance are relational, for they only become fully realised in the relationship that exists between performer and audience. There has to be an alliance between them, a commitment on the part of the performer to care enough about the audience to *want* to communicate with them; and a willingness on their part to be open to what might happen, the possibility that they may be touched and moved and changed. Both parties take responsibility for this alliance, but I suggest that the preacher has to initiate it. For preaching is a pastoral as well as a rhetorical art. It cares for human beings and how they respond.

Let me illustrate this from Bunyan's *Pilgrim's Progress*. You recall how Christian comes carrying his burden to the House of the Interpreter. As he steps inside, he is shown a painting. It depicts a man "with his eyes lift up to heaven, the best of Books in his hand, and the Law of Truth writ on his lips; it is to show thee that his work is to know and unfold dark things to sinners, even as also thou seest him stand as if he pleaded with men." This man, says the Interpreter, is the guide Christian must follow on his journey. It's of course a portrait of Christ, depicted as both travelling companion and destination, the Interpreter *par excellence* of our pilgrimage. He "knows and unfolds dark things to sinners", says the Interpreter, and at once we are clear where the Interpreter's authority comes from. What Christ does, the preacher-as-interpreter does, unfolding dark and wonderful things, emulating in his preaching the movement of Christ the Word into the heart of the world.

Bunyan is saying that faith-sharing is an invitation to step inside the House of the Interpreter so as to be shown Christ—precisely the way Chekhov's student does it. For preaching is not a *telling* but a *showing*, just as the sacraments are not telling but showing; "visible words", Augustine called them. And this is how the Interpreter deals with Christian. He takes Christian through his house and shows him a series of tableaux, strange little dramas like the room where the dust never settles, where a servant throws water on a fire that won't go out, where a man crouches like a frightened animal in a small iron cage. They are images that have to be puzzled over before they make sense. Emily Dickinson says: "Tell all the truth, but tell it slant." This is the way of preaching: not to tell, but to show by posing questions that lead to a deeper awareness of God and a true encounter with Christ. Calvin says that the function of the scriptures is to give us spectacles through which the world suddenly comes into focus. You could put the preacher's mission in the same way. When he leaves the House of the Interpreter, Christian sees where to go. He comes to the Wall of Salvation and finds the cross; and there the burden he has carried for so long falls off his shoulders, and he is free.

—

Let me next say something about the preacher in his or her environment. How is a sermon *grown*? Where do sermons come *from*? And how is a *preacher* made—both the preacher on this specific Sunday morning in this particular local church with these given texts to work with; and, more generally, the identity of the preacher as inhabiting a way of life?

I am going to take my cue from the Book of Jeremiah, from the letter the prophet writes to the exiles in Babylon. "Build houses and live in them", he says; "plant gardens and eat what they produce. Take wives and have sons and daughters: multiply there and do not decrease. But seek the welfare of the city where I have sent you into exile, and pray to the Lord on its behalf, for in its welfare you will find your welfare" (Jeremiah 29:4–7). It's a remarkable act of faith to believe that the future of the exiled community could lie away from their homeland, and still more remarkable, not to say seditious, to think, let alone pronounce, that the God of Israel could be alive and active in a place regarded as ritually unclean, that it was possible to "sing the Lord's song in a strange land".

Walter Brueggemann explores this theme in his book, *Cadences of Home: Preaching among Exiles.* He argues that exile means the loss of a structured, reliable world and being transported into one where treasured symbols of meaning are mocked and dismissed. It means displacement and failed hopes, inarticulate longings, and loss of direction. This, he says, is the postmodern world in which we have to speak of God, a world Stanley Hauerwas describes as peopled by "resident aliens". And in this world preachers need to be bilingual. They have to understand the language of empire which is the language of exile, the alien forms of speech, culture, and habit that Jeremiah asks the exiles to learn.

The prophet told the exiles to plant gardens and eat their produce. No doubt this included vineyards. We're lucky enough to have a small house in Burgundy, near the great vineyards of Chablis to the north and the Côte de Nuits and the Côte de Beaune to the south. As the seasons turn, we watch the vines sprout in the spring, when the fear is that a late frost will blast the vines and wreck all prospect of a harvest. In summer, when the grapes begin to ripen, all eyes are on the sky, praying for enough sunshine to make sure that the balance of sugar content, acid, and water will grow a grape that develops the complexity that's needed for a great wine. Then, and up to the autumn harvest, the big threat is hail, for a single storm can wipe out months of painstaking work and put a *vigneron* out of business. Only in winter, when the vines are pruned and tied up, is it time to relax, until the cycle begins again.

The French have a word for which there is no real English equivalent: *terroir.* It means the environment of a vineyard that gives it its unique character. It includes the soil and its underlying geology, how well watered it is, its altitude, the direction it faces, whether it is on a hillside or in a valley, the way the soil has been worked historically, how near it is to a main road, and its microclimate. The wines of the Chablis Grand Cru, for instance, owe their greatness (and their price) largely to the fact that the vines are grown on a soil known as Kimmeridgian, found in only one other place in Europe, at Kimmeridge Bay in Dorset; this is the defining ingredient of their *terroir.* Move a hundred metres off that geology and the wines are mere *vin de table.* One degree of latitude reverses the whole of viticulture. To make good wine, you need to know the *terroir,* besides being proficient in all the practical crafts of viticulture. This means being a geologist, meteorologist, botanist, chemist, physicist, cultural historian, and economist, as well as having the patience and good judgment to know when the time is right to harvest. It is a skilled occupation.

I find this a rich and suggestive analogy of how a preacher is formed, and not, perhaps, too far away from the biblical use of vineyard images. A preacher is like a vineyard and the sermon the wine that is poured out and shared. Vineyards don't grow overnight. A new vineyard won't produce great wine for many years; it won't get its quality mark, its *appellation controlée,* until its *terroir* begins to be established, until all the variables that go into making it stabilise and begin to react creatively. Well, preachers don't grow overnight either. And they too have their own *terroir,* their own ecology that constitutes their unique preaching environment. And, like a vineyard, part of this ecology is interior—personal to the preacher; and part of it is external—an aspect of the given setting in which a preacher is working.

Let's take the external environment first. This is, if you like, the climate and the soil, factors over which we have no control, for they are given. Some of them are global, and you heard me sketch out just now in a sentence how a cultural critique of our age might describe the world we live in today. *Terroir* for the twenty-first-century preacher is, I suggest, largely the environment of exile. But there is the local aspect too: what belongs to our city, town, suburb, village, neighbourhood where we preach week by week. The word "parish", *paroikia*, literally means "those who live around", and the preacher is one of these. We are part of the local *terroir*, not spectators but participants, learning to speak with the local accent, and with a nuance that enables our words to be recognised as a genuine attempt to speak not only *to* the place and its concerns but from *within* it.

In the media they talk about "self-embedded journalism", which means going incognito into a situation, often at great risk, in order to report on it from inside. Preachers too are "embedded", or, to put it more theologically, "enfleshed", incarnated in the place to which both preacher and parishioners belong. To be genuinely embedded in this way and not merely be a bird of passage with a bird's-eye view means reading the "text" of the place and of its people as well as the "text" of the Christian story. It means taking the time and trouble to understand the issues that belong to this place rather than that, to know the community to whom we shall deliver the sermon. Some of us have tried to take on some local issue of justice from the pulpit, only to find afterwards, to our embarrassment, that because we didn't do our homework properly, our case was flawed or fell on deaf ears. Understanding the grain of a place's story, having the judgment to know when to affirm it and when to criticise it, is a demanding assignment, one that is well chronicled in the Old Testament's record of both wisdom and prophecy, where knowing how to listen well and discern truth from falsehood was a continuous challenge for the faith community.

Equally testing is the inward aspect of *terroir*. By this I mean the preacher's own interior formation, what the poet Rilke called "heart work". At the core of this is the spiritual discipline that forms us as theologians. The Benedictine Rule to which we owe so much here at Durham emphasises the importance of a balanced regime of prayer, study, and work; and the "work" of preaching can only take place effectively if prayer and study are constantly informing it. Perhaps we are never more theologians than when we preach; and if the liturgy is the crucible of theology, as I believe it is, then the development of a theological mind is not just a desirable quality but an essential one. But the discipline is not simply intellectual.

George Herbert says that the only sermons worth preaching are those we have first preached to ourselves. So there is a task of ingestion here, making the text our own. Too many sermons are like a wine that has been opened too soon: the rawness shows. I believe it's required of us that we "grow" our sermons during the week, so that they reach maturity through a week's interaction between prayer, thought, meditation, our personal lived experience, and the continuous exposure to human life that flows out of pastoral ministry. It means that we do not speak until we are ready to. Only when this has happened and the unconscious has been allowed to do its work (always a key part of any creative process) will the sermon be properly formed within us.

In a larger sense, *terroir* means the task of nurturing not only our spiritual and intellectual selves, but our cultural and emotional selves as well. This is the work of a lifetime. Part of this is self-awareness, for if preaching is intended to heighten other people's awareness of God, of one another, of the world, of justice, truth, beauty, and love, then our own self-awareness, including our understanding of the complexities and vicissitudes of our own selves, is not only a prerequisite of preaching but also one of the gifts we have to offer. This is what makes preaching honest and gives it integrity. Henri Nouwen coined the familiar phrase "wounded healer", which he applied to the pastor, but it applies equally to the preacher, for preaching is a pastoral act. John Wesley may not have meant precisely this when he said "I preach as a dying man to dying men", but it is an aspect of the fact that we always speak as vulnerable, broken people. Only this degree of spiritual intelligence enables the miracle of preaching to take place, which is that as we speak of God out of the text and out of our lived experience, our community begins to know its own soul.

To do this well we need "hinterland". This was the quality Denis Healey complained that Margaret Thatcher lacked: feeling for history, literature, poetry, art, science—whatever helps us read the human landscape and position ourselves in it with insight. It's often said that the poets, the dramatists, the painters are the prophets and the wise of our time. We should read lots of novels, go to concerts, theatre, the cinema, keep a book of poetry by our bed. A colleague of mine in the Diocese of Durham theologises on TV soap opera. A previous Archbishop of Canterbury famously found enjoyment and inspiration in *The Simpsons*. Whatever turns you on.

All this is part of our personal *terroir*. It's crucial, if we want to make real connections both with people and for them, to touch one end of the chain and feel it quiver along its whole length. This is not in order to impress congregations, for most people would be profoundly *un*impressed by lengthy quotes from Dante or references to Caravaggio, the Dreyfus affair, or string theory—not to mention the semiotics of *EastEnders*. Hinterland should be exactly that: what lies behind the visible coastline, unseen, even unguessed at in its details, but a constant source of stability and depth. It's to recognise in our own hearts and minds the sheer scope of God's involvement in human life, to which we have committed ourselves in baptism and ordination. It's to return to the fundamental point that we are participants in life, not observers, whose task is to distil what we have glimpsed in a way that can help others glimpse it too. Jesus says that it is "out of the abundance of the heart that the mouth speaks". Cultivating this *perisseuma*, this abundance of God-given things, is the work of our formation as preachers.

—

I have tried to explore two analogies for preaching that I find helpful. We are artists and interpreters who do things with words; and our art is nurtured in our personal and public *terroir*, which is the environment within which we live and preach. Let me end by taking us back to the beginning and to Chekhov's little tale.

What happens to the student and his hearers as he speaks is transformation. This is always the goal: our expectation that as we talk about God, something life-changing happens, for preaching is to collaborate with God's movement of generosity and embrace towards all human beings and all creatures. It is odd to think that our faltering efforts in the pulpit could be part of this great project of grace. But this is precisely how St Paul speaks of his ministry in the Corinthian letters. Here is preaching in a nutshell: "We are ambassadors for Christ, since God is making his appeal through us: we entreat you on behalf of Christ, be reconciled to God" (2 Corinthians 5:20). But this ministry of reconciliation is an act of foolishness. It eschews lofty words and arcane wisdom, dramatic signs and pseudo-wonders. Instead, the preacher comes in weakness and fear and much trembling, with the modesty of a fragile earthen vessel. They say that the preacher has little presence and no gifts as an orator. Yet the preacher is determined to know nothing but Christ crucified. He or she comes with the confidence that is born of hope in Jesus who died and was raised from death. And this is where the preacher's authority comes from, "so that it may be made clear that this extraordinary power belongs to God and not to us".

How do we remain confident and hopeful in the face of this extraordinary calling to preach? Preaching is certainly our duty, and it is often our joy. But duty and joy are not by themselves enough. The answer must be, always, to see our preaching as an act of *love*. We preach out of love for the scriptures where the story we tell was first borne witness to. We preach out of love for our hearers, and for the rich, complex, and bewildering variety of human life they embody. We preach out of love for the world in all its beauty and brokenness, which we love because God loves it. We preach out of love because we are to be living symbols of God's love, and preaching is his work before it is ours.

Ultimately, we preach out of love for God. For all preaching, because it is theology, is ultimately doxological. It begins and ends in adoration, in wonder, love, and praise. It is part of the offering of our life to God. Let me end with two composers and two of the greatest sacred works I know. On the score of the *Missa Solemnis,* Beethoven wrote: "From the heart; may it go to the heart." When Elgar completed his oratorio *The Dream of Gerontius,* he added: "This is the best of me." As preachers, we offer the best of ourselves for the greater glory of God. We hold our nerve as we continue to believe in preaching as an aspect of God's mission to his world. And we do not lose heart.

Afterword 1: Work in Progress

I am due to preach the sermon at tonight's evensong. This is in no sense a masterclass: I don't claim any more for this sermon than I would for any other, which is that I shall try the best I can to do justice to the occasion. But in the light of what I have been saying, I thought it might be interesting to say something briefly about how I have gone about this assignment, which, since my lecture falls in between my sermon's preparation and delivery, has something of the character of "work in progress" about it.

The "givens" for tonight's office are readings from Zechariah and Revelation, both swarming with angels. Today we also remember one of the great women of thirteenth-century Europe, Elizabeth of Hungary; all this in the setting of this clergy conference whose theme is communication.

When I saw that the Revelation reading was the story of Michael and the angels, it was too good to resist. Given my name, it's a text I've pondered all my life. What is more, I was an incumbent in a parish dedicated to St Michael and then worked at a cathedral which is also dedicated to him. There, every day for eight years, I prayed beneath the great Sutherland tapestry of Christ in Glory, from whose side Michael hurls the devil out of heaven. So I have preached maybe a dozen sermons at Michaelmas, a season, like Ascension and Trinity, where too many preachers fear to go.

The temptation of course—I admit it—was to go to my sermon drawer and pull out something I could reasonably deduce none of you would have heard. I am not against recycling sermons provided they really are refreshed with the needs of a different time or place in mind and provided that we are still able to say something new, even if it is based on previously laid foundations. If it was good once, why waste the work that went into it? But, apart from the opening paragraph of one of them that I wanted to rework, none of my Michaelmas sermons seemed to fit the bill, and I wasn't satisfied that they would easily translate to mid-November and a diocesan clergy conference.

So it was back to the drawing board. And it was one of those cases where, by allowing the text to take me where it wanted, I found myself in a wholly unexpected place. This called for some waiting for the themes to coalesce, something that would not be hurried. I thought I would be preaching to you about angels, or good and evil, or the apocalyptic vision of death, judgment, hell, and heaven. Instead, I found myself led on to a rather different path, a more intimate one, which is perhaps more directly germane to your being here in conference, and where St Elizabeth (who is not the topic of my sermon, by the way) could fall naturally in place as a "for instance" of my main theme.

Of course, themes interweave with one another; like the carpet pages of the Lindisfarne Gospels, everything is connected to everything else. Good and evil, and the four last things, are, I suppose, folded into my sermon somewhere. As to the ending, I often conclude where I began, as a kind of verbal trigger to remind people where I started out, but with a slight twist. But we can never anticipate what may happen when we get there. Preaching should have the capacity to spring God-given surprises, not least to the preacher.

Afterword 2: Ten Deadly Sins of Preaching

1. **Speaking too soon.** The fault is preparation that is too thin, too hurried, or too late. Put the sermon to bed before Saturday night and spend the evening watching football. Tweak early on Sunday morning.
2. **Being too long.** The twenty-first century calls for the art of the miniaturist. Twelve to fifteen minutes is long enough for the parish communion; any longer and the liturgy will drift. Lengthiness is the sin of sloth in those who can't be bothered to refine and sharpen up the content.
3. **Jokiness.** Don't subvert the faith with throwaway lines that suggest you don't believe what you are saying any more than your hearers do. Humour and irony are one thing, cynicism quite another.
4. **Not taking the text seriously.** Don't undermine the sermon by closing the gospel book after reading from it and then changing the subject. Your task is to preach the word of God.

5. **Playing to the gallery.** Don't preach to impress, or try to be clever, especially on big occasions. People will see through your insincerity. Be yourself, and they will respect you.

6. **Moralising and thought control.** It's not your job to control what people think or how they behave. Your task is to proclaim good news and invite people to consider their lives, attitudes, behaviour, and thought in the light of it.

7. **Lack of shape and direction.** Without structure, a sermon falls at the first post. Avoid stream-of-consciousness soliloquising. Know where you want to go and take your hearers with you. Pay attention to how you begin and especially how you end.

8. **Cliché.** Don't fall for pat sayings, either those in common use or your own, or even thoughtless biblical quotations. Cliché is the idleness or cowardice that avoids having to say something new, at least to yourself. An entire sermon is cliché if it's just another variation on what you're said a hundred times before. Be original.

9. **Being boring.** The biggest sin of all. Boredom comes from sermons that are too long, too verbose, too simplistic, too didactic. It thrives on lack of narrative, metaphor, and symbol, or just on dull delivery. If you're bored by your own preaching, be sure your hearers will be too. If you suspect you're incapable of being interesting, imaginative, and inspiring, get some training fast or stop preaching.

10. **The unlived sermon.** Never preach to others what you have not yet offered to God and preached to yourself. Your sermon goes on in your life and character long after you have left the pulpit.

Who Is Like God?

Here goes: the Wakefield clergy sermon as delivered
following my lecture. The proof of the pudding . . .

My name is one of my treasured possessions. It is part of me, for I can't think of myself other than as "Michael". It is, I know, only a word. Its two ordinary syllables belong to millions of others besides me, for it's a common name. And yet no one else hears it as I do, for it carries a unique set of memories and associations. I hear my parents calling me by name from the dawn of consciousness; my grandmother lovingly pronouncing it in her German-Jewish way; my schoolteachers, doctors, neighbours, friends, priests . . . my name brings so many echoes to mind. I hear myself called to by name, cared for, told off, taught, looked up to, looked down on, judged, affirmed, loved, baptised, confirmed, married, ordained—in a word, *known*.

It features in tonight's reading from Revelation: "Michael", the mighty archangel. That name asks a question in Hebrew: "Who is like God?" It is a question, not a statement. And this is of a piece with how angels often ask questions in the Old Testament. When the angel appears to Daniel and strengthens him, it is with a question: "Do you know why I have come?" When the shadowy figure wrestles with Jacob in the dark, he asks him his name. And the unnamed angel in our reading from Zechariah pesters the bemused prophet with a full-scale catechism: "What do you see?", "Do you not know what these are?", "Do you not know what *these* are?" In Saxon folktales, Wotan the divine wanderer walks the earth asking riddles that clothe the cosmic issues of human destiny. In the same way, Yahweh's visitants puzzle mortals with questions that are bigger than they seem. And here is the biggest of all: *mi-cha-el*: "Who is like God?"

A lot of ink has been spilled on what Genesis means when it says that human beings are made in God's image. Physical likeness to God was an early candidate. Self-awareness, moral perception, living in relationship, differentiation into male and female, recognising beauty, capable of thought and speech—these and a thousand other explanations have been canvassed, and who is to say that they are not partly right? But most likely, I think, given the way Genesis tells the story, is that it is linked to the idea of authority and dominion. Human beings are charged to fill the earth and subdue it; not autonomously, but on behalf of the Creator to whom it all belongs. Our dominion is God's.

And this fits with how the archangel Michael is depicted in Revelation. He "takes dominion" as a warrior against evil. He represents God's stand for salvation, truth, and justice against the illusions and lies that falsify human life, symbolised by "the deceiver of the whole world", the adversary Satan. By throwing the dragon out of heaven, Michael re-enacts the primordial creation battles of ancient myth, where the world came into being through the defeat of the monsters of the deep, like the dragonish figures of Rahab and Leviathan we meet in the psalms. So there is a new creation here; the universe is restored to the order and goodness it had at first. The slide from cosmos to chaos is reversed. Because of Christ, what was lost in the fall is recapitulated, restored, put right.

But the question "Who is like God?" looks beyond the archangel, for it is not Michael alone who takes the victor's crown. That belongs, says the text, to "our comrades", that is to say, those whom the adversary Satan had accused night and day before God. It is they "who have conquered him by the blood of the Lamb and by the word of their testimony, for they loved not their lives even unto death". It's a beautifully drawn contrast between the apocalyptic events taking place in the sky and the human scale of what is happening on earth. For the vast canvas on which the angelic conflict is fought out is mirrored in the intimate, personal victories won by individual people, the martyrs of Christ. We can imagine how this picture of evil defeated in dimensions unseen and unknown would strengthen those facing persecution at that time. So the question "Who is like God?" is answered in those who follow Jesus into the fiery ordeals of passion and death, who "bear witness" at the cost of their lives. In their suffering we see the truest meaning of dominion. "This is the victory that overcomes the world, even our faith." Discipleship, said Jesus, is to be so free within yourself, so given up to God, so focused on the kingdom of heaven, that you can contemplate losing your life in order to find it, indeed, in a sense, have already said goodbye to those things we imagine mean "life" for us.

And whatever the way of the cross holds, it means having the inner soul of a martyr. I can't make the New Testament mean anything else.

The formation of a martyr in each of us: what does this mean? It's a hard truth for us to hear, and I am as ambivalent about it as you are, wondering how on earth I have got myself into this, not only as a Christian but as a public representative of this way of living. Yet it seems to me that even if we are a long way yet from being able to say "yes" to losing our lives for Christ's sake, there are lesser martyrdoms that are still real and costly enough, and to these, most of you will not be strangers. I say this not to cheapen the cost of discipleship, but to encourage us to consider that if we can be faithful in the small things Zechariah speaks about, maybe we can find it in us to be faithful in larger ones too.

In the early church, when persecution subsided, many chose the way of "white" martyrdom, that is, to enter the religious life as a way of dying to the world. Perhaps secular ministry in our postmodern world is a kind of white martyrdom, for you know better than anyone the costs of ministering to declining congregations with next to no resources in a part of England with one of the lowest churchgoing rates in Europe. What else might you have done with your lives—how much might you have earned, what glories might you have had—and you have chosen this! In renunciation, the soul of the martyr is formed. It's St Francis embracing the leper; it's St Martin giving his cloak to the beggar; it's Elizabeth of Hungary, whom we honour today, leaving the castle of the Wartburg one wintry night and giving her life to the care of the sick and needy.

Kierkegaard said that "purity of heart is to will one thing". And that one thing is to be like God, to imitate Christ in his *kenosis*, his self-offering for the world. So the question "Who is like God?" must be *the* question for our church, *the* issue that faces anyone who wants be serious about Christianity, particularly all of us who are ministers and publicly represent the gospel in our time. How do we live up to our name and bear good *martyria*, faithful witness to Jesus? For if the demons that stalk this world are to be conquered, and the storms that threaten to overwhelm it are to be stilled, if people are to feel after God and find him, then much turns on how we as ministers embrace discipleship, how ready we are not to love our lives too much. You know as well as I do that Jesus calls us to nothing less than this. It is the angel's question to each of us, God's question as he walks the earth and looks for those who will bring the just and gentle dominion of Christ, his wisdom, truth, and love to this generation. His question clothes our entire destiny: who we are, why we are here, what will become of us. The questions the angels put to us are profoundly disturbing. Yet *Mi-cha-el* is the name of all of us to whom it matters that we ask, "Who is like God?" And it will not let us go.

19 November 2003
Zechariah 4; Revelation 12:7–13

Part 2: To Be a Fool for Christ

Following our opening exploration of what preaching is, this section gathers up sermons on Christian ministry and loosely poses the question of who the preacher is and how vocation is formed. The final address, "Anointing Jesus' Feet", is included here because without extravagant generosity and—yes—passionate love, preaching will never take wings and fly.

I have mentioned already how my installation as Dean of Durham was overshadowed (at least for me) by the outbreak of the Iraq war. Events were developing by the hour throughout that March day. I knew I must not dodge this unlooked-for context of a sermon I had been thinking about for many weeks. Yet, even an hour before the service began, it was not clear what was happening and what it could mean. There came a point at which I had to turn the radio news off and settle on a final text. Sometimes a preacher can be taken to the very edge.

A War, a Cathedral, and St Cuthbert

An Installation Sermon

We shall all remember St Cuthbert's Day 2003 as the day the war began. It is a sombre moment in our history. We have prayed that this cup might pass from us. Now we are compelled to drink it, and its taste is very bitter. We gather here with sadness that it has come to this and with fear for a future we cannot know. Many of us have pleaded not to go to war without United Nations backing, but we are where we are. We must pray that the conflict will be brief, with as little suffering and loss of life as possible. We must pray for relations between the faith communities both in the Middle East and here, for this war will ratchet up tensions that are already very strained. We must pray for our leaders and support those serving in the armed forces. We must pray for the Iraqi people. We must love our enemies, for this conflict will make many more of them. And because war always erodes truth and brutalises people, we must pray, in the words of tonight's gospel, that the darkness may not overtake us. While this conflict lasts, a large candle will burn each day at the centre of this Cathedral, with the invitation to all comers to light candles to stand for our thoughts, longings, and prayers.

This is not the first time a new chapter in my ministry has coincided with larger events on the world stage. I was ordained priest in June 1976, the same week that hundreds of people were killed at Soweto. I asked myself then how we could celebrate while so many lived in fear, what it meant to have faith and be a priest at such a time as this. Religion, as we know, tends to be used as a bolt-hole at times of crisis: a safe place from the shocks and alarms that threaten us. Well, when waters are turbulent, we need a haven to recover ourselves for a while. Yet to follow Christ is always to be drawn back out into open seas. Faith is a way given to us not to escape from the troubles of this world but so that we can face them with courage and equanimity, and in the belief that God is in all this, however mysteriously. The prayer of Jesus in tonight's reading is an apt comment on today's events. He is facing his own crisis of suffering and death, and does not flinch from it: "Now is my soul troubled. And what should I say—Father, save me from this hour? No, it is for this reason that I have come to this hour. Father, glorify your name."

For us here in the North East, St Cuthbert is the great example of this way of living. His profound awareness of God, his rule of life, his learning, his compassion for people, his missionary fervour, and his dedication to the church—these qualities were forged in a crucible of passionate engagement with the world around him. His was a hard age marked by poverty, barbarity, and plague. When he left Lindisfarne to live as a solitary on Inner Farne, it was not to escape the trials of his day in order to etherealise and think beautiful thoughts. It was to do battle with evil. And he chose an island in full view of the seat of the Northumbrian kings at Bamburgh, as if to say that hermitage and holiness have a political and social context, that the world and its struggles are God's concern, and that even the principalities and powers have to reckon with their maker and their judge.

Like the Lindisfarne Gospels, created in honour of "God and St Cuthbert", Durham Cathedral is the legacy of Cuthbert and his community of wanderers who so faithfully carried his body around the North of England until it came to rest on this peninsula. That band of refugees, dislocated by Viking raids, knew all about fear, invasion, and war. Next year we mark the 900th anniversary of the placing of Cuthbert's shrine in this Cathedral in 1104 where it has remained ever since. There is a paradox in his ending up in a building like this, so formidable a statement is it of temporal as well as spiritual power, "half church of God, half castle 'gainst the Scot", in the well-worn words. Yet the very history of this marvellous cathedral points us beyond itself to the ultimate questions about God, the world, and our human condition: a bastion erected in violent and cruel times, yet down the centuries a place numinous with the presence of God, where prayer has been valid and where the vision of Christian living and service has been lived out. We need sacred space to stretch our horizons, enlarge our imaginations, and help us re-envision the world and how God wants it to be. In Hilary Davies' poem, quoted in tonight's service sheet, it is rock and stone bent to "shape our thoughts of heaven in a human space".

So we need to continue to discover how Cuthbert and this incomparable church help us to speak intelligently about God in our own day. We do this as we learn and live the gospel together in word and sacrament, witness, *koinonia*, and service. A new dean brings no formulae, no templates. In this Cathedral, this present-day community of St Cuthbert, we build on the work of our predecessors by continuing the journey of discernment together in a common life of prayer, study, and work that honours the Benedictine tradition of the great Priory of Durham. We know what is God's work and ours as we practise hospitality and friendship, as we suffer and rejoice with one another, as we share our faith and serve the poor.

And we do this in the company of a great cloud of witnesses. To celebrate Cuthbert and the saints is to keep the flame of faith and hope alive, to recall that even in turbulent times there are points of light to help us navigate a path across dark seas, as if by the stars. The saints speak to us across the ages about how we do not trust God in vain. They tell us of a way of living that is based, not on power, violence, and greed, but on love, joy, and peace. They invite us to act in the name of God for all that is honourable and just, to do our part to help build a gentler, kinder world. They encourage us to an artistry of personal and public life based on goodness, service, and trust. They urge us to pray and not to lose heart.

In tonight's reading from the Fourth Gospel that Boisil, Cuthbert, and Bede loved so much, we are to believe in the light and walk in the light. Soon it will be Passiontide, and who knows what passion our world may be passing through by then? Yet it is the season not only of pain but of glory, as St John speaks of it. There are tears in things, but mercy too. If we can embody in our life together the passion and resurrection of Jesus, be sensitive to the agonies our world is going through, yet confident in the hope God sets before us, then we shall be true to Cuthbert, true to Christ, and true to the unceasing movement of God's love into his world. The chroniclers tell us that Cuthbert sang psalms as the waves of the sea broke over him. The waters may yet overwhelm us, but we will still praise God. Like Cuthbert, we will say our prayers and ask that our sins may be forgiven, and trust to the end in the love that moves the sun and the other stars.

St Cuthbert's Day, 20 March 2003
John 12:27–36

What Kind of Bishop?

*Bishops of Durham have come and gone during the last twelve
years; I have worked with no fewer than four, all very different. The
announcement of a new bishop is understandably always a matter of
keen interest in a diocese whose cathedral will have a formal role in
"electing" him or her to the office. It is an opportunity to reflect on what
it means to be a bishop in the church; hence this sermon, preached
not long before the name of the present bishop was announced.*

Tomorrow is St John the Baptist's Day, the forerunner of Jesus. He did
not know the name of the one who would be revealed as the saviour of
the world. But he was to look for the man "on whom you see the Spirit
descend". This is what he recognised in Jesus. He spoke of him as the
promised Lamb of God and people began to follow him. They called
him *Rabbi*, "teacher". St John the Evangelist, who tells us this, seems
to be saying that four things mark Jesus out: his spiritual charism, his
sacrificial vocation, his teaching, and his insight into human nature. Four
marks of messiahship.

And perhaps they are four marks of leadership in the church in any
age, although we do not look for, or need, little messiahs. Next Saturday
we shall ordain new priests here at the Cathedral. So what do we look
for in the church's leadership as we pray for them? We also await the
announcement of our next bishop. The Commission which recommends
the appointment has finished its work. We can expect a name within a
few weeks. Whoever he will be (and I wish I could say that it might be a
"she"), we have been praying for him long before he himself has realised
that this is his destiny. But perhaps it will help our prayers if we think
about those qualities John the Baptist saw in the Christ who was to come.
What *kind* of person should occupy the See of Cuthbert? What kind of
men and women does the church need as its priests? Obviously, people
who put the imitation of Christ above all, who will do what Jesus tells the

healed demoniac in our gospel reading: tell everyone what great things God has done.

I don't suppose our new bishop needs me to tell him what bishopping is about. But it may help us as we prepare to welcome him, we hope this time for a period of many years, to think about these marks of anointing that a spiritual leader should emulate.

First, *charism*. "The one on whom you see the Spirit descend and rest." It goes without saying that we need a man of prayer, reflection, and inwardness, whose vision is shaped by a deeply nurtured relationship with God. Yet it needs affirming that this is fundamental to spiritual leadership. There are plenty of good theologians, people who are well read, tough, financially shrewd, articulate, kind and caring, expert strategists, and passionate for justice. These qualities are all important in a bishop. But, like patriotism, they are not enough. What is remembered in great church leaders is the charism of spiritual wisdom born of a deep and rich inward life. I wonder if it is becoming harder for senior appointments in the church to be made with regard to this *sine qua non*. We don't know if the next bishop will be a well-known figure with a large following, or whether he comes to us as one unknown, not yet burdened by high office. Whichever it is, we pray for this charism in him, for under the constant scrutiny of public gaze, only the Spirit of God will set his priorities in order, stop him from thinking of himself more highly than he ought to think, save him from burning out. Only the Spirit will be his safeguard against the cult of celebrity that bedevils public life today. Only the Spirit can save him from himself. And this goes for priests too.

Secondly, *vocation*. John says: "Behold the Lamb of God who takes away the sins of the world." There is a kind of dying to oneself in leadership that is part of its vocation. Priests and bishops know the cost of bearing public office in the church. Sydney Smith, that nineteenth-century clerical wit, said that what bishops loved most about their role was a dropping-down deadness of manner in other people because bishops had favours to bestow. I hope we shall have a bishop who is free of the need to receive deference or to give it. The truth about a privileged position is that it can often mean being laid on the altar of relentless demand. The new bishop will need to see through the glamour of the job to be a servant of the servants of God. He will need to model to an often demoralised and discouraged church the real nature of vocation, how it is self-offering for the building up of Christ's body and the service of the world. He will be blamed for many of the church's ills: its decline both in numbers and influence, its waning finances, its fragile morale. It would be unfair to blame anyone personally for these realities, whose causes are complex and not always well understood. But leaders often find themselves cast into the role of sacrificial victims. That requires patience and humility when a bishop's leadership is strange and baffling to some, and marginal to almost everyone else. A strong sense of calling is necessary.

Intelligence. When Jesus comes, he puts a question to those waiting for him: "What are you looking for?" They say to him, "*Rabbi* (which means teacher)". I don't hesitate to say that the next bishop must be a good *rabbi,* literally in Hebrew a "great one", like a *guru,* literally a "heavy one", or, as we might say, someone with *gravitas.* This means he must be a good theologian; that is, someone who constantly asks the questions: how do we speak of God in the modern era? How do we read the signs of his presence and activity? What account do we give of Christian faith in a complex world of many faiths and meanings, and in particular, this secularised western society of ours? What does God want for North East England and for this diocese? How can religion be offered as a credible and attractive path for scientists, philosophers, economists, historians, artists, politicians, thinking people in all walks of life? It seems to me that these are inescapable tasks for a bishop today, and, no less importantly, for priests in parishes too. How the church engages in apologetics and evangelism in this climate will have far-reaching consequences for the intellectual survival of Christianity as public faith in this century. Our leaders need finely nurtured Christian minds, need to be immersed in the Bible and Christian tradition yet to also wear their learning lightly. There must be simplicity in their depth. That calls for real religious intelligence. It's what it means to be a *rabbi.*

Insight. St John says that one of Jesus' first acts is to look at Simon and say, "You are to be called *Cephas.*" Later in the gospel he records that Jesus "knew what was in the heart of everyone". The gifts of insight, perceptiveness, discernment cannot be overrated in public life. A bishop has to move among the great and powerful of the land without losing his integrity. He sits at the apex of a complex, disparate institution and has to understand why it is what it is. At times he must speak for a wider public, even the nation, if not in Durham, then in the House of Lords. He will face difficult issues to do with the future of the establishment, relations with other faith communities, women bishops, gay marriage, and human sexuality, where he must hold the ring amid fractious disputes. More intractably, he will be a senior public representative of religion at a time when many people see no place for faith, as I've said. He will not be able to arrest the devastating slide in church attendance, but he may perhaps help the church not to despair. He needs to be a "dealer in hope", as Napoleon said about leaders. He will need to be a shrewd politician, know the art of the possible, temper vision with reality. But he will also need to be unafraid of change, of taking risks, of thinking the unthinkable, of being a prophet for our times. And, more intimately, he will need to have insight into the daily lives of parish clergy and the communities they serve, and this of course is the special task of our parish priests. To do this pastoral task, priests and bishops must listen carefully to many disparate voices, be present to them, commit themselves to them without reserve.

"Who is sufficient for these things?" asks Paul in one of his letters. Who is sufficient to lead us in telling what God has done and to lead the church to be the kind of society Paul speaks about in today's epistle, the transforming and transformed life where there is no longer Jew or Greek, slave or free, male or female, for we are all one in Christ Jesus? It is an impossible job, of course. Anyone offered it would surely respond instantly by saying, as bishops of old used to when they were dragged off to be consecrated, *nolo episcopari*: I do not want this. Only a fool would want it. But to be a fool for Christ is also at the core of the job description. For our next bishop, and for our new priests, this may be food for thought and prayer in the days that lie ahead.

23 June 2013
Galatians 3:23–end; Luke 8:26–39

Digital Lambs

And here is an afterthought that followed the departure
of a bishop suffragan whose farewell service prompted
this sermon on a Sunday dedicated to vocations.

The other night there were two lambs standing here in the crossing of this Cathedral. They were digital lambs on a screen at the farewell service for the Bishop of Jarrow. It posed a liturgical dilemma for us in procession: how were we to acknowledge the high altar beyond? I proffered a dip of the decanal head, but wasn't sure if I *ought* to be reverencing lambs. The semiotics were puzzling: the hymn we were singing was "Thy hand O God hath guided thy flock from age to age". Hardly a flock, this; rather, two lost sheep that had strayed from the ninety and eight. How very postmodern, I thought, this layered liturgical riddle carrying bits and pieces of possible meaning. I trawled for remembered insights from that great classic of toilet literature, *Buddhism for Sheep,* and began to deconstruct. Were these creatures on-screen for their innocence or their foolishness, as objects of admiration or of pity? Were they gazing at each other or at us in amiability or suspicion? Was the expanse of grass and sky an image of beauty or bleakness? Was the implied allusion to the Good Shepherd, Little Bo-Peep, or *One Man and His Dog*? Was there a sinister subtext about the slaughterhouse and dinnerplate? Was it a warning, or just an elaborate tease with the joke at our expense?

Well, the Archdeacon helpfully suggested that what I was bowing to was in fact our two bishops as we'd never seen them before. Then it began to fall into place. The focus of the service was the ministry of a bishop. And while ordained ministry is often spoken of in terms of the *shepherd* because of its *pastoral* character, what was on-screen offered a suggestive image in its own right. The picture of two innocents standing apart from each other and apart from life, puzzled, bewildered, even forlorn, exposed to the elements, not knowing what they were for and not *capable* of knowing—that is the picture some people have of the clergy.

Take it further and think about being driven by others against your will, being extinguished, roasted, eaten up, devoured—these are all metaphors anyone in a caring profession will recognise at times. I don't want to press this too far. But when I was a parish priest in Northumberland, where there are more sheep than people, and used to roam the high and lonely Cheviot hills, I sometimes thought that being a vicar was a bit like wandering lonely as a sheep.

I am musing in this vein because today is being kept across the Church of England as a Sunday on which to highlight *vocations*. Vocation, of course, means "calling", *any* calling, not simply one to an explicitly *religious* role like ordination or entering a religious community. Baptism involves each of us in an inescapable vocation to discipleship, being faithful followers of Jesus Christ, and in every aspect of life to emulate his own living and dying and rising again. The New Testament reminds us that we are "called to be saints", called to live before God in the world, called to the offering of our life in its totality of work, leisure, and relationships. I can't emphasise enough the importance of this. And if Christianity is to be credible in the modern world, then it depends on our grasping hold of this insight and living it consciously, and, through the authenticity and integrity of who and what we are, giving a reason for the hope that is within us.

But what about vocation to *ordained* ministry? Many meanings can be given to ordination, but one of them is to be *a public sign of the spiritual dimension in the world*. This is what the Anglican theologian Austin Farrer meant by his happy phrase "walking sacrament". He said that a priest was, so to speak, an outward and visible sign on legs of inward and spiritual grace present and at work in the world that God loves. Of course, every baptised Christian is already fulfilling that vocation. But the ordained do it publicly and officially. For if we are going to have organised religion, and it is inevitable, then it needs its spokesmen and women, its representatives who will speak and act for it, and, in speaking and acting for the church, speak and act for the God who is present to and at work in all of life. The *Common Worship* Ordinal says:

> The Church is the Body of Christ, the people of God and the
> dwelling-place of the Holy Spirit. In baptism the whole Church

is summoned to witness to God's love and to work for the coming of his kingdom.

To serve this royal priesthood, God has given particular ministries. Priests are ordained to lead God's people in the offering of praise and the proclamation of the gospel. They share with the Bishop in the oversight of the Church, delighting in its beauty and rejoicing in its well-being. They are to set the example of the Good Shepherd always before them as the pattern of their calling. With the Bishop and their fellow presbyters, they are to sustain the community of the faithful by the ministry of word and sacrament, that we all may grow into the fullness of Christ and be a living sacrifice acceptable to God.

Today's gospel is part of that great passage in St John's Gospel in which Jesus speaks of himself as the Good Shepherd. In it he says: "My sheep hear my voice. I know them and they follow me." Could it be that those lambs on the screen here in the crossing were not lost but *listening*? One way of speaking about ordination is that it is about helping the church, our society, and individual people hear and recognise that voice that calls to us in judgment and mercy. That requires a quality of attentive listening and spiritual focus which in turn entails being willing to live *contemplatively*. If you ask people what they look for in their clergy, they often say that they expect us to be at our prayers, to give an intelligent account of religious belief, and to be passionate for God. They do not want bishops and clergy to be in a flurry of relentless activity with time for nothing and nobody. They want us to be reflective, to be able to speak from an inward spiritual wisdom. The spiritual tradition knows that it is precisely this quality of being, grounded in relationship with God, that leads to radical personal and social transformation. The vision of God always includes our vision of a world and of human life renewed in the light of God's kingdom. "After Sunday" is as important a dimension of being disciples as our praise and prayer on this first day of the week. "What matters for prayer is what we do next." This is what Christianity means. It lies at the core of what it is to be ordained. If ordained ministry looks uncomfortably *churchy* at times, this is only so that it can become a truly *worldly* vocation.

It's heartening that a number of people in this Cathedral community are exploring the possibility of ordination. I hope there may be others. After more than thirty years as a priest, I can honestly say that there is nothing I would rather have done with my life. But I would not be standing here with any integrity were it not for you, for our life together here and in the other Christian communities that have been part of my formation. Our partnership in the gospel, the praise of God, and the pain of the world is the real privilege here. So I ask you to pray for your ministers as we pray daily for you. Pray too that God will call men and women of depth and wisdom to serve in the ordained ministry. And, whatever your vocation, lay or ordained, think of those digital lambs and carry on listening.

29 April 2007
John 10:22–30

The Duty and Delight of Vocation

In 2005 I was privileged to preach at the ordination services in the Cathedral. In the retreat addresses, I took as my theme the role of wisdom in Christian ministry (my reflections were later to find their way into my book Wisdom and Ministry). At this service, the Old Testament reading was from Proverbs where wisdom plays before her Creator. I wanted to say that ministry was not only a solemn and awesome commitment but that it must always be motivated by the same delight God takes in the world he has made.

Ordinations often coincide with the Wimbledon finals. Perhaps there should be strawberries after the service. I once preached about tennis at an ordination—no small achievement for someone with my athletic prowess. I said that it was the most theological of sports because not only do you *serve* in tennis, but every game, set, and match starts out from *love.* My attitude to sport was deeply coloured when, as a nine-year-old on my second day at prep school, I was frogmarched with twenty-nine other boys out on to a rugby pitch one baking hot September day. We sat down on the parched ground to listen as the master in charge of us, "Old Marsey", taught us the rules of the game. "Boys," he began, "the object of a game is to enjoy yourself." Within a week, the misery of endless cold, wet, muddy games afternoons confirmed my view that this was the biggest lie I had yet been sold. School has a lot to answer for. Yet he was right about the theory. Playing is fundamental to living. We need enjoyment, recreation, laughter; we are *homo ludens,* people who play. It's how we learn and grow. It's how we spontaneously experience what it is to be free. It's how we tap into our creativity and enlarge the imagination, which is why we speak of *recreation.* Far from being a way of escape, to play well is to enter into reality. The great Thomas Aquinas said that God wanted human beings to be "well-turned", maintaining a right balance between gravity and laughter, holding together the tragedy and the comedy of life. So even theologians want us to play.

This is the theme of our reading from the Book of Proverbs. But it makes the extraordinary claim that playing isn't simply a human activity, but belongs to the nature of God himself. Wisdom is pictured as being with God at the beginning, as if she is the mind and imagination of God, fashioning the heavens and the earth, giving birth to its life. In the famous painting of creation in the Sistine Chapel, where the spark of life passes from God's finger to Adam's, Michelangelo has placed a beautiful woman by God's side. You might think she is Eve. But more likely she is the figure of Wisdom, God's helpmeet in creation, contemplating the goodness of what is coming into being. But the text goes further. It seems to say that creation was not, after all, *work* but *play* on God's part. "I was his delight daily, playing before him continually, playing in his inhabited world, and my delight was with the human race." It's an image of laughter in heaven and creation as an act of playfulness and joy. God did not have to make the world or make us. It was his choice; *we* are his choice. And if we could open our eyes to this sunrise of wonder at our own existence, we too, like God, would dance and play.

Why am I telling you all this at your ordination as priests? Because the gospel is an invitation to be re-created and to find in Jesus our delight. In the cross and resurrection of Jesus there is a new creation. Paradise lost has been restored to us and made more glorious. Jesus says that receiving the kingdom of heaven is to embrace this new world God is making; it's to dance when he pipes to us; it's to leap for joy because we are being healed; it's to sing when anyone turns back to God; it's to feast at his table like royals; it's to assist at a wedding; it's to become like little children. These are all images of pleasure and play. You could say that the church is called to be a community of delight, who are discovering what it means, as the *Shorter Catechism* puts it, to glorify God and enjoy him forever. Like Thomas in the gospel reading, we acclaim the risen Jesus as our Lord and our God, and pass from the shadows in the full light of day. We are an Easter people and alleluia is our song.

And the priesthood of the church is a visible focus of all this. Priests are there for many things. Much of our ministry concerns the dark and desperate places of human life where people are overwhelmed by tragedy, suffering, and pain, struggling with failure, facing death, longing for purpose and meaning. Into these places the priest comes in the name of

Christ himself. And because the church dares to stand for public faith, the priest is a public sign of God's judgment and mercy in the wider world, where the gospel word needs openly to be spoken into the issues of our time: conflict, poverty, saving our planet. At the time of the G8 Summit, when history may be made for good or evil, we are deeply aware of our responsibility to millions of people in the developing nations. For every priest, ordination is a sacred and inescapable vocation to be immersed in the pain of the world.

But if you ask what is at the *heart* of priestly ministry, I say that it is to preside over the church's praise of God. The church is never more a community of delight than when we gather, as we do now, to offer our praises in the eucharist. The word *eucharistia* means thanksgiving. And we offer praise not only on our own behalf but, we believe, for the whole human family, indeed, for the whole of creation. In the eucharist, we celebrate the love shown us in Christ and we anticipate the promised new creation. We come to the table of God as equals at his banquet. Whether we are rich or poor, clever or stupid, weak or powerful, old or young, Christ invites us here as his honoured guests, makes us kings and queens as we feast on the bread and wine of heaven. The liturgy is godly play. It opens our eyes and makes us wise. It imagines that the kingdom of God is already among us and invites us to live as if it were. In giving shape and voice to the play of God's people, priests have a uniquely privileged role.

In our retreat together over these past few days, we have been exploring the nature of wisdom. We have talked about integrity and insight, about faith and trust in God, about discerning purpose in a perplexing world, about standing with those who suffer: serious issues, and all necessary if priests are to be wise themselves and help others on the path to wisdom. But it is not enough to be solemnly dutiful about these things. They must be underpinned by celebration and delight. Your ordination today charges you with the responsibility to keep faith alive against the relentless undertow of its melancholy long-withdrawing roar. It is hard to be a priest in an age so uncertain about religion. But, as Napoleon put it, a leader is a dealer in hope. That is profoundly true of the ordained ministry in a world so devoid of hope. Why else be ordained? So take up the heavy–light burden Christ lays on you today, reawaken joy, consecrate everything by thanksgiving. Like Lady Wisdom, never leave the side of God where your life belongs, and where the healing and salvation of humanity springs. Be his helper in bringing new worlds to birth. Delight in him and in the human race. Be glad that he calls you today. Never lose heart.

3 July 2005, at the ordination of priests
Proverbs 8:22–31; John 20:19–39

An Ordination Anniversary

The year this book appears, I shall have been ordained for the biblical span of forty years. Here is what I said on the occasion of my thirtieth anniversary. If only I knew in 1975 what I know now, especially about myself. Ministry, like life, can be full of "if onlys". But if they lead us to right-minded regret, how much more ought they to bring us to a point of thanksgiving for what has been and is and may yet be to come!

In the gospel for today, Jesus says: "Whoever welcomes you welcomes me, and whoever welcomes me welcomes the one who sent me." He goes on to speak of those who give "even a cup of cold water to one of these little ones in the name of a disciple". I have a special reason today for lingering on those words of hospitality, compassion, and care—words that are summed up in one of the greatest New Testament words of all, *diakonia,* servanthood. For on St Peter's Day 1975, thirty years ago this Wednesday, I was ordained deacon, the ministry that carries the office and name of servanthood. Serendipitously, I find myself this year leading the ordination retreat for the new deacons and priests, and preaching at their ordinations here next Saturday and Sunday.

How do I distil into a few minutes what thirty years of ordained ministry have taught me? How do I do justice to the heights and depths of being a deacon and a priest, the sacrifice and delight of this vocation, which is sometimes an unimaginable privilege and sometimes an almost unendurable burden? How do I honour the places where this ministry has led me, the people whose lives have been folded together with mine in Oxford, Salisbury, Alnwick, Coventry, Sheffield, and Durham? And how do I encapsulate what is so extraordinary about ordained ministry, that deacons, priests, and bishops should exist at all and still be largely welcomed and wanted in a society such as ours?

In one way, of course, the ministry of the ordained is not different from the ministry of the whole people of God. The fountain and focus of everything is Christ himself, who as servant of the Lord washes the feet of others and lays down his life for his friends. From him, crucified and risen, we are born as the church, his body that celebrates the love and the goodness of God in Christ and lives out his incarnate, self-emptying life in service to the world. Only then comes the ordained ministry that focuses and represents the ministry of all the baptised. What I am saying is that an ordained minister can never speak about *my* ministry or *my* vocation as if these were private possessions apart from the ministry and vocation of the church and of Christ himself. Ministry is for others and for God. The ordained are there publicly to represent God's church; we are collective people and not just individuals. A deacon, a priest, a bishop is what he is or she is because of what the church itself is called to be and what Christ for ever is.

Yet, in another way, the ordained stand apart. We are anomalous, paradoxical people, like clowns and jesters, who live an alternative lifestyle, who don't quite fit the rules. Clergy fascinate and make people nervous. What are we paid to do? Is it a job or isn't it? What does it mean to stand both for the paraphernalia of organised religion and at the same time for the contradiction of the cross, not least in a setting like this? And how do we come to be here at all? For the experience of vocation is that it often happens somewhat against our will. Perhaps ordained ministry becomes more elusive the more we inhabit it—just as a long-married couple can be hard put to it to say what lies at the heart of an experience so rich and rewarding, like a fine wine that becomes more complex with age.

An old answer is that the ordained minister is *alter Christus,* standing as Christ towards others and to the world. This is what today's gospel is saying: "whoever welcomes you welcomes me"; where we go, Christ goes. Another is that a minister is a "walking sacrament" of the grace of God, in Austin Farrer's memorable phrase. To me, words like "awareness" and "presence" matter; it is what we *are* as ministers, the human and spiritual *quality* of our lives that is the fundamental thing. Jung said that a society without clergy would be the poorer, for who then would reawaken in people the spiritual, the imaginative, the humane, the compassionate, and the prophetic dimensions of life? Who would be *there,* in Blake's words, to open in people the doors of perception? Who would publicly help people celebrate the goodness of things or lament in the face of injustice or pain? Who would care for the *soul?*

I have vivid memories of thirty years ago. I am not being nostalgic when I recall that it was a glorious summer. I was ordained under a Norman arch in the parish church where I was to serve as a curate. My incumbent, a good man and an excellent trainer of priests, but a bit of a liturgist's nightmare, decided to throw in a confirmation service as well. He preached about how the Son of Man came not to be served but to serve, how confirmation was the "ordination of the laity", how all of us, lay and ordained, were called to the same servant ministry of living out the love of Christ. The following year, during an even hotter summer, I was ordained priest in the Gothic Revival chapel of my Oxford college. That week we learned, most of us for the first time, about a place called Soweto. There was to me a deep connection between Soweto and being ordained priest. On the very day that I was celebrating the eucharist for the first time, people, mostly young, were being brutally battered to death: broken body and shed blood not only in the bread and wine of eucharist, but in Soweto's streets and squares. I knew I must never forget this, how ministry means both celebrating with and suffering with, how it connects us with the whole of life. I glimpsed the particular vocation in ordained ministry to be there for victims, to *feel* within myself something of the pain of the world, never to forget how surprisingly prominent in the scriptures is the genre biblical scholars call *lament*.

Strangely, society still welcomes men and women who choose this way, who are chosen *for* this way that involves immersing themselves in the glory and the pain of life. Next weekend, in this Cathedral, men and women will be ordained deacon and priest. Pray for them. Pray for those being called to this ministry, and who are training for it. Pray for all of us who are ordained. Pray that as the years pass and we grow old in vocation, our love may not grow old. Just before today's gospel, Jesus speaks of loving him in such a way that nothing is held back, nothing kept in reserve: "Whoever loves father or mother more than me is not worthy of me; whoever does not take up the cross and follow me is not worthy of me." Who am I to speak of this to you? We can only listen again to the words of Jesus: "Where your heart is, there will your treasure be also." That was said to me before I was ordained. It is all I have to say to this year's deacons and priests, for it is the distillation of everything. It is all I have to say to you. It is all there is to say.

26 June 2005
Matthew 10:40–42

Anointing Jesus' Feet

The extravagance of the woman who anointed Jesus' feet has always fascinated me. It clearly intrigued the gospel writers too, for all four include the story and link it to their accounts of Jesus' passion and death. How hard it is for us British to treat religion with extravagance! As I have already said, this is a vital quality in any preacher.

On the Sunday before a new Archbishop of Canterbury and a new Pope are anointed for their ministry, the gospel tells how Jesus is anointed at the house of Lazarus. The timing is suggestive: just as Jesus is anointed for burial, so two new Christian leaders embrace the vocation to take up the cross. When Donald Coggan was installed as Archbishop, a secretary mistyped "enthronement" as "enthornment" in the draft service order. She typed more wisely than she knew, said Coggan. Archbishop Justin Welby and Pope Francis will be in all our prayers this week.

Back to Bethany, where Jesus loved to go. There, a woman spontaneously does what prophets and priests do in the Old Testament: anoint a king for a royal vocation. This is what Christ literally is, the *mashiah* or anointed one who has come into the world, says St John, to bring a kingdom that is not of this world. What prompts this extraordinary, extravagant gesture, so disapproved of by tut-tutting Judas, emptying a pot of scented oil almost above price over the feet of Jesus? It's worth a king's ransom indeed, and that is what it is, for this is a King above price, at least to Mary, for whom her anointing symbolises all the passionate devotion she feels for him.

Tim Rice in *Jesus Christ Superstar* assigns to a different character (how confusing all these Marys are in the New Testament!) the song "I don't know how to love him". But her precious ointment shows that she does know, in her heart of hearts. She knows how to love in a way few of us ever have. And Jesus knows it too. That touch of hers, so physical, so erotic that it cannot fail to shock; the perfumed scent that fills the house like incense: both freight this story with powerful, sensual images. Of all the senses, touch and smell are the most pervasive and long-lasting. The sense of smell is the last to leave a dying person; it has the capacity to evoke long-forgotten landscapes, recall long-dead people, reawaken long-lost memories. So it is not surprising that this aromatic episode is associated in St Mark with an act of memory: "wherever this gospel is proclaimed, what this woman has done will be told in memory of her"—*anamnesis,* the same word that Jesus uses when he commands us to take bread and wine "in memory of me".

In St John, this episode opens the passion narrative, and sets the scene for what he will go on to tell us in the following chapters about the suffering and death of Jesus. It is six days before the Passover, Jesus' last Sunday. So this is a last Sunday meal, perhaps meant as a pre-echo of the last supper in the upper room on the coming Thursday, just as the bathing of Jesus' feet with oil also looks forward to the upper room where he himself will wash his disciples' feet. The previous chapter has ended ominously with the threat of Jesus' arrest. Now, says Jesus, Mary has anointed him with oil for the day of his burial. From now on, St John will be concerned with one thing above all else: how Jesus will be lifted up on a cross so that all humanity may be drawn to him. For in the Fourth Gospel Golgotha is not tragedy but triumph. Jesus' life is poured out on the cross just like precious oil so that the aroma of divine self-giving and grace may fill the world that God so loves.

Maybe Mary intuited this in her act of anointing, maybe not. For her, it may simply have been the offering of her devoted service and passionate love; or an extreme act of courtesy to honour a guest in her home; or else the recognition of a royal presence on the part of a loyal subject. It is Jesus who turns it into preparation for his death and burial. John tells us that after his death, women bring spices to anoint Jesus' body before laying it in the tomb. We are in the realm of the symbolic; this is more than simply an anticipation of what will happen in six days' time. What does it mean?

The word I want to use is "consecration". This little drama at Bethany is nothing less than Jesus' consecration for the work he has to do: to achieve the salvation of the world. The idea of a set purpose and of accomplishment is strong in the Fourth Gospel. Early on, Jesus says that his food is to do the will of the one who sent him and to accomplish his work. And his last word from the cross will be the triumphant cry of accomplishment that all is now done: *tetelestai,* "it is finished!" So Mary consecrates Jesus by anointing him for this awful but glorious task. On Passion Sunday, I want to suggest that we too must consecrate Jesus in our hearts as we prepare to celebrate the coming days of awe, the Passover of our crucified and risen Lord. In the next chapter of St John, it is Jesus himself who washes the feet of his disciples, consecrating them for service and commanding his disciples in every time and place to wash and anoint one another's feet. But just as we do this for one another and for the world, we also need to do it for Jesus, to come to him with all the love we can find in our hearts to break open the container of our heart and pour at his feet all its wealth and treasure.

Perhaps something like this lies behind the puzzling saying about always having the poor with us, but not always having Jesus. Judas' angry outburst about waste, and how the money saved could have been given to the poor, misunderstands the gesture. For it is precisely as we pour out all that we have and anoint the Messiah's feet that we begin to grasp what our obligation to the world truly is. The Torah says in Deuteronomy that we always have the poor with us, so we must open our hand to our neighbour in need. In a sense, this is precisely what Mary does for the poor Christ who has nowhere to lay his head, who has to rely on the kindness and generosity of those like her who receive him into their homes. What we do for Christ, we do for one another, just as St Matthew says: what we do for the hungry and thirsty, the stranger and the naked, the sick and the prisoner, we do for him. We wash Jesus' feet and we wash him in his poor companions.

As I approach the threshold of Holy Week, I ask myself: how have I consecrated Christ in my heart for this celebration of his passion and resurrection? How will I honour him, love him, serve him as he goes to the cross for my salvation? Will it be by doing the works of mercy to the poor who bear his image and who are always with us? Will it be by some act of generous giving to the church which is his body that we love and care about? Will it be by time spent in prayer and reflection in this holiest of seasons? Might it be in all three ways: consecrating Christ by serving the poor, giving to the church, growing as disciples as we walk the *via dolorosa* with him? We have six days to think about it before Holy Week begins and we sing about the love that is so amazing, so divine. For love is the issue today: loving Jesus and not being afraid of extravagance in the treasure we open up and lay at his feet. The question we face is simple: if he has so loved us, how will we show our love for him? How will we consecrate him within our own selves for the work of love he comes to do? And how will we become "as Christ" to a world that needs him so much?

Passion Sunday, 17 March 2013
John 12:1–8

Part 3: Singing the Lord's Song in a Strange Land

The next few sermons explore the different ways in which we preach, so to speak, in exile. They visit some of the dark places of life, both public and private. Like the Hebrew prophets of the exile, the task is to try to interpret the meaning of what disorientates or threatens, even overwhelms, us human beings, whether in collective ways as nations and societies, or more personally. What is important, I believe, is to avoid the easy answer (which will certainly be wrong). Instead, we must peer into the complexity, even when it baffles us, as it so often does. I find that preaching is often more about asking questions than stating resolutions, yet always with the perspective of faith in an ever-loving, suffering God. We are on holy ground when touching human pain.

Face to Face with the Angel of Death

*This sermon was preached out of my personal history as
the son of a German Jewish Holocaust survivor.*

Tomorrow is Holocaust Memorial Day, the anniversary of the liberation
of Auschwitz in 1945. It's a day to remember the millions who perished
at the hand of the Nazis and in the other genocides and acts of ethnic
cleansing of modern times. We need it to strengthen our resolve to build
a more peaceable world in which every member of the human family is
equally valued and where prejudice has no place. We need it to reinforce
our prayer that what happened in Armenia, in Germany and in Europe,
in Cambodia, Uganda, Rwanda, and Bosnia, and is still happening in
Southern Sudan, the Central African Republic, in parts of the Middle
East will not happen again, anywhere, ever.

In the Nazi Holocaust, two-thirds of all the Jews in Europe perished.
Survivors carry the physical and emotional scars with them in memories
that can never fully be healed. It is part of my own psyche too, as a "second-
generation survivor", as we are called. Almost too late, my grandparents
got my uncle and my mother out of Germany before the borders were
closed. But for that, they would have been transported to Treblinka,
Dachau, or Auschwitz with other members of the family. This country
took them in. Thank God for British kindness to the stranger, the refugee,
the asylum-seeker.

The Holocaust was a defining event in the life of Jewish people. That
memory is deeply embedded in the Jewish consciousness today, and always
will be. It has become part of the long story that defines that community
and its capacity to survive extreme persecution. The Passover *haggadah*
tells of how the Hebrews were resident in Egypt. Pharaoh made slaves of
them, piled on the oppression until they managed to flee for safety across
the Red Sea at the hands of Moses and Aaron. Escaping to a land of safety
across the water was precisely my mother's experience. The Festival of
Purim recalls how Queen Esther, the Jewish consort of a pagan king, acts

with supreme courage to save her people from extinction. Yet another feast, Hannukah, commemorates a fierce persecution of the second century BC when a Seleucid king, Antiochus Epiphanes, desecrated the temple in Jerusalem and exacted a terrible price from Jews who would not bow to his will and abandon their covenant. This time it is Judas Maccabaeus, the "hammer", who saved them. These are not the only holocausts written into the history of Judaism.

This background helps us to see why "holocaust", *Sho'ah,* literally a whole burnt offering of flesh, stands as a symbol of genocide. Our question must be: what do we say and do in the face of it? I don't mean the Jewish holocaust only, but every genocide where the same story gets acted out in new places and new ways. The inventiveness and dark imagination of evil seems to know no limit.

In the Hebrew Bible, the "Old" Testament as we call it, many texts try to grapple with the question of why human beings suffer. The greatest of them is the Book of Job. It tells of a devout, religious man who finds himself progressively afflicted with terrible diseases, has his house and home destroyed, loses all his children. Mrs Job asks how this could possibly have come about: "Curse God and die!" But this is precisely what he will not do. He is baffled, like she is, but he chooses to stay with the unanswerable questions while all along knowing that he has done nothing to deserve this personal holocaust of his. And then, says the story, his friends come along to keep him company as he sits among the ashes. Although they will utter plenty of thoughtless nonsense later on, they are at least wise enough to stay silent to begin with, not just for a few minutes but for an entire week, "for they saw that his suffering was very great".

There is something we can learn in that picture of friends standing by silently. When we are in the presence of suffering, it's not that the words fail us, or not only that. It's how best we stand in solidarity with suffering human beings, honour them in their ordeals. Silence is not passivity. When we go to the site of a terrible atrocity, we know that we are not simply onlookers, sightseers of history. There is "work" to be done here: mental, heartwork, spiritual work that should change us, transform our attitudes to suffering and injustice, empower us to act for the victim, the voiceless, and the weak.

A few years ago my wife and I went to the Bay of Naples to visit Pompeii, the Roman town destroyed by the eruption of Vesuvius in AD 79. It was a human disaster on a vast scale. To see the moulds taken of men, women, and children found in the rubble, showing them bracing themselves helplessly against a relentless, unpitying power, is deeply moving. But with millions of people visiting the site each year, you now have to run the gauntlet of a "shadow" money-spinning city of fast food outlets, hawkers of tacky souvenirs, and lurid entertainments of every kind that has grown up outside the gates. It does not prepare you to visit the site of a tragedy. Our guide took us round in an irritating jokey way that was far more interested in erotic paintings inside the prostitutes' house than in human suffering and grief. We wanted somewhere to be silent, like Job's friends, to try to take in what a momentous place it was, this arena of suffering and grief. The least we could do was to remember silently.

As we commemorate the victims of holocaust today and tomorrow, I hope we can find some way of being reflective and thoughtful; perhaps, if we are people of faith, saying a simple prayer like *Kyrie eleison,* "Lord have mercy", or the Lord's Prayer, "Save us from the time of trial and deliver us from the evil one". If our nation could be quiet, like it is on Armistice Day, if we could collectively stand alongside the victims of every place, it would help us to act with more compassion and justice in the future, to speak out for the voiceless, to take in those who flee from terror like my mother, to do all we can to make this world a better place for our children and grandchildren.

The gospel reading spoke about how Jesus began his public ministry by calling people to repent, to turn away from what was dark and destructive and turn towards the light of grace and truth dawning on the world. He spoke of it as the kingdom of heaven drawing near. He called people to follow him, to say yes to this world made new. Perhaps those who felt the heavy hand of imperial Rome crushing the life out of them found a new hope rising up before them. And we say: if only those who still harbour cruelty in their hearts could hear this, could feel the stirrings within of another, better, kinder way to live!

At the end of St Matthew's Gospel from which we read, Jesus prays in agony from the cross, "My God, my God, why have you abandoned me?" That is the cry of so many who suffer, not least those who, like him, are victims of other people's cruelty. But St Luke tells the story differently. He has Jesus utter one of the most extraordinary prayers ever breathed. While he hangs there, mocked and ridiculed by his persecutors, by the bystanders, even by the man dying on the cross next to his, he prays: "Father, forgive them, for they know not what they do." Face to face with death, another voice, kind and merciful, invites us to turn back towards the light. There is light and hope for those who sat in darkness, a redemption so universal in its scope that it includes even the perpetrators of evil who sit in the darkness of their own making. And we who stand in silent solidarity with victims, bearing witness to all that is wrong, need to be fortified by the announcement that the kingdom of heaven is near. Faith says that the long-awaited dawn the prophet foretold is breaking. *Christus Victor*, our Redeemer, has overcome the world. So be of good cheer.

St Chad's College, Durham, 26 January 2014
Isaiah 9:1–4; Matthew 4:12–22

This Thing of Darkness I Acknowledge Mine

The figure of Judas fascinates us, not least how the gospel writers
come to terms with him. But until preaching this sermon, I had
never tackled the subject before. It links with the previous sermon
in that, as I explain, anti-Semitism has historically been fuelled
among Christians by the Judas story (Judas = "the Jew") of betrayal.
It is a topic the church still finds it difficult to grapple with.

"Concerning Judas . . .", says our reading. The lectionary spares our feelings. We heard in the Acts about the vacancy among the apostles, how the gap left by Judas Iscariot was filled, but the verses describing his death were cut out. You do not want too much detail on a Sunday morning; this is family viewing and it is not a nice story.

I want to say something about Judas, this man whom the gospel turns its face against. In St John, "Judas went out; and it was night." That says it all. He is the dark face of apostleship, the shadow over that happy band of pilgrims. He deserves his place in his icy pit at the centre of Dante's hell with the other two arch-traducers of antiquity, Brutus and Cassius, where he keeps company with Satan himself. One of the excised verses in our Acts reading quotes the psalm that elaborates on the fate of those who betray their friends: "Let his homestead become desolate, and let there be no one to live in it." That is not the worst of the catalogue of disasters the psalm brings down on the reprobate. In Thomas Hardy's *The Mayor of Casterbridge,* there is a memorable scene following Henchard's downfall. He goes into a tavern where the choir has gathered after church (an honourable custom still observed here at Durham). Out of the window he sees his arch-rival Donald Farfrae. He orders the singers to perform the metrical version of Psalm 109 to curse his enemy. The bandmaster is horrified. "Twasn't made for singing. Whatever Servant David were thinking about when he made a Psalm that nobody can sing without disgracing himself, I can't fathom."

Who was this figure whom the tradition makes the object of the psalm's fierce curse? One of the puzzles in biblical scholarship is why Judas should have handed Jesus over to his persecutors. The modest price of thirty pieces of silver doesn't seem to explain it. For when he had succeeded in having Jesus arrested, he did not hold on to his gains but threw them down in a burst of self-recrimination. So what did he want to achieve by this elaborately hatched plot with its night-time encounter in the garden and a treacherous kiss? For twenty centuries. writers have speculated. An early gnostic codex in Coptic, *The Gospel of Judas*, portrays him as Jesus' closest friend and ally. He secretly asks Judas to betray him so that through his death, his spirit can be released and the world be saved. So Judas, far from being the traitor, is the willing midwife of salvation, an idea taken up in a great novel by Nikos Kazantzakis, later made into a less great film by Martin Scorsese, *The Last Temptation of Christ*. More credible is the idea that Judas was indeed a fervent follower and friend, perhaps a zealot who believed that Jesus had become diverted from his true vocation, which was to free Judea from the Romans by leading a violent uprising. His arrest would drive Jesus to orchestrate an insurrection, or else his death would force God's hand into a spectacular intervention that would herald the kingdom of the saints. Or perhaps he was simply a disappointed man, disillusioned at the apparent failure of Jesus' mission. In *Jesus Christ Superstar*, he is the real hero of the musical, who concludes that, sadly, Jesus is, after all, "just a man". Judas doesn't want Jesus to risk attracting Roman persecution that will result in a Jewish massacre. Or he comes to think that he is a false messiah. So he hands him over, as he believes he must.

What do we do with this enigmatic figure who has come to symbolise all that is ambivalent, treacherous, or just plain bad? Well, for one thing, we should remind ourselves that whoever we are and whatever we do, human motive is a complex thing, hard to be sure about even in ourselves, let alone in other people. Why on earth did I do that? What got into me? It would take a lifetime of analysis to uncover and understand the ambivalences deep within us. One of Shakespeare's most opaque villains, Iago, finds that his burning jealousy of Othello leads him into acts of betrayal that even he himself does not understand, let alone his victim. "Why hath he thus ensnared my soul and body?" asks the wounded Othello. "O my people, what have I done to you?"

Our story in Acts tells of how the "bad" Judas is replaced by the "good" Matthias. After the ascension, all seems set fair for a new paradise-era when the Spirit of truth is given. Yet Luke's Gospel does not paint the first generation of Christians as untainted by human deceit: think of the story of how Ananias and Sapphira played false to the faith hard on the heels of Pentecost. In the earliest New Testament documents, Paul's first letters, we see the shadow that lies across the primitive Christian communities, like a cancer dispersing secondaries into every member of the Body of Christ. Dissent, division, pride, greed, the lust for power, "envy, malice and all uncharitableness", the things we pray to be delivered from in the Litany—these are among the ways in which the church has continued to betray Christ through its entire history. They come from the very heart of Jesus' own society of followers and friends. And they are still among us to this day.

One aspect of this malevolent capacity for evil that has dominated the twentieth century, and still casts a long shadow over the twenty-first, goes back to Judas' name, "the Jew". An early, ugly, reading of the gospels identified Judas as the chief culprit of Jesus' crucifixion. So history has demonised him and often the people whose name he carried, "the Jews" who cried to have Jesus put to death. Anti-Semitism originates in the blame ascribed to Judas, who took money to betray the Son of God. "Blood-guilt" has coloured some Christian readings of the gospel; some scholars even find it in the New Testament itself. Once established, it spawns a thousand other evils: the Nazi Holocaust is only one of them. Compromised as Judas was, he was flesh and blood like us, capable of good and bad like us, in need of forgiveness and redemption like us. As Paul says, there is no distinction: "all have sinned".

If we put ourselves inside Judas' skin for a while, we may emerge with new insights about ourselves. Our betrayals of Christ are a way of talking about our sins: "our great refusals", Dante calls them. What evil might we be capable of if time and circumstance were different? If we had lived as respectable German citizens in the Nazi era, what might we have found ourselves colluding with? Yet however bad or mixed our motives may be, providence can do redemptive things with them. "You meant it for evil but the Lord meant it for good," says Joseph to his brothers after that story of betrayal and capture leads tortuously to its marvellous outcome of forgiveness and reconciliation. *O felix culpa!* Where life was lost, there life has been restored. At the end of *The Tempest*, Prospero has an unforgettable line as he renounces his magic arts. He turns to his rebellious, misshapen slave Caliban, who had tried to displace him, and says: "This thing of darkness I acknowledge mine."

This is what we need to do with the lost, dark side of ourselves that is capable of doing harm; and with the lost, dark side of the church; and with the lost, dark side of humanity. We need to acknowledge it, embrace it rather than banish it, as the father did his errant prodigal son, and Joseph his wayward brothers, and Jesus too, in accepting the kiss of his betrayer. For this is how the risen and ascended Christ always is. He embraces us and acknowledges these things of darkness as his, whoever we are and whatever shame we carry. He pleads the glorious wounds in his hands and side for the lost souls of humanity. God has infinite time to complete his wise and loving project for creation. And he gives us these pledges of love in the eucharist to persuade us that it is true.

Sunday of Ascension, 20 May 2012
Acts 1:15–26

9/11 Ten Years On

I was due to preach on Sunday, 11 September 2011. However, a family bereavement intervened, so a colleague took my place. But my planned sermon would not go away, even a month after the tenth anniversary of an event that shook the whole world. There is more of the preacher's autobiography in this sermon, for on the very day this shattering event took place, I was down to preach at a special service . . .

The media coverage of the tenth anniversary of the eleventh of September 2001 reinforced my sense that ten years ago we lived through a defining moment in our history. It was one of those days we instinctively know mattered and would go on mattering for decades to come. And my own bereavement—so different from what was experienced by the loved ones who perished that day, because it was long expected—still seemed to connect me more closely with the heartbroken families of the victims who perished in New York.

I was on the rota to preach on the evening of Tuesday, 11 September 2001, at a service in Sheffield for the licensing of new ministers. It was a day to tear up what I had prepared and start again. Here is part of what I said:

> With these images of burning and destruction in our minds as we gather here to worship God, what can we say to one another that will help? What can we say to God? In one sense, we can say nothing for we need time to take this in. We simply stare, appalled, at the spectacle we have witnessed and are silenced by what human beings can do to one another . . . Today is a time to be silent when the fragility of life and the reality of death feel very close. When we begin to speak again, what we shall say is that the praise of God and the pain of the world cannot be kept apart. And whether the pain of the world is felt in the tears of a solitary sufferer or in the anguish of an entire nation, it is what we are about as God's people and it is what God himself is about.

Therefore, it is what the ministry of each of us must mean if we are to be true to the crucified One who sends us into the world in his name. I would have wished that we would remember today, 11 September, for happier reasons than we undoubtedly will. But this is the cruel reality of the world in which we are called to ministry. We always knew it was a broken world into which we were sent in the name of Christ our healer.

Before 9/11, I had contributed to a book of essays *Calling Time: Religion and Change at the Turn of the Millennium*. My piece was called "A Threshold of Fear and of Hope". It explored the idea that entering the new millennium might be like crossing a frontier to another country: they do things differently there. This seemed to me more than just turning over the calendar and writing "2" at the start of each year. It would mean crossing a significant threshold. I conjectured that we were far from clear what the next century would look like, half optimistic (blindly so?) about the new possibilities it would open up for civilisation, half fearful of the risk that we could be running headlong into unimagined disaster. "We do not yet have a map to guide us," I said, "only a few compass bearings to suggest a general direction." So was the advent of a new millennium an unambiguous celebration?

At the time, some thought this a bit far-fetched. Yet this first decade of the millennium has surely brought us into a strange land where we do not always know how to sing the Lord's song: the calamity of 9/11, our recognition in the West that there are those who hate us and everything we stand for; the war on terror, security pervading our daily lives on an unheard-of scale, making us feel even more insecure; and, if that were not enough, a global economic crisis that is probably the worst for more than a century and which will take years, maybe decades, to recover from. The world is not the same as it was. We have all had to learn to live in this unwelcome exile where it feels as though "things fall apart, the centre cannot hold", where precarious times make us very afraid for the safety of our world and the future of our children.

If any good came out of 9/11, it is perhaps that there is now a greater awareness of how Christianity, Islam, and Judaism are one family of faiths. Paradoxically, as radical fundamentalists of all three monotheistic traditions try to erect ever higher barriers of hatred, thinking people increasingly want to give recognition to Christianity's origins in Judaism and Islam's debt to both; and how these Abrahamic faiths, committed to the worship of the one true God, impart a set of values and ethics and a concern for justice that is unique in religion. We should not collude with the gloss often put on acts of terrorism that they are primarily about religious hatred. Religion (by which I mean the wildly distorted readings of it by radical fundamentalists) is the pretext, not the cause. This hatred we have now come to experience has many different and complex origins: some historical, some contemporary. It's a noxious cocktail of unhealed memory, powerlessness, dislocation, and envy. These can take on the mantle of a plausible religious rhetoric, but it is spurious. Intelligent religion sees through it and names it for what it is.

In today's New Testament reading, St John speaks of what lies at the heart of religion. "God is love, and those who abide in love abide in God, and God abides in them." And again, "There is no fear in love, but perfect love casts out fear . . . whoever fears has not reached perfection in love." Is this a clue about how our world could become a better place? It is important not to be simplistic about this: John is writing about personal relationships, not the clash of civilisations. Yet our future and the world's must depend on learning how to live in open, unafraid relationships of giving and receiving, where we truly love our enemies and do good to those who hate us.

I would not be a Christian if I did not believe that faith holds out the promise of a better future. This promise belongs to the kingdom of heaven that is not yet among us. But, even as we long for it and wait for it, we glimpse its life-changing effects, motivating and energising us so that we do not capitulate to helplessness and despair, but are aroused to give ourselves to God's work of justice, truth, and love in the world. This risks sounding rhetorical and grandiose, the sort of impossible ideal preachers like to talk up. This is where today's reading helps, because whenever we embrace the kingdom of God and live its path of truth, we make a difference. It is costly to love in the way the gospel requires of us, but we have no choice about it. If we heard the voice of wisdom calling out to us in our first reading, we know that it is folly to live any other way.

This means trying (and I like that humble little word) to imitate the one whose words and works were life-changing for those on whom he turned the light of truth and looked with the gaze of love. For then we find that as his heart speaks to our hearts we begin to face the future with equanimity, and even with hope. In bewildering times, we are right to be suspicious of easy speeches, grand designs, quick fixes. If we think this is Christianity, we have not been paying attention. Yet we can be sure of Love's great ways. We are more than conquerors through him who loved us. We do not lose heart.

16 October 2011
Proverbs 4:1–18; 1 John 3:16–4:6

After the Tsunami

*9/11 was the result of human agency. The Indian Ocean tsunami
of Boxing Day 2004, with its dreadful loss of life, was caused by a
catastrophic natural event. When we try to speak about "the problem
of suffering", events like this are often the hardest to understand.*

I need to return to the tsunami. Three weeks on, our initial sense of shock
is subsiding a little, though not our prayers and profound sympathy for
its victims. If there is a crumb of comfort in the aftermath, it is the sense
of common purpose running through the relief effort, which is truly a
global expression of care.

We have always lived in world full of threat and risk. The universe,
necessarily, is a violent place. Its huge energies, unleashed in the births
of galaxies, stars, and planets, have made our earth what it is, capable of
sustaining and cherishing life, sustaining and cherishing *us*. In its long
history over billions of years, it has experienced tectonic convulsions, solar
flares, volcanic eruptions, impacts from meteorites, abrupt climate change
the like of which human beings have never seen in the microscopically
brief time we have been here. Some of these global events have been
so catastrophic that they have extinguished millions of living species,
abruptly changed the course of evolution; we would simply not be here
now without them. The message is that only a universe that is what it is
could give birth to us: a place of dangerous flux, energy, and liveliness.
And these risks are always with us, because that is the price we pay for
our existence. We are, almost literally in terms of the earth's crust, walking
on eggshells. We do not live in a specially privileged era, except that for
the million and a half years we humans and our ancestors have walked
this earth, it has been a relatively quiescent place.

For most of that time, we have understood that nature is vaster, more
capricious, and, most of all, more powerful than we are. From time to
time, we are put in our place, together with the *hubris* that imagines we
can somehow tame these awesome forces. We are reminded of our own

creatureliness, how we are not gods, cannot do all things or know all things. There is no Canute who can rule the tsunami. So it is futile to try to "make sense" of horror and calamity on the scale we have seen in the past three weeks, ask pointless questions about its meaning in the divine scheme of things. The worst thing we can do for its victims is engage in pious speculation. It will always be facile in the end. As in the Book of Job, we know that the victims of this and every other disaster did not deserve this. There is no logic to it, no fairness. We simply cannot speak about *why* it happened, other than in terms of natural causes we can understand. We demean the dignity of those caught up in this disaster if we try to explain it. There are no words we can utter. We have to live by the truth of Wittgenstein's dictum: that whereof we cannot speak, thereof we must be silent; and, at the same time, do what we must do to help; not make easy, speculative speeches about what God was doing on Boxing Day, but speak the concrete, incarnated, practical words of care, support, relief, compassion, and prayer.

Inevitably, as the Archbishop of Canterbury wrote in his thoughtful piece in the *Sunday Telegraph,* cataclysmic disaster makes you go back to the foundations of your faith, ask who and where God is in all this suffering and pain. He recalls that he was a teenager at the time of the Aberfan disaster of 1966 and how the vacuous words pouring from the lips of some religious people at the time contrasted with the substance of what the Archbishop of Wales said:

> I can only dare to speak about this because I once lost a child. I have nothing to say that will make sense of this horror today. All I know is that the words in my Bible about God's promise to be alongside us have never lost their meaning for me. And now we have to work in God's name for the future.

I have never forgotten how a preacher I heard at the time asked that very question of where God was in Aberfan. Not at the top of the slurry heap pushing it down on to that school and those children who died, he said, but underneath it, in the midst of the grief and pain.

And this is what we must say to one another about the tsunami: that God is its victim too. And because of this, he is not far from all who have suffered or died or been bereaved. The hands of those bringing relief and help are his hands too. Why do I believe this? Because of the memory of Christmas, and the ringing affirmation of the Christmas gospel that the one who made the cosmos and walks among the galaxies has come among us to live in our midst; more than that, to be given as victim for the life of the world. Victimhood is his meaning and his vocation. St John never loses sight both of the cosmic significance of the Word made flesh and of his call to walk the way of the cross for us all. In this morning's reading, John the Baptist points to the Lamb of God who comes as saviour of the world. *The world*—that is where I want to lay the stress—*cosmos* in Greek, this beautiful, mysterious, ambiguous, compromised, dangerous, life-giving, and life-taking world that is our home.

Since Christmas, I have pondered the psalms that speak often of the terror the Hebrews felt for the sea, so sustaining, yet always threatening to unleash demonic, chaotic forces that would wrench the land from their fragile hold. In my prayers, I have drawn strength from one of the best-loved of them all, a psalm that rises to the very height of faith in the midst of calamitous watery disaster. "God is our hope and strength: a very present help in trouble. Therefore will we not fear, though the earth be moved, and though the hills be carried into the midst of the sea. Though the waters thereof rage and swell, and though the mountains shake at the tempest of the same." There is no easy comfort there, only a faith hard-won in the storms of human experience, and a hoping against hope. It continues: "The Lord of hosts is with us; the God of Jacob is our refuge . . . Be still, then, and know that I am God." Yes, I am saying that if we do not speak when we should be silent, if we dare to be still in the face of this terrible pain, then we shall glimpse the awful yet compassionate face of God; and, far from being paralysed, we shall know what we need to do, and how we ought to do it.

16 January 2005
John 1:29–42

Britain and Germany: Healing Memories

The title is an echo of Tacitus. The event was the anniversary of the allied bombing of Lübeck in 1942. The church in north Germany has a long-standing link with the Diocese of Durham. Lübeck Cathedral is a magnificent building in one of Germany's most beautiful cities. I preached in faltering German and gave an English précis as I went along for the sake of British guests. I believe that our church and nation would be so much richer if we entered in a more committed way into what it means to be citizens of a common European home.

It is a great honour to be here in Lübeck today. I bring you the warm greetings of your partner Cathedral and Diocese in Durham. At this solemn time when we enter Holy Week, we are strengthened by the knowledge that we celebrate these "days of awe" together, whatever our nation, our history, our culture, or our race. As Jesus is lifted up in glory and draws all humanity to himself, so he also draws us closer into relationship with one another. We are one in Christ Jesus at the cross and at the empty tomb.

This is not my first visit to your historic and beautiful city. I last came here in 1987, with the choir of Coventry Cathedral, to take part in the dedication of the newly rebuilt Petrikirche. We sang too in the Marienkirche, and visited this Cathedral. Today I come to you on the anniversary of the allied air raid on Lübeck in 1942. This time of year, I am sure, brings painful recollections to mind for many of you. For those of my generation, born after the war, there is pain too. It is not the unforgettable images and experiences you have when you know at first hand death and injury, and see the destruction of beauty with your own eyes. It is more the sadness, the anger, the bafflement that comes from realising that civilised nations like yours and mine could inflict this on each other: nations made up of human beings like us who loved and laughed and longed for happiness; Christians like us who worshipped and prayed and celebrated the sacraments and heard the word of God.

The healing of memories is a long and difficult process. We must not underestimate how even now there are those for whom it is not yet possible to love their enemies and pray for them in the words from the cross, "Father, forgive". Yet I glimpsed a miracle once, in the ruins of Coventry Cathedral, when an elderly German man who had been a Luftwaffe pilot and taken part in the "Moonlight Sonata" air raid on Coventry laid a wreath at the altar and wept openly at the recollection of this terrible waste of human life. In that moment, the peace of the world seemed possible. There have been other moments when peace seemed within reach. The end of apartheid in South Africa was one. The collapse of communism was another, and with it, the reunification of Germany. Those years were a time of great hope and expectation for people across the world. The breaking down of walls between people, the new freedoms enjoyed by millions of citizens, the opening up of new economic, cultural, and political possibilities across Europe, seemed as close as anything in my lifetime to an image, a metaphor, of the kingdom of God. We give thanks that so much has been achieved on this common journey of reconciliation, understanding, and friendship.

But now, in this first decade of the new century, the future looks darker and hope is more elusive. As a convinced European, I am bitterly disappointed that Britain has stood aside from full participation in the European Union, for a united, democratic Europe is our best hope for peace in a world increasingly at risk from a clash of civilisations. Here, Germany has had to face the hard cost of integrating East and West. The enlargement of the Union later this year, potentially a great enrichment not only to the new member states but to all of us, has been beset with controversy and alarm. Added to these difficulties is perhaps the biggest threat we now face to our common European home: that of international terrorism, with the damage it inflicts on so many human lives, and the destabilising effect it has on our political and economic, and maybe even religious, institutions. It is many years since fear stalked the western world like this.

What does Christian faith have to say to all this? On Palm Sunday, Jerusalem welcomes her Messiah. Who is this strange king who is greeted with joy yet who weeps over the city? Who is he who is acclaimed the Son of David yet is carried by a lowly donkey? Who is he to whom the crowd shouts *hosanna* today yet by Friday is clamouring for his death? Our preaching text for this Sunday tells us how we are to see him. It is the beautiful *Carmen Christi,* the Christ-hymn from the Letter to the Philippians, perhaps one of the most moving testimonies we have to how the first Christians understood the Lord's coming to our world. It speaks of the Christ who laid aside his glory and took the form of a slave, becoming obedient unto death, even the death of a cross. The text calls this *kenosis*: self-emptying, abasement, a voluntary, chosen act of impoverishment. It is the true meaning of Christ's kingship; this is the path of renunciation and taking up of the mantle of the servant. This is of a piece with how Jesus is portrayed throughout the gospel, from his birth at Bethlehem to his crucifixion at Golgotha and his resurrection in a garden early in the morning. "I am among you as one who serves," he says to his disciples, as he turns his words into actions and washes their feet.

This is the beginning and the end of our salvation: a divine transaction or exchange whereby Christ became poor so that we in turn might become rich. And on this Sunday of the Cross, we need to establish where our treasure really lies. It is easy in our society to collude with the project of gaining wealth, power, possessions, influence, gratification of every kind. No western nation is immune from these longings, no family, no man, woman, or child. The more insecure we are, the more we crave them to protect us from harm and danger—so we imagine. These things are pervasive in the west, and, to the extent that we cannot give them away, as Albert Schweitzer put it: it is not we who possess *them*; it is *they* that possess us. The gospel is offered to us as the way of being delivered from this burden of being possessed. And its emblem is the lowly king of Palm Sunday, the Son of David who empties himself, the slave who washes our feet out of mercy and love.

As he has been to us, we must be to one another, says the gospel: "Love one another as I have loved you." St Paul introduces this famous song from the Letter to the Philippians by saying: "Be of the same mind, having the same love, being in full accord and of one mind. Let each of you look not to your own interests but to the interests of others. Let the same mind be in you that was in Christ Jesus." This is the heart of reconciliation: *having the mind of Christ.* It means not only asking what Christ would have us do, but actively discerning the Christ who is in each of our fellow human beings, those who, in the parable, he calls his brothers and sisters. It means staking our lives on the generosity of God, whose gospel is large enough to include even those who regard us as enemies because of our history, practices, or beliefs. We must not, in Europe, give in to the easy certainties of fundamentalists, of any religious persuasion, whose mission is to cut down and destroy, for our history tells us that to apply the principle of "an eye for an eye" means that one day soon everyone will be blind. On the contrary. The inclusive, generous openness of a way of life built on the God-given ideals of peace, justice, and service should be our vision for the future of Europe: *having the mind of Christ*. The part this historic Christian vision has played in shaping our continent should be written into the preamble to the European constitution.

This service, then, is a sign of grace and hope. It is wonderful to know that there are with us today men and women who are celebrating fifty years of church membership since their confirmation. They remind us of our Christian calling: to be faithful to Christ in bearing witness to peace and love in the world in which God has set us. As a community that transcends national frontiers, the church needs once again to hear the urgent summons put to it during the last war and in times of crisis since then: to have the mind of Christ, to act not out of fear but out of love, in peace, generosity, and gratitude, and to be the soul and conscience of our world in these demanding, even dangerous, times in which we live.

Lübecker Dom, Palm Sunday 2004
Philippians 2:5-11

Fear and Love in West Africa: Ebola

*Researching a sermon can teach you a lot. Here is
one example from my recent experience.*

The name Mabalo Lokela may not mean much to you. He lived in a
place called Yambuku in Zaire, now the Democratic Republic of Congo.
At the end of August 1976 he suddenly became ill and was admitted to
the local mission hospital. At first, the staff thought it was malaria. But
he failed to respond to the usual drugs. In a week he was suffering from
uncontrollable vomiting, diarrhoea, and terrible pains. Then he started
bleeding from his nose, gums, and eyes. No one had any idea what these
frightening symptoms meant. On 8 September he died. Within days, his
family and those who had treated him developed the same symptoms.
Soon, hundreds of cases were reported. The mortality rate was nearly
90 per cent.

You'll have realised by now that I am talking about EHF, Ebola
haemorrhagic fever. It is one of the deadliest diseases to have emerged
in our time. Many of us remember the rhetoric of the 1950s and 60s, when
we were told that, thanks to modern drugs, epidemics were a thing of the
past. But for every disease eradicated like smallpox, others have sprung up
like the Hydra's heads: Lassa fever, Lyme's disease, Legionnaire's disease,
and of course HIV-AIDS. Ebola is one more in the litany of names to
strike fear into human hearts, and, as we are learning daily, it is perhaps
the most lethal and most frightening of them all. In Sierra Leone, Liberia,
and Guinea, it is rapidly getting out of control. Thousands have perished;
the attrition rate is doubling each month. "With war you know to avoid
the enemy," says one Christian sister who is well used to violence and civil
conflict. "With Ebola you just don't know." And now, thanks to global travel,
it threatens people across the world, not only those who have travelled to
West Africa or been with those who have, but all of us, wherever we are.

Why am I disturbing the tranquillity of Cathedral matins by reminding
you of this? Because I believe that every threat our world faces is our

business as human beings and as churches. Because of that, I believe that it is God's business too. God cares about the victims of Ebola. God cares about those who are caring for them, at great risk to themselves. God cares about the panic that is running through populations in West Africa. God cares about those who are researching the causes and cure of this disease. Perhaps the most important thing the preacher can say today is that whatever ordeals humanity faces, we are not alone. And that should give us courage as we try to find ways of responding to what is rapidly becoming a worldwide health crisis.

In previous ages, disease was seen as divine punishment for wickedness, unleashed by the pale green Horseman of the Apocalypse whose name was Death and who had authority to kill with sword, famine, and pestilence. Retribution was the most plausible explanation. It has a long and ugly history that goes back to the ten plagues visited upon Egypt in the Book of Exodus. In the early days of AIDS, you frequently heard reckless and cruel talk about a gay plague sent to punish homosexuals. You might have thought that the Book of Job had put paid to this idea of reward and punishment for all time. Not so. But, as with all suffering, it is unexplained and unexplainable. Why does God allow it? It is beyond our understanding. Elie Wiesel asked whether even God understood it. When victims ask "Why me?" and cry out that it isn't fair, they are right. It never is. The best we can do is acknowledge the risk that is built into our universe that is the price of existing at all. But civilisations have been here before. When the Black Death swept across Europe and arrived in Durham in 1349, people's hearts failed them for fear. This was final judgment. It wasn't, of course. But it took generations for England to recover, not least from the economic and social fallout. I don't want to frighten you, but I've read that it's even possible that the Black Death was not bubonic plague but a haemorrhagic disease like Ebola. Whatever it was, it haunted the European imagination and left it overwhelmed with foreboding, as you can see in Dance of Death wall paintings that have survived in a few churches from that era. It was not until the Great War that Europe suffered another shock comparable to it.

So what do we think God wants us to do in the face of Ebola? We all need to recognise, and name, and deal with these atavistic fears that are taking hold. We need to know that this epidemic is not an apocalyptic event sent to punish us. We need to understand the causes of Ebola and how the virus is transmitted. We need to throw everything we can at it by way of scientific research, hospitals, beds, drugs, and everything else that the best health care needs. We need to support relief efforts going on across West Africa. I mean not only the medical emergency but its social consequences: failing economies, food and water harder than ever to come by, orphaned children whose schools are closed.

If you want a twentieth-century novel that charts the impact of an epidemic, read Albert Camus' *The Plague*. It's a rich exploration of how the contagion of fear spreads through a society and paralyses it; how panicky self-interest, the survival instinct, dominates all else; how preachers try to make sense of the catastrophe that is happening. This epidemic, set in a North African seaside town, was fictional; writing during the Second World War, Camus meant it as a metaphor of enemy invasion and occupation, and how a terrorised society reacts. But I think we can also see in it a metaphor of another occupying power that holds sway over humanity: the corruption of our motives by self-concern, putting ourselves first, protecting ourselves from harm at all costs. That turning in on ourselves is what Christian faith calls *sin*. In an important way, it is fear that spreads a spiritual plague, not because it's unnatural or wrong to be afraid, but because of how we respond when it takes hold of us. Like prayer, what matters for fear is what we do next.

The stories coming out of West Africa point in the other direction. Even non-religious observers have noticed that in some places, it is only imams, priests, and members of religious communities who are willing to take supplies into stricken villages, because only they are willing to put themselves at risk. I wonder how we could emulate that response here in the West. We can be pleased that the UK is putting resource and muscle into fighting the epidemic on the ground. The World Health Organisation, the United Nations, and *Médecins Sans Frontières* all tell us that this is where the battle to contain Ebola will be won or lost, not in our own countries where even the toughest of portcullises at airports and railway stations will avail little. But all that is being done is not yet enough. We must multiply our support twentyfold if we are to contain the disease and bring proper medical support and health care to many thousands of victims. That means pledging what we can to meet a grave emergency, not to save our own skins, but to care for our fellow human beings who are in such desperate need.

I recognise the part fear plays in our response to Ebola—and whatever else makes us afraid. I feel it in myself. But I have good news. In today's lesson, St John takes us to the source of what makes us Christian. At its heart is love, "not that we love God but that he loves us and sent his Son". Now he addresses the consequences of this for how we are with one another, how we live in community. "Since God loves us so much, we also ought to love one another." And he faces the issue of fear itself, and its paralysing effect. What is the antidote? John tells us. "There is no fear in love, but perfect love casts out fear." So what must we do? Again, John has the answer. "Beloved, let us love one another not in word only but in deed and truth." *In deed and truth.* We can bring love to our comrades in suffering by holding them in our minds and hearts, by giving financial support to the relief agencies, and by raising awareness of a real crisis where it might make a difference to how western nations respond. And in all this, falling on our knees and saying our prayers.

19 October 2014
1 John 4:1–18

Global Terror and Christ the King

We are all learning, painfully, that, like the poor, terrorism is always with us. When I preached this sermon in 2006, no one had heard of ISIS. Now, it seems, terror is everywhere, and when it is not threatening our towns and cities and transport systems, it is taking root in our heads. If ever there were a time for preachers to insist on the gospel command "do not be afraid", this is it. Perhaps there is some strange comfort in finding that these threats that are so real to us today have a long history, not least in the Bible.

How do we respond to terror? I don't mean the strategies governments resort to in the so-called "war on terror". I doubt if the many-headed hydra of terrorism will be defeated in our time; the best we can hope for is that it can to some extent be contained. What I mean is the effect it has on us, all of us probably, in generating anything from a low-level unease when stepping into an aeroplane or an underground train to a much keener sense of fear when some outrage yet again destroys innocent lives and reminds us that we are living on eggshells. I guess we are leaning to live with fear, and to be prudent in the face of it.

There is nothing new in this. Bloodshed, violence, terror are as old as the race. Those who wrote the Book of Daniel, from which we read in the Old Testament lesson, knew this for themselves. The era was the mid second century BC, when the Jewish community had come under the rule of the Seleucid kings. Antiochus Epiphanes' programme was to impose all things Greek on this beleaguered Semitic community. The terror was relentless in its operation and ruthless in its scope. Jewish religion was proscribed under pain of death: practices such as circumcision, possessing the Torah, observing the Sabbath and the festivals, taking part in temple worship. The crowning insult was the offering of swine's flesh on the altar of the temple, what the writings called "the abomination of desolation". Those who would not conform suffered terribly: they were tortured without mercy and then slain. Their stories are told in the Books of the

Maccabees. It isn't too much to say that this was the first Jewish holocaust. It was not to be the last.

How does a community live with its fear? The Book of Daniel responds in two ways. The first is by telling stories of heroic survival to inspire faith and perseverance. Daniel and his three friends, depicted as exiles in Babylon, undergo all manner of ordeals because they refuse to obey the royal command to worship the tyrant's golden image, and, indeed, the tyrant himself. Shadrach, Meshach, and Abednego are thrown into the burning fiery furnace for their loyalty to God (an eloquent image of the fires of persecution), yet they sing a *Benedicite* from the very heart of the cauldron and emerge unscathed as a testimony to how the God of Israel protects his own. Daniel too is hurled into the den of lions; he too is unharmed. The message is: the worst that others can do to you is as nothing if you remain faithful to God and to his covenant. To do this, says Daniel, is what it means to be *wise*.

But, of course, for most of the faithful living in times that must have seemed like the end of the world, there was to be no deliverance. So the second part of the Book of Daniel draws out of those tales of deliverance their fundamental truth. It does this by using the colourful, dramatic imagery of what is called apocalyptic writing. The threats to the community are presented as terrifying monsters, catastrophic floods, global conflagrations. Amid ordeals such as these, where was God? What was he doing to protect his people? Why was he so absent from their suffering? And the answer apocalyptic gives is to say that, despite appearances, God is indeed king. In our Old Testament reading, the Ancient of Days "has dominion and glory and kingship, that all peoples, nations, and languages should serve him". And "his dominion is an everlasting dominion that shall not pass away, and his kingship shall never be destroyed." The persecuted author, perhaps on the threshold of death, can say that God is the Lord of history. Only, it is not yet time for him to intervene to rescue the faithful and claim his true sovereignty. But that day of the Lord is coming. When it does, the righteous sufferers will be vindicated. Evil will be banished. Chaos will be returned to cosmos, just as it was at the creation. The universe will regain its right order.

When we turn to today's gospel from St John, we seem to be in an entirely different world. We are in the presence of Christ before Pilate in the Praetorium, one of the great scenes not only in the Bible but in all literature. Their encounter turns on the meaning of kingship. Jesus has been arraigned as "king of the Jews". *Are* you a king, asks Pilate? You say so, says Jesus. But he goes on to explain carefully what this means and what it *doesn't* mean. "My kingdom is not from this world; if it were, my servants would be fighting that I might not be delivered up to the Jews." So this kingdom is not founded on human power, imperial hegemony, and the force of arms. Rather, it is a kingdom of truth. Jesus has come into the world to bear witness to the truth. His subjects know the truth because they listen to his voice. There is a power that brings people into this kingdom, but not the coercive power Pilate understands, rather the power of self-giving love.

Now, for the Fourth Gospel, it is not a case of saying that whereas Daniel's Ancient of Days has a worldwide glory and dominion, Christ's kingship is hidden, inward, known only to those who follow him. On the contrary, St John's Gospel tells a story that leads to a climax that is visible, public, and cosmic in scope. That climax is what he calls Jesus' "hour" of glory, when he is acknowledged as the world's true king. Where is his throne, his place of transfiguration? The answer is: Golgotha. The cross is where he reigns, where he takes the dominion and glory of the Ancient of Days, where he is lifted up and draws all people to himself so that peoples, nations, and languages may serve him. Here, his dominion is everlasting, his kingship never to be destroyed. The cross is where he acclaims in triumph that greatest of the eight passion words in St John: *tetelestai,* "it is accomplished!"

How can I transfer the extravagant apocalyptic language of Daniel to the gentle Good Shepherd of St John? Because for John, the true glory of Jesus is that he lays down his life for the sheep. John tells us, as Jesus begins his journey to the cross, that "having loved his own who were in the world, he loved them to the end". It's this "love to the end" that proclaims Jesus' glory, which the Christmas gospel will tell us we have beheld in the face of the only begotten of the Father, full of grace and truth. And because love is his meaning, we find the hope and strength we need to go on living with our fear; for we know that the cross is not only the sign of the love that sustains us through the ordeals we face, but is the demonstration that God knows from within the pain and suffering of his children. He too is their victim, for he too has given his life and known the cost of bearing witness to the truth.

Christ the king calls us his subjects and invites our allegiance and our love. It isn't much of a kingdom: nobodies, peasants, fishermen, prostitutes, tax-gatherers. Yet the common people heard him gladly, and were the first to recognise what shone out of this man. This king does not promise that if we go with him, his way will be glorious, or lead to wealth or success or even personal fulfilment; it leads only to afflictions and trials. Yet he also promises that we can discover a new way of living that is not driven by an oppressive sense of dread. And this is the answer to our fear: not a palliative religion that denies fear's reality, but a faith that takes away its *power* over us and gives us the courage to live by hope and by the truth that sets us free. Christianity is to acknowledge that Jesus is the king who has overcome the world. It is to live as subjects of this kingdom "not from here", whose law is the perfect love that casts out fear.

The Feast of Christ the King, 26 November 2006
Daniel 7:20–27; John 18:33–37

At the Grave and Gate of Death

Preachers need to be careful about drawing on personal experience. What happens to us is indeed constantly shaping and moulding us as people of faith and as Christian ministers; it's when and how to speak about personal history in public. Often it is not appropriate; sometimes it is. I don't know if I got this right, but something in me impelled me to try to find the words on this Sunday in the joyful Easter season. The question must always be: am I preaching not myself but Christ crucified?

Death visited our family two weeks ago. The partner and best friend of one of my daughters, Clive, drowned while he was on holiday in Turkey. On the day he arrived he had gone swimming in a rough sea with someone he met on the beach. They both got into difficulties and Clive was pulled under. He did not survive. He was 39.

At times like these, when we stand at life's raw edges, we struggle to find the right words. That Sunday we worshipped in our local church in France. We felt a long way from our daughter. I tried to sing *alleluia* at the graveside, so to speak, as Christians should. But the words did not come readily. Easier—though never easy—when life has come to its proper end and someone dies, as the Old Testament puts it, full of years. This death of a kind and caring young man seemed so wrong, so cruel. The next night, as the Hull ferry pitched and rolled towards England across a dark and choppy sea, I thought about how in the Hebrew scriptures the chaotic deep was a symbol of threat and destructiveness whose demons only the power of God could tame and still. This sea may be our parent, I mused, but it is a violent and capricious one, like Cronos swallowing his own young. It seemed more like an enemy than a friend. I could understand why, in the vision of John's Apocalypse, there was no more sea.

Back in the rhythm of daily prayer, I found the Eastertide response powerful: *Death is swallowed up in victory; where O death is thy sting?* It felt as though the liturgy was a stabilising influence, a place where your feet could touch the ground again and you weren't floundering any more like a drowning man. At one of the services we sang:

> Jesus lives! Thy terrors now
> Can, O death, no more appal us;
> Jesus lives! By this we know
> Thou O grave canst not enthral us.
>
> Jesus lives! Henceforth is death
> But the gate of life immortal;
> This shall calm our trembling breath
> When we pass its gloomy portal.

I was much moved by those words, so familiar yet, that day, strangely new and life-changing. I found them difficult to sing, not because I struggled to believe them, but because I realised how deeply they had embedded themselves into me. It was almost—a strange thought, this—as if I believed them too much. Yet how could I doubt that it is by such words that we live and die and live again if we hold the faith of Christ crucified and risen, as we look for the resurrection of the dead and the life of the world to come?

At the Stations of the Resurrection last Sunday afternoon, we processed into the Galilee Chapel to stand at the Easter Garden and meditate on how the risen Jesus appeared to the women on the first Easter Day. I had not seen our new Easter Garden, though the Precentor had told me how good it was. Encountering things for the first time within the liturgy brings a heightened awareness, like switching on the Christmas Tree lights during the Crib Service, or carrying in the great cross on Good Friday to *Sing my tongue the glorious battle.* I can't explain this little epiphany. I can simply say that this stark, unadorned cave with a huge millstone rolled away, three crosses superimposed over the windows, the grave cloths in a neat and poignant pile, the flasks of burial oil, and some understated bushes at the side to hint at new life and growth—these all struck me with great power and moved me deeply. Here at last was an Easter garden to believe in, not a pretty toytown model of a happy ending, but a truly eloquent symbol whose profound simplicity and disciplined composition drew you inside and made you ponder the mystery of resurrection.

As we left the Chapel, we sang one of the most radiant of Easter hymns:

> Lives again our glorious King
> Where O death is now thy sting?
> Dying once, he all doth save
> Where thy victory O grave?

I thought: we have to rediscover the resurrection afresh each Eastertide. The calendar generously gives us fifty days in which to do it, for, like Thomas in the upper room or the disciples on the Emmaus Road, we can be slow of heart to believe, and Easter takes time to become real. Sometimes it takes the sharpness of death and the dull ache of bereavement to summon us back to the heart of our faith and of our humanity: what it means to be alive and be a man, a woman, a child; what it means to love and cherish; what it means to believe and trust in God's mercy with a sure and certain hope in the resurrection of the dead.

I wonder why some people disparage a faith that brings real hope to those who walk in dark and desolate places. I am thinking of Christians who are reluctant to speak about the grave and what lies beyond it, as if the kingdom of God is only a hope for the future of this world and Christ's reign over it. Only! It's a big enough hope to embrace. But I do believe that New Testament Christianity is about even more than this. In the fifteenth chapter of St Paul's first Corinthian letter, he spells out how Jesus' resurrection has overturned our human perspective on life and death. Paul's Easter faith is about more than the renewal of the world and of our lives now. "If for this life only we have hoped in Christ, we are of all people most to be pitied," he says, and embarks on a long discourse about what it means for the last enemy, death, to be destroyed, for us to be made alive in Christ and our mortal bodies put on immortality. "Behold I show you a mystery", and it is a mystery whose meaning can never be plumbed. Paul struggles for words to do it justice. But behind these words lies the conviction that God has raised his Son in triumph and has given his victory to mortals. It was this that utterly transformed the lives of those who first believed, who we read about in the first reading, gave them a reason for living and a hope with which to die. It is not an evasion to believe life transcends the grave. "This world is not a conclusion," said Emily Dickinson. It is what Christianity means.

In today's gospel, the Good Shepherd lays down his life for the sheep in an echo of the twenty-third psalm: "The Lord is my shepherd." That psalm contains some of the most precious words in the Bible: "Yea, though I walk through the valley of the shadow of death I will fear no evil: for thou art with me; thy rod and thy staff comfort me." For the Good Shepherd loves us to the end, and walks beside us on the dark path because he has already walked the sorrowful way and gathers us into his movement of dying and rising again. What else "takes its terror from the grave and gilds the bed of death with light"? What else can do this?

We are always on the boundary between worlds, the threshold that links this world to the next. We tremble at that dangerous, precarious place: who is not afraid at the gate of death? It takes a lifetime to learn to stand on the edge of the deep and troubled waters we know we have to cross and face them with equanimity, courage, and hope. Yet death is swallowed up in victory. Christ will carry us safely over, and, like in *Pilgrim's Progress*, all the trumpets will sound on the other side. We dare to sing *alleluia* even when there are tears in things. And then, "sweet is the calm of paradise the blest".

15 May 2011
Acts 2:42–end; John 10:1–10

Pullman Pilgrimage

*The last sermon in this "Strange Land" series was preached soon
after we got back from a pilgrimage to Santiago de Compostela. The
Camino across France and Spain was medieval Europe's greatest
pilgrim route. Northern Spain proved a "stranger" land than I had
expected: the journey raised uncomfortable questions about relationships
between Christianity and Islam that have by no means gone away.*

This is my first sermon since Easter. So I am out of practice. Most of you
know that I have been on sabbatical leave for the last few months. Getting
back into your stride is not just a matter of discovering how the place has
changed while you have been away but also how *you* have changed. On
the Cathedral front, re-entry has meant no big shocks, I'm glad to say,
and I do want to say thank you to my colleagues and to you for sparing
me. As to how this period of leave has affected me, only time will tell.
A sabbatical is not simply a chance to study and write—though I have
done that. "Sabbath" means a change of pace, refocusing, the renewal of
perspectives and horizons. And that changes you.

While I was away, I made a physical journey that I hoped would
be emblematic of an interior, spiritual journey. Jenny and I wanted to
follow the line of brass cockle-shells set into the road outside our house
in France. They point down the hill towards a place a thousand miles
away. In the Middle Ages, our village of Vézelay was a starting point of
the great pilgrimage to the shrine of St James at Compostela in northern
Spain at the westernmost tip of Europe. Its symbol was the cockle-shell
or *coquille*. Each year thousands of pilgrims undertake all or part of the
Camino, on bicycle, horseback, or foot, and converge at Santiago with
half of Spain for the Feast of St James on 25 July. For many of them, it's
an opportunity to renounce, at least for a time, rapid and polluting forms
of transport, re-connect with the soil beneath their feet, gain a deeper
spiritual perspective, perhaps take time to come to terms with some

life-crisis, and allow the slower, gentler pace to give a sense of what the human journey is *for*.

One of my colleagues unkindly dubbed this adventure "Pullman Pilgrimage", for we decided to drive there and back. Yet driving offered surprising perspectives of its own. For one thing, it enabled us to do the entire journey there and back as a single event, which is how those who completed it in the Middle Ages experienced it. Because the car is an archetypally modern form of transport, to put it to the service of pilgrimage raised questions about being pilgrims of our own twenty-first century. Not to race along motorways, but to drive slowly, stop at churches and shrines to pray and meet pilgrims, to treat the car as sacred space and home for this little community of pilgrims—perhaps there could be something redemptive in such an approach. And if pilgrimage is meant to include ordeals, we encountered those in a strange land whose language we did not speak and whose city centres were seething with aggressive Latin drivers for whom two innocents abroad sporting a UK registration plate were fair game.

Those seventeen days of pilgrimage proved a remarkable experience. I don't think we were expecting to feel the "pull" of the *Camino* so strongly, and the fellowship of its travellers moving in a purposeful procession across Spain. The spirituality of the churches, the beauty of the landscapes, the stories of the people we met, the knowledge that pilgrims had been making this journey for hundreds of years, all made for an unforgettable adventure. Arriving at the magnificent Cathedral at Santiago was profoundly moving after that immense journey. I have not experienced anything quite like it.

But pilgrimage is not simply about etherealising. Santiago, like Jerusalem and Rome, and for that matter Durham too, raises questions that can be disturbing. In the Cathedral there is a monumental sculpture of St James on horseback, brandishing a sword. Underneath are hapless Muslims being massacred—for St James is *matamoros,* the moor-slayer adopted as the patron saint of the *Reconquista*, that project of seven centuries to drive Islam out of Spain and reclaim it for Christendom. The Cathedral authorities have the decency to hide the lower part of that sculpture with flowers. But it opened my eyes to what I had not appreciated before, that making the pilgrimage in the Middle Ages was a political act. It stood for the church's power over another faith community, a power that was brutally expressed in battle and bloodshed. Soldiers of Christ, indeed, as in the hymn we have just sung and the reading from Ephesians—but with literal shields and helmets and swords. It was thought-provoking that I was writing a book at the same time about St John's Passion Narrative, where Jesus says, "My kingdom is not from this world; if my kingdom were from this world, my servants would be fighting." And we should recall that here too, our great church of Durham was not only built as the shrine of a saint. It was an unambiguous statement of Norman power. It belonged with the Conqueror's ruthless policies in this part of England and his massacre of the native Saxon people in the infamous Harrying of the North. To associate gentle Cuthbert with that act of ethnic cleansing is perhaps more paradoxical than making James the Son of Thunder the symbol of the reconquest of Spain.

I am saying that political realities and the dark side of our human condition are never far away, even in the most uplifting sacred spaces. In today's gospel, Jesus speaks of himself as the living bread that came down from heaven. He is the source of our life: without him we die. Just before this, he has fed the hungry crowd with the loaves and fishes, and they have threatened to grab him by force and make him king. By evading capture and going on to teach about this living bread, Jesus renounces political power for himself and his followers; his kingship is "not from here". It is not that politics and power are of no concern to him—the opposite, in fact, for the embrace of the Word made flesh is nothing less than everything: all that belongs to our human condition belongs to him. Rather, his exercise of power points to a kingship beyond all human authority and rule. He came, he says to Pilate, "to bear witness to the truth. Everyone who is of the truth hears my voice."

Pilgrimage, if it is real, must always be a journey into truth. It is not enough to overcome ordeals, have beautiful experiences, return home with travellers' tales to tell. There must be some glimpse of truth: about ourselves, our world, our God. No one who is aware of the threats we face in our century can go to Compostela without a sense of sorrow for the destructiveness of the past and present and without realising afresh that the language of hegemony and conquest can have no place in today's world. Like the crusades, the story of *Reconquista* calls for a healing of memories. Today's gospel points us to its source. Peter speaks for a world hungry for hope: "Lord, to whom can we go? You have the words of eternal life." St John says that we see the glory of God in the one who is lifted up on the cross and draws all humanity to himself; there we see love poured out for the world. The cross brings healing and reconciliation; and food for the long march towards the kinder, more Christ-like world we long for. We bring to this eucharist of living bread our longing, our hope, that the crucified and risen Lord will soon gather up the fragments of our broken world and of our broken lives so that nothing may be lost.

27 August 2006
John 6:56–69

Part 4: In Galilee

Part 4 includes sermons on Christian faith in the contemporary world. In the Gospels, "Galilee" stands for both faith's origin and its destination. It's where Jesus first called his disciples and invited them to follow him, and it's where he promised to be with them as their risen Lord. In Durham, medieval services often began and ended in the Galilee Chapel as the place of both gathering and sending out. I find this symbolism both eloquent and beautiful.

On St Mark's Day

St Mark's resurrection story in its authentic (i.e. shorter) version makes for a baffling conclusion to the Gospel. But the clue is "Galilee".

It's been an odd spring. Very few people alive today have lived through one like this before, and none of us will ever see its like again, not even the youngest chorister. What am I talking about? Not the arctic weather we in the north have been enduring, with the snow regularly deep and crisp and even. Rather, the date of Easter itself. This year, 23 March, was the earliest since 1913. It will not happen again until the year 2160, in our great-great-great-great grandchildren's time. The astronomy does actually allow Easter to fall one day earlier, should the paschal full moon fall on the day of the spring equinox when that day is also a Saturday. Easter fell on 22 March in 1818, and will do so again in 2285. (Those who are alive in the middle of the twenty-third century are even luckier than we are. In 2258, Easter will fall on the latest possible date, 25 April, and only twenty-seven years later, on the earliest possible day, something that happens only every 10,000 years.)

This Friday, 25 April, is St Mark's Day: the latest date Easter can fall, when we remember the writer who gave us the earliest of the gospel accounts of the resurrection. And not simply the earliest, but, for me, the most powerful. It consists of just eight verses. They tell of the empty tomb, the young man's message that Jesus is risen, the command to tell the disciples that he has gone ahead to Galilee, and the promise that they will meet him there. The story ends with the women's flight from the tomb, "for they were afraid". And that's all. There's no meeting with the risen Lord, no gift of peace, no great commission, no restoration of fallen or doubting disciples, no promise of the Spirit, no triumphant ascension. It's a *lean* story, spare, understated. It leaves so much unsaid, so many questions unanswered.

True, our Bibles print a longer ending to the Gospel. But it's not found in the best and oldest New Testament manuscripts. It's an inept tidying-up job. It has none of the vividness we've learned, by chapter 16, to expect of St Mark. Instead, there's the familiar tendency of well-meaning religious people to spell everything out and tie up loose ends, and that should make us suspicious at once. I for one am glad that my Easter faith does not depend on handling deadly snakes or drinking poison. And as for theories that Mark died before he could finish his Gospel, or that the last page was lost, these are theories of desperation. No, we can trust the manuscripts, and let the short ending stand.

But what does it *mean*, this edgy story that leaves us uneasy, bewildered? However powerful Mark's theme, its music is in a minor key. If it is spring, the memory of winter is still recent; if it is dawn, night has not long fled. It subverts the happy endings we like so much, sits uneasily alongside Easter bunnies and chocolate eggs and the mistranslated line at the end of "Thine be the glory", *No more we doubt thee*. Suppose we had never read the other Gospels, never heard of Mary in the garden or the Emmaus Road, or of Thomas, or that breakfast by the lakeside we read about this morning. Suppose all we had was Mark. What kind of Easter would that leave us?

Mark was writing for Christians at a time of persecution. To them, the words of the young man at the tomb would be deeply significant: "Do not be alarmed. He has been raised; he is not here. He is going ahead of you to Galilee." Mark's fragile, suffering church would not have misread the message that despite the resurrection, the risen Jesus wasn't coming to rescue them from their time of trial just yet. But they were to cling on to the promise that he was going ahead: "There you will see him, just as he told you." So Mark's Easter is about the Christ who is promised, even though he is not yet present. And the symbol of that promise, that certainty of meeting, is Galilee. Galilee stands for all our futures, our hopes, our longings. At the empty tomb they are hinted at, but not yet realised. Its full meaning is *eschatological*. It lies ahead. It can't be fully known for now.

Mark invites us to look again at what we mean by the truth of Easter. There are those who are agnostic about the empty tomb, but tell us that Easter means meeting and knowing the risen Christ. St Mark, however, turns that round. His reticence is not about the empty tomb but about the presence of the risen Jesus. The tomb is empty, to be sure; we affirm that he is risen. But we don't yet meet him, know him face to face. So

I *believe* that Easter is true, even if the full experience of it eludes me. Instead, I am silenced by this awesome demonstration of God's power. Easter, far from banishing my bewilderment, plunges me deeper into mystery. I need to wait for the future, for whatever "Galilee" may come to mean. Mark warns against expecting that the joyous recognitions of John's lakeside or Luke's Emmaus are for all of us all the time. But he says that there is more than one way of being an Easter people: our alleluias may be whispered rather than shouted. For him, Easter's new beginnings are promised, not yet fully present. At the empty tomb, hope is all that is left to us. But it's all we need.

The poet R. S. Thomas talks about a "fast God", reminding us of the familiar experience of entering a room the moment after someone else has just left it. This is Mark's empty tomb, a place of bafflement where understanding only comes with waiting. In the story, Mark shows himself as the great New Testament theologian of faith, what the Letter to the Hebrews calls "the assurance of things hoped for, the conviction of things not seen". Mark's Easter is about things hoped for but not seen: "he is not here". His Easter faith is in the gaps, the silences, the hints. For him, the place of God's power is an empty space, like the holy of holies at the heart of the temple. And in his story of absence and longing, I learn that most of life is lived on this threshold between emptiness and meeting, between fear and hope, between darkness and noon, between Golgotha and Galilee. I learn that it is not knowledge that counts, but faith.

So there is no happy ending in St Mark, no closure—for adult life does not consist of closures and happy endings. Rather, it consists of open ends, and risk, and crossing thresholds. That is why we need a message as stark and tough as Mark's; not for nothing is traditionally the lion among the evangelists. For it requires us to believe in a way that sheds false hopes and illusions. It calls us to obey in faith and hope the summons that first rang out by Galilee and reverberates on every page of St Mark's Gospel: *follow me*. Mark's great gift to us in spelling out the nature of true discipleship is to refuse to make it too easy. He reminds us that the empty tomb is not the answer, but the question. It leads towards the edge of things, where the unpredictable leaps out at us, and we emerge shaken, silenced, and changed.

It's a story, I think, that is peculiarly in tune with our postmodern age, with its open-endedness that makes us not spectators but participants. Like the Marys, we bring to the empty tomb our own confusion, emptiness, unbelief. We hardly know why we come, except that we are driven by some instinct that here is the clue to human life where meanings are uncovered and new possibilities open up before us, where hope, dread, wonder, fear, and longing meet. And this is Mark's faith. Sometimes, the veil is lifted, and my spirits soar; and then I can sing, "No more we doubt thee, glorious Prince of Life." But not always. Much of life has a more sombre hue. I need an Easter faith for ordinary days that can embrace my questions and my doubt as well as my joy and love. So I go back to the empty tomb and try not to run away like Mark's frightened women. Something compels me to stay, even if, as the story insists, Christ is not here. For I hear a word that penetrates fear and longing, that speaks of promise and hope, and that rolls away the stone at the portal of the human heart. It's a word we in Durham particularly cherish as a sign that a new day is dawning. What is that transfiguring word? *Galilee!*

25 April 2004
Mark 16:1–8

The Gift of Tears

*This sermon was prompted by hearing on the news about a terribly
abused child in Coventry, a place where we had once lived. Alas, such
stories are distressingly common. Inspired by Jeremiah, I wanted to
say something about weeping with those who weep. When they come
and are authentic, tears can be a true gift to others and to ourselves.*

"The one good thing about being shut in a coal-hole is it prompts reflection."
That child lived in an allegedly Christian household: her mother was a
fervent Pentecostal. Jeanette Winterson's autobiography, *Why Be Happy
When You Could Be Normal?*, tells a scarcely believable story about an
oppressive religious upbringing, fictionalised in the novel and TV series
Oranges Are Not The Only Fruit. She was, by her own account, an oddball
in her schooldays. One day her class was given the project of embroidering
a text of their choice. Jeanette chose words from Jeremiah: "the summer
is ended and we are not yet saved", given us in our first reading.

In the light of what we have learned about the cruel abuse heaped on
young Daniel in Coventry, and thinking of my grandson Isaac baptised
here three weeks ago, who, by contrast, is so much loved and cherished,
it's tempting to speak about childhood and how we love and don't love
children. But that must wait for another day. I need to stay with this
Jeremiah. There is a link, I suppose: Jeremiah, called to the impossible
task of being a prophet, pleads he is "only a child": how can he find the
words or have the courage to utter them when there is no hope that they
will be heard or understood?

"The harvest is past, the summer is ended, and we are not saved." Apt
words for the weekend of the autumn equinox. I have always found them
haunting. The summer has been glorious, but its long, golden days are
becoming a memory. The Lindisfarne Gospels will soon leave us again
for their southern exile, not to return home for many years. The flowers
that glowed in our marvellous festival are dead. Summer has too short
a lease; its light is being overtaken, and soon we shall be lighting fires in

cold, dark places. Jeremiah's autumnal farewell to good times captures the mood of fall. And maybe his elegiac outpourings of two and a half millennia ago can speak to us who also find it hard to take our leave of light-filled health or happiness or hope.

This is one of the so-called "confessions" of Jeremiah, in which this most passionate of prophets exposes something of the agony and self-doubt going on inside. This was a young man who had never sought to be a prophet, never wanted to speak out as prophets must, never contemplated the pain and misery it would bring him. "My joy is gone, grief is upon me, my heart is sick." In another place he cries out like Job, "Cursed be the day on which I was born! The day when my mother bore me, let it not be blessed! Why did I come forth from the womb to see toil and sorrow, and spend my days in shame?" And out pour the relentless questions: five of them in this short reading. "Is the Lord not in Zion? Is her King not in her? . . . Is there no balm in Gilead? Is there no physician there? Why has the health of my poor people not been restored?"

What strikes us about these cries of pain is their honesty. They don't pretend. Jeremiah is telling the truth about his condition: that it is unbearably hard to be hurt, misunderstood, in pain, in despair, and, above all, without a friend. And like others in the Hebrew Bible, he is not afraid to acknowledge the reality of dark times. Many of the psalms are in the same minor key; there are more laments in the Psalter than any other kind of psalm. It is a courageous thing to do, to turn suffering back to God and argue with him. It's what we find at the cross when Jesus cries in the words of one of the most desolate psalm laments: *Eloi, Eloi, lema sabachthani?* "My God, my God, why hast thou forsaken me?" All of life has a dark side, a night that overtakes the day, a winter that dispels summer. Sometimes we expect it, often it takes us by surprise. True religion recognises that faith is not a pain-killing escape from that shadow, but a way of facing it truthfully. Faith helps us stop pretending. The job of the church is not to sell comfort but courage. Life is hard. We need the virtue of fortitude. Faith points us in the right direction.

But Jeremiah's confessions are not just his own personal outpourings. They belong to an entire people. At the end of the sixth century BC, an ominous cloud hung over Judah, the threat of being overrun by Babylon, their overlord amassing soldiers and weapons on their borders. Those with eyes to see understood that the life they knew was at an end; ruin was imminent, and those who survived would be deported to a strange land where it was not obvious that they could ever again sing the Lord's song. Jeremiah never wavered in looking this prospect in the eyes and speaking about it as God's work, though it cost him dear. Neither did he walk away when he had spoken such hard words, but stood with his people, imploring God's mercy, yet knowing that he and they would not escape judgment. As a victim himself, his destiny embodied theirs. He talked of being a lamb led to the slaughter—precisely how he also saw Judah. To make other people's sufferings and fears your own is the mark of true ministry, *compassion*. It is the image of Jesus who emptied himself so as to take the form of a slave and share our human condition. It is how God is, who, says the passion story, always stands with us in our darkness and our pain.

Sunt lachrimae rerum: "there are tears in things", says Virgil in a beautiful but untranslatable line. This lament ends that way. "O that my head were a spring of water, and my eyes a fountain of tears, so that I might weep day and night for the slain of my poor people!" It sounds like a cry of despair. Yet the strange thing is that lament opens the way to a new perspective. It purifies the gaze, helps us see differently. The desert fathers spoke of the "gift of tears" as a kind of baptism, meaning not just what we call self-awareness, emotional intelligence, but a cleansing of the soul. At the lowest point of lament, where we have nothing else to rely on or trust in, things become clearer; and faith senses that, in ways we can't understand, God himself could be in the midst of our ordeal: a crucified God who knows pain and darkness; a God who, says our psalm, though he has his dwelling on high, yet humbles himself to behold things that are on earth; who not only sees but acts, by taking the lowly out of the dust and lifting the poor out of the mire.

Psalm laments usually end on a note of confidence, even thankfulness. There is a turning-round, a belief that we are heard. Sometimes it is feeble and tentative, barely glimpsed before it is snuffed out again, as in other laments of Jeremiah. Sometimes, it transfigures despair, as in the *miserere* psalm Jesus quotes on the cross where faith wins through to a radiant sunburst. But when we find ourselves shedding tears for the tragedy of Syria, or the victims of Nairobi, or little Daniel and so many children abused in literal or metaphorical coal-holes, or for the friend we love who has a terminal illness, or for ourselves in the fear or pain or shame that haunt us: we are in a place where prayer becomes possible. And when we are overwhelmed and can't find it in ourselves to pray, we can at least weep for others and for ourselves. We can hold out empty hands as we do in this eucharist, to receive what mercy and love want to give. This is not a happy ending, but the hard, exacting journey through the vale of soul-making that lasts a lifetime. Is there any other path to walk?

22 September 2013
Jeremiah 8:18–9:1; Psalm 113

Back to Booths!

*The elliptical reference in the opening line is to the Cathedral's
development project, Open Treasure. This focuses on the transformation
of the buildings round the cloister into exhibition spaces in which
to interpret the life of the Cathedral as a living community of
faith past and present. As this sermon suggests, buildings are
never an end in themselves; however wonderful, they must always
point beyond themselves. "Open Treasure" means the treasure
of a Christian community and the gospel it bears witness to.*

When you are embarking on an ambitious development project, it
consumes a great deal of your time and energies, as we know well, here
at the Cathedral. Nehemiah, governor of Judah, has set himself the task of
rebuilding the walls of Jerusalem, ruinous since the Babylonian invasions
over a century before. A man of energetic character who brooks no
opposition, he achieves this task despite the Machiavellian tactics of his
opponents. They allege that this huge act of reconstruction is to cover up
a conspiracy to rebel against the Persian Empire. Why build walls unless
your intention is to declare independence?

If this were all there were to the story, it would hardly be worth
telling. But the next part of the book shows that a deeper purpose lies
behind it. When the wall is finished and families have settled into their
homes, a great assembly is convened. The people tell Ezra the priest to
bring out the book of the law and read from it. For a whole morning he
reads aloud at a ceremony marked by both tears of sorrow and shouts
of thankfulness: sorrow for the years they have been alienated from this
torah, God's instruction for sound and healthy living; thankfulness to
have their covenant with God given back to them. And they see how the
renewal of buildings, temples, walls, houses is a symbol of something
deeper: the renewal of their vocation and resolve to live purposefully in
obedience to God's rule.

Nehemiah sees that the ancient book requires them to do something specific to mark their obedience. It's the autumn, the season of harvest. Nehemiah realises that, according to the law, a long-neglected festival needs to be reinstated. So he instructs everyone to go out into the fields, gather branches of whatever trees they can find, and construct leafy booths in the open air: on their housetops or in streets and courts and public squares, even in the temple precincts. Then they are to go and live in them for a week. All this the people do. The text goes out of its way to say that they did it gladly: "there was very great rejoicing."

Here's an odd thing: to celebrate the end of a building project not by occupying the newly created buildings, but by deliberately quitting them to live outside. Clearly, the people understood what this meant, because the text doesn't explain why it was important, only that it was part of being thankful. We have to look back into the Torah, the books of the law, to understand the significance of the festival of Booths. If there are gaps in the law-codes, we shall need to use our imaginations a little. Here is how I read it.

First, the feast was as an act of celebration. How better to mark the ingathering of the harvest than going out to live in the very fields where you have sweated and toiled all summer to garner the fruits of the earth? It is God's harvest, but it is also the work of human hands. There is something endearing about this command to go out and be at home in the open air. It is our natural environment, a memory of how, once upon a time, a man and a woman lived without fear or shame in a garden where the Lord God walked and enjoyed the company of his human friends. What we love about Cuthbert and Francis is that they were so much at home in the natural world. By contrast, we see around us ever more evidence of how alienated we have become from good earth, so estranged from it that we can contemplate the planet burning because of our contempt for the environment. Tabernacles reminds us how our own health and the earth's renewal depend on our learning to reconnect with the natural order, learning to treat all things living with courtesy, to "discover our place in God's creation", as the Cathedral's purpose statement puts it. It looks forward to the day when nature and humanity are reconciled and, in Isaiah's vision, the wolf dwells with the lamb, the child plays over the hole of the asp, and nothing hurts or destroys in all God's holy mountain, for the earth is filled with the knowledge of the Lord as the waters cover the sea.

Then this exercise in *al fresco* living was meant to teach the Jews something important about dependence. It's precisely at the time solid structures are completed that Nehemiah says: don't depend on these beautiful stones and beautiful buildings. Depend only on God. Let your faith in him be re-energised by having to live for a while without the securities you are getting used to again. For this was precisely how your ancestors lived in days of old: "a wandering Aramean was my father", says one of Israel's oldest creeds; nomads and fugitives in the barren wilderness for all those years they trekked, often despondently, towards the land of promise. Yet, despite their obduracy and lack of hope, God did not forget the Hebrews, but prepared a table in the wilderness for them, as Ezra puts it in his magnificent covenant-making speech in the next chapter. Tabernacles was a way of going back to that story, rekindling the memory of far-off days when the Hebrews had no houses, no temple, no abiding city. "You shall dwell in booths seven days, so that your generations may know that I made the children of Israel dwell in booths when I brought them up out of the land of Egypt." It reminded them how life's changes and chances threw them on the mercy of the covenant. It told them not to vest ultimate security in anything they could see or touch. It threw them on the mercy and goodness of God. We no doubt expect to learn this lesson in other ways. But learn it we must, if faith means anything.

And there is a third theme running through this observance. How often does the Torah instil the habit of being generous and compassionate towards the wanderer and stranger, the outcast, the disadvantaged, the poor. The more prosperous and successful you become, the easier it is not simply to forget those who need your help, but actively to choose not to remember them. The feast of Booths is a kind of enforced homelessness, having to live in temporary accommodation, discover what it is like to live in the cold and the wet and the dark. When people with a social conscience decide to live for a week on unemployment benefit, perhaps sleeping rough in parks or doorways, it's easy to disparage this as the token gesture of the comfortably off: *acting* a part rather than truly *taking* part. But this is what Tabernacles calls the people to do. I imagine that it is physically and emotionally costly to live in a booth for a week. I have never done it. I like to think the Jews of Nehemiah's day discovered that by taking up roles and acting out rituals their meanings become more real, are understood in new ways. That leads to the transformation of attitudes and perspectives, in this case a deeper sympathy with and compassion for those for whom living in streets and squares and the open country is not a matter of joy and will not come to an end next week.

The renewal of a people's mind and heart is what Nehemiah wanted to achieve. He knew that building the walls was the easy part. Much harder to rebuild a community on the values of justice, loving-kindness, and truth. This great communal celebration of an ancient festival was only the beginning. But it sowed the seeds of the future when, under pressure and at times of terrible persecution, Judaism's covenant would remain steadfast to the God of Abraham, Isaac, and Jacob, who had called them into this privileged life and promised that in their seed all the peoples of the world would bless themselves. In Jesus, Christians believe that promise to be coming true. This is why we pray as he taught us, "thy kingdom come", and look with eager longing for the day of God when the rich promises foreshadowed in one of the old pilgrim feasts become nothing less than a new heaven and new earth.

20 October 2013
Nehemiah 8:9–end

Intimations and Announcements

In the Christmas story, Joseph isn't forgotten, exactly, but I don't think he is given enough recognition for his extraordinary courage in staying with the pregnant Mary. His "be it to me according to your word" was every bit as heroic as hers. This sermon explores the spirituality of taking such life-changing risks and what happens when we run away from them, as we so often do.

Among the people who walked in darkness was Joseph. He knew the bewilderment of the dark when paths were obscured, the secrets the night hours held. He had dreams. We know it was night because the text says that "Joseph awoke from sleep". If your name is Joseph, it is assumed that you have Important Dreams. In these two opening chapters of St Matthew, he dreams no fewer than three times. Like his namesake in Genesis, these dreams not only touch the core of his personal life but the direction of history itself. By doing three times what the angel says, he makes sure that Jesus is born into a family that can care for him and is kept safe from the dangers that threaten the Infant King.

There is a whole mystical theology in this story of darkness and dreaming. Ancient wisdom was right to prize dreams. We should learn from it. We don't pay nearly enough attention to what happens when we let go of rationality and intellect, and allow ourselves to be opened up to new dimensions of awareness and the Spirit's work in our unconscious selves. The great French poet and mystic Charles Péguy addresses the night as a friend who shrouds us "in silence and shadow and in healthy forgetfulness of the mortal anxiety of the day". Self-abandonment in the journey into God is a risky path to take. But the teachers and writers of all the world's spiritual traditions tell us that if we are to know God, there has to be a process of "unknowing", letting go of all that we can understand and name, in order to cross the thresholds of new and unknown horizons.

That is why faith is faith. We can expect to be unsettled when we leave the safety of harbour and strike out across the wide ocean of faith, where knowledge stops short. So Joseph has our sympathy. To be faced with the news that his betrothed is carrying a child that is not his will have shaken him to the core. In a long, dramatic poem by W. H. Auden, *A Christmas Oratorio*, there is a section called "The Temptation of St Joseph". Auden has the chorus question Joseph, articulating the argument raging inside him. There is Mary's story, and there is what everyone else will say, knowingly pointing the finger, putting two and two together. How is the poor man to know? We imagine him swinging this way and that. Like Abraham going into a far country, tormented by the thought that God is commanding him to bind his beloved son Isaac for sacrifice, this is a terrible dilemma: divorce her and let honour be saved—his own honour, that is; or believe somehow that God might be in this, however absurd it seems?

What matters for annunciations is what we do next. "Joseph did as the angel of the Lord commanded him; he took Mary as his wife." It says *commanded*, but if Joseph is at all like us, that word conceals the complex, twisting path towards knowing what is required. In the scriptures, patriarchs and prophets, seers and apostles are told to do strange things and go to strange places, pluck up and destroy, build and plant. It is the story of the Messiah himself, from the temptations of the wilderness to the ordeal of Gethsemane. And human experience tells us that it is our story too. And not simply in the big decisions of life where we long for illumination, for unmistakable clarity about the direction of travel: whom shall we marry? What will our life's work be? Where shall we live? What shall we believe? What values will shape and guide us? In a thousand lesser ways, which sometimes turn out not to be lesser, we find we are baffled not so much by the absence of annunciations as how to recognise them when they come, and how to test and trust them.

Anyone who has taken up what we call a vocation to ordained ministry or the religious life, or to a role in a caring profession such as healthcare, education, or social support, understands something of this language of discernment, as we call it. But we should not privilege some forms of human activity over others. If we believe that all of human life matters to God, then it follows that we can all expect to be faced by annunciations that have the potential to change our lives, as they did Joseph's. And even if we did not know at the time that it was such an intimation from another world, we shall probably know it with hindsight and tell a story about how we said either "yes" or "no" to what the angel said. In a fine poem by Denise Levertov, she contrasts the "yesses" and "noes" of the choices we make, the relief we can feel when we decline a summons to take a risk, how we are not necessarily punished for it but yet life is subtly narrowed as a result: "the gates close, the pathway vanishes."

So the question for each of us must be: how we can retune our ears to listen better, anoint our eyes to see with greater insight, prepare our hearts to say "yes", by recognising God's time when it comes. That time may come Moses-like as earthquake, wind, or fire, though more often it is the still, small voice that it was for Elijah, or the whisper of the angel of both agony and ecstasy who visited Joseph and Mary. It may come through the scriptures or in the eucharist; it may come through our prayers or our dreams, in art or poetry, in the silence of remote places, or by listening and talking to those who know us and love us.

It's never easy. If the annunciation stories we hear before Christmas tell us anything, they reveal just how difficult it is to discern the voice of God calling to us amid the babble of noises off that distract and confuse us. Often we get it wrong, or find reasons for not paying attention, or throw up every obstacle we can to turn in another direction: "I am only a child"; "I am a man of unclean lips"; "How can this be, for I am a virgin?"; "Let this cup pass from me". If we turn away, God does not smite us, or stop loving us; but a path vanishes. Yet have the confidence that providence gives us, learn to listen to and trust our instincts, and things miraculously shift within us. We walked in darkness but begin to see a light. We sense a destiny, and that opens our mouths to say yes, however tentatively. A door opens that no one can shut. We know he is Immanuel, God with us.

In this season of Advent, we ask ourselves once more: how will the birth of a Child touch us this year? What new insight will Christmas bring? And if the Infant should knock at the door not just begging our shelter, but bringing some new work that only we can do, what then? It could be a disconcerting Christmas, but more wonderful too. Sidney Royse Lysaght's poem haunts me at this time of year. Let me end with it:

He wakes desires you never may forget.
He shows you stars you never saw before,
He makes you share with him, for evermore,
The burden of the world's divine regret.
How wise you were to open not! and yet
How poor if you should turn him from the door.

22 December 2013
Matthew 1:18–25

"The Dangerous Edge of Things"

*I had to read some of Browning's longer poems at school, and even
at that age was struck by his unflinching way of facing complexity
and paradox. We may want to think of Galilee as the hymn writer
does, beguiled by "sabbath rest" and "calm of hills above". But
it wasn't like that in Jesus' day and it is not like that now.*

"Our interest's on the dangerous edge of things," says Bishop Blougram
in Robert Browning's great poem. Paradoxically, we human beings are as
fascinated as we are repelled by danger. We are increasingly risk-averse,
more and more obsessed with our own safety and protection, less and less
inclined to have real adventures or allow our children to have them—yet at
the same time we celebrate and even envy, from the comfort of the fireside
or bed, those who scale heights and plumb depths, who face extremes or
penetrate remote places where old maps say there are dragons and it is
unwise to go. The internal landscape of the human soul has its dangerous
edges and scope for adventure too, as Gerard Manley Hopkins knew:

> O the mind, mind has mountains; cliffs of fall
> Frightful, sheer, no-man-fathomed. Hold them cheap
> May who ne'er hung there.

Most good stories provide the frisson of risk and danger. So today, St
John's Gospel obligingly drives the story out towards two dangerous
edges, places on the margins of existence where people are exposed to
basic human fears.

The first of these dangerous edges is the mountain: specifically, the
uplands that form the eastern shore of Galilee opposite Tiberias, what
we now know as the foothills of the occupied territory of the Golan
Heights. While this is grassy terrain, not yet desert, it holds risk because
it is on the margins of civilisation, a kind of liminal threshold to the
wilderness where the securities of ordinary life collapse and existence

has to be fought for. In the wild places, says the mythological tradition picked up by St Mark, lurk angels, demons, and wild animals. This is why Jesus underwent his ordeal of initiation in the desert, for it is a place of truth and self-discovery. And now it is the crowd that is facing the truth of its own hunger and wishing that stones could be turned into bread. For St John, there is a memory in this story, for had not their ancestors, condemned to wander the lonely desert sands for forty years, demanded of Moses, "Can God spread a table in the wilderness?" And perhaps an older memory of creation when the dry land became fertile and food-bearing to sustain the life formed out of the lifeless dust of the ground?

The second dangerous edge is the sea, specifically the waters of deceptive Galilee, normally so placid, that can be whipped up into a frenzy in an instant by ferocious blasts of wind slamming down from the snowy heights of Hermon into the rift valley of the Jordan. Like the wilderness, the storm is another dangerous edge where life clings on against the probability that it will be overwhelmed. Here, again, mythology locates sea monsters and demons, for the Hebrews feared the sea even more than they feared the desert. They told stories, as ancient civilisations did, of Rahab and Leviathan and the great primordial battle in which they were slain and the floods subdued so that life could appear. And again for St John, there are archetypal Old Testament memories in Jesus walking on the sea in the darkness and speaking the words I AM; Moses leading the Hebrews through the waters of the Red Sea; and, behind that, an older story of how the Spirit of God had swept over the face of the chaotic deep that was *tohu wa vohu*, "without form and void", before there was light and the dry land appeared.

Two stories, then, of how Jesus delivers people from ordeals at the dangerous edge of things. He feeds a crowd where there is no source of food. He delivers his disciples from a storm that threatens to engulf them. Like the first two Gospels, St John sees these episodes are closely connected; indeed, his story of the storm on the lake is folded into the great sixth chapter of the Gospel, where the single theme is the feeding of the crowd and Jesus proclaiming himself as the living bread from heaven. And no doubt the connection John wants us to draw is how God has the power to rescue even at the dangerous edge. Jesus is another Moses, the longed-for prophet who is now here to deliver his people through water and nourish them with manna in the wilderness. Jesus is the embodiment of the Creator, at whose word food is brought forth and the storm stilled. Perhaps there are echoes in this story of wilderness-and-water of how Jesus, like Moses, underwent ordeals of water and wilderness in his baptism, fasting, and temptation; and there are resonances too, surely, to the sacraments of the church, for we too are saved through the water of baptism and fed with the living bread of the eucharist.

But underneath the many layers of today's gospel, there is a simple truth about trust and faith in God. When a previous Canon of Westminster arrived in Durham as Bishop in 1890, he had already written a great commentary on St John's Gospel that many still regard as a classic of New Testament scholarship. I mention it because today, 27 July, is kept in the Church of England calendar as his commemoration: Bishop Brooke Foss Westcott, whom Durham remembers with great affection for his commitment to the poor of this diocese and for his mediation in the bitter coal strike of 1892. Westcott says of our gospel reading: "Effects are produced at variance with our ideas of quantity and quality. That which is small becomes great. That which is heavy moves on the surface of the water. Contrary elements yield at a divine presence. Both signs prepare the way for new thoughts of Christ, of his sustaining, preserving, guiding power."

So the first insight of today's gospel is the invitation to look again at what is big and what is small and consider how they are redefined, resized, by faith in God. In the first story, there is a great crowd and a great open space, and a great and primitive human need: hunger. Yet the text emphasises the small things: the boy, the five barley loaves, the two fish, the twelve baskets with the fragments gathered up afterwards. In the second story, there is a great sea and a great storm and a great darkness and another great, raw, primitive human experience: fear. And again the text highlights the small things: a fragile boat, its few occupants pitted against these huge elemental forces. In both stories, deliverance comes, not in big demonstrations of power but through what is humble and scarcely to be noticed, the small things that the prophet says we must never despise. There is a lovely cameo of the incarnation in Jesus being among the people and distributing the few loaves and fishes; and again in his coming across the water and getting into the boat with the disciples so that together they reach the dry land where they would be.

This is the way of St John's God, who steps low enough to become flesh and blood as we are.

And a second insight from our story is to reflect that however lost I feel in the face of life's hungers and storms, their power to hurt and to harm is limited. For faith understands that there is another power at work in this world. It is the power of love. For love, nothing is ever lost or wasted. Love sits with us in our places of need and gathers up the broken fragments of our lives. Love journeys with us through the storms that terrify and says to us "do not be afraid". Love is that traveller unknown who is always at our side in life's dangerous edges where we are unprotected and exposed. It is precisely here that love comes to us, that breadth and length and height and depth of which the epistle to the Ephesians speaks so beautifully, the love of Christ that passes knowledge. We learn what this means when there is nowhere else to turn, no hiding place left, no use in pretending any more that we can help ourselves.

So the question this gospel puts to us today is, quite simply: will we, dare we, trust this power of love we glimpse in Jesus? Will we allow his presence to transfigure our way of being in the world, make us less afraid, less mistrustful, less cowardly as Christians, embody a vision of Christianity that is as generous, fearless, and free as love itself? To hold out our hands this morning and receive the living bread is to say yes to this mysterious yet wonderful God whose works are often strange to us, whose silences we fear, whose words can make us tremble, yet who beckons us with love. To say yes to him is the act of faith that matters. It defines Christianity, the faith Kierkegaard said had never yet been realised in the history of the human race. Could we, could I, begin to realise it? Every eucharist is another opportunity to try the experiment of faith. For we walk the dangerous edge with safety when we know love's nature and love's name.

27 July 2003
Ephesians 3:14–21; John 6:1–21

Catching the Eye of Love

*I was goaded into preaching this sermon, as you will see. I had
been made to think—always a good thing. I won't "out" the
person who challenged me: he is now with his Maker. It helped
me to get beneath the service of Mark's brilliant but elusive
gospel and to ask myself why he never says that God loves us,
only that we must love God. Are we uncomfortable to learn that
there is only one human being that Mark says Jesus loved?*

Some years ago I was preaching in another place from St Mark's Gospel.
It was Advent, and the text was one of the fiercest passages in the Bible,
where Jesus speaks about the cataclysms that will engulf the world before
the Son of Man comes. I did my best to open up a difficult passage and
try to make sense of apocalypse for contemporary believers. Afterwards,
a well-known writer whose books many of you will certainly have read
came up to me and rather stuffily said: "Michael, I didn't hear the central
word of the Christian vocabulary mentioned once in your sermon."

Well, the fault, dear Jim, lies not in the preacher but in the text. You
will not find that central word "love" anywhere in Mark chapter 13. And
if you're looking to hear that God is love, I'm afraid you won't find that
anywhere in Mark either, nor in Matthew or Luke for that matter. Only in
one short passage do you find Mark making anything of the word. There,
it's not that God loves us, but that we must love God and our neighbour as
ourselves. To hear about God's love for us, you have to turn to the writings
of St John, his incomparable Gospel and his three letters. And it's true
that there is no greater affirmation in all religion than to know that God
so loved the world that he gave his only begotten Son. This is why, for me,
St John is the most important and original writer in the New Testament.
He, above all the others, speaks the word of love most directly into the
longings of human hearts in this and every age. He gets to the very core
of Jesus' message. He uncovers the heart of Christianity.

Of course, love can exist even if the word is absent. And we continue our journey through this year of St Mark with amazement at the Second Gospel's freshness, its vitality, its toughness, how it cuts to the chase and challenges our easy assumptions. Here is the rich young man who wants so much to follow Jesus and find eternal life. Surely he will be the model disciple, this wide-eyed youth who has loved the Torah and kept the commandments so well. We need to remember that this central section of St Mark focuses on what it means to be a good disciple. Mark does this by highlighting the failures of those close to Jesus: they couldn't grasp his mission, argued about who was greatest, failed in the basic tasks of teaching and healing. Will this man outshine them? Will he say yes, leave everything behind to become a disciple? Well, sadly, no. With unnerving accuracy, Jesus exposes his Achilles heel. "'You lack one thing; go, sell what you own, and give the money to the poor, and you will have treasure in heaven; then come, follow me.' When he heard this he was shocked and went away grieving, for he had many possessions."

But there's a little detail in the way Mark tells the story that we mustn't miss. As he tells of how the man's face fell at the cost of following Jesus, he says: "Jesus, looking at him, *loved him*." There is that word, so rare in Mark's Gospel that it leaps out of the page at us. It's the only time in the synoptic gospels that it's used of God or Jesus. Mark never says that Jesus loved his mother. He does not say that he loved Peter, James or even John, or the Canaanite woman, or Jairus' daughter, or the thieves at the cross. Only this young man. The Jesus of St Mark catches his eye and knows that there is a charge, a connection, perhaps like the woman with the haemorrhage who touches him in the crowd where again, says Mark, Jesus *knows*, It was a meeting we can confidently say the young man never forgot. I wonder whether he may have been the young man who follows Jesus when he is arrested but runs away naked, leaving his loincloth behind; and the young man dressed in a white robe who is in the empty tomb on Easter morning. But in today's story, he wasn't the only one who was sorrowful. Jesus goes on to lament how hard it is for the rich to enter the kingdom of God. And beneath these words is the undertow of sadness that this young man had turned his back not just on the kingdom but on Jesus too.

It seems that this detail was an embarrassment later on. Matthew and Luke both tell the same story and follow Mark's account closely. But they leave out this reference to Jesus loving the man. Is this because it wouldn't do to have Jesus' heart going out to someone so simply and directly, like the king's son Jonathan loving the gifted but wayward David? Do we already see Jesus being taken away from us, removed from the ordinary world of tender yet messy human encounters, and elevated into a safer, more impassive realm, untroubled by the complexities of attachment and loss? As the iconography of the church develops over the Middle Ages, you see how the face of Christ becomes increasingly regal, the *Pantocrator* whose divine gaze scans the entire universe but captures no one in particular. And even when the conventions begin to be loosened at the Renaissance, paintings like Piero della Francesca's *Resurrection* have the risen Lord staring serenely yet inscrutably out of the canvas, not *at* you so much as *into* you and *through* you, in a perspective that is disconcerting, as if the realm in which his gaze meets ours is far removed from the flesh-and-blood world of the dazed soldiers by the empty tomb.

We need to remember the wider setting of this painful encounter. This story of the rich young man, like all these cameos of failed discipleship, is framed by episodes in which a deaf and then a blind man are healed. It's Mark's way of saying that turning away, as the rich man did, is a way of *not* seeing, *not* hearing, *not* understanding, *not* grasping hold of what is offered when Jesus comes to find us. And it also comes in the setting of the three predictions of the passion, where Mark underlines that it's the destiny of Jesus to suffer and die. So discipleship, learning to *see* and *hear*, to take our true bearings and find our direction in life, means losing our life to find it. It means shedding wealth, the love of power, ambition, success, whatever it is we build our existence on, abandoning them all for the sake of something greater: what Jesus calls the kingdom of God. "When Jesus calls a man," said Bonhoeffer, "he bids him come and die." I wish I could soften today's gospel and say that it doesn't mean that. But I can't make it mean anything else.

So where is the good news? Not so much in the rewards Jesus promises to those who follow him—though they are real. More, I think, in that wonderful reassurance that what is impossible for mortals like the rich young man is possible with God. But what lifts my spirit most of all is that telling detail, this unique occurrence of the L-word in relation to how Jesus dealt with human beings. Jesus didn't love a successful disciple. He loved a flawed, broken man for whom the cost of following was too much. He loved the failure for whom it was all too hard. He loved the man who wanted so much to say "yes", but couldn't bring himself to do it. So I dare to hope that he did not despair as that nameless but remembered young man turned sadly away and went back to what he knew. And I dare to hope that he does not despair of us. It is enough that there are those miraculous moments, even after a lifetime of disappointment and failure, when he comes to us again, and his gaze catches ours, and "we see him when we greet him, and bless when we understand".

Oh, and Jim, if you're reading this on the web, I make that seventeen occurrences of the word you missed last time.

15 October 2006
Mark 10:17–31

Transfigured Love

It's probably important to follow the last sermon with this one.

St Valentine's Day, and a gift to the preacher, for our thoughts turn to love: love given, love received, love longed for and love unrequited, love disappointed and love fulfilled, the memory of love and the hope of love, "love's endeavour, love's expense", "immortal love for ever full", "the love that moves the sun and the other stars", God's love. And as I speak like this I ask myself whether I want to add to the millions of words spoken about love down the centuries, whether I *can* add anything. Well, perhaps I should try. For today is not only St Valentine's Day, but the Sunday before Lent, Quinquagesima. In the *Book of Common Prayer*, "charity", or love, is today's word in the epistle reading and the collect that is based on it, one of the most beautiful in our liturgy. The reading is Paul's great hymn to love in the thirteenth chapter of the First Letter to the Corinthians: "now abideth faith, hope, charity, these three; but the greatest of these is charity." The collect prays: "send thy Holy Ghost and pour into our hearts that most excellent gift of charity, the very bond of peace and of all virtues without which whosoever liveth is counted dead before thee." *Caritas* never fails because it is divine.

This theme of love made the perfect portal for Lent, and I miss the Prayer Book on this day more than any other. If Lent is to mean anything, it should surely be that our love for God is reawakened, or rather, our awareness of how God so loves us. Lent should be a journey in love, a new discovery of it each day as we walk towards the cross and resurrection of Jesus. It should be a daily transfiguration, a life-changing encounter with the beloved Son whose voice we have heard and whom we love because he first loved us. Without love we are nothing, says St Paul. But once touched by it, we glimpse glory, we see into the face of the divine. Life is not the same after that. What we once thought it was worth burning out for we are learning to see in a different way. Like the journey of the magi and their return home, we are no longer at ease with these old gods. The epiphany we have glimpsed has lit up something within us, made us see the world in a new way. We feel and know that we want to turn away from dead things to seek after the living God. It is disquieting and disturbing; but it is transfiguring too.

Among many guides to the landscape of love profane and love divine, let me draw on just one. He was one of the most fervent lovers in history, and also one of the profoundest interpreters of love's meaning. That man wrote: "Give me a lover, he will feel that of which I speak; give me one who longs, who hungers, who is a thirsty pilgrim in this wilderness, sighing for the springs of his eternal homeland; give me such a man: he will know what I mean." He is depicted in a stained glass window in the north transept of this Cathedral as one of the four doctors of the church: St Augustine, Bishop of the North African city of Hippo Regius at the turn of the fifth century. Augustine is usually blamed for the church's obsession with sex. As an Augustinian, I want to defend him. Yes, he crusaded against the degrading lusts he saw all around him in the dying Roman empire, in thrall to violence and bloodshed as well as to sex, and this led him to think that all humanity was locked into a system that was fundamentally disordered and from which it could never save itself. This is what we call original sin, and my own experience of life and what I know of myself does not lead me to question it.

Yet this is precisely where Augustine's awareness of the beauty of God shines as a transfiguring vision. We find in Augustine's writings a spirituality of love that is joyful, celebratory, and rich. His conversion in AD 386 and the part played in it by his mother Monica's prayers is perhaps as important a story for western Christianity as the conversion of St Paul, for these two were, in many ways, its theological architects. But Augustine's *Confessions* was not written for theologians, but for fellow travellers on the journey of faith. This is what makes it one of the greatest classics of spiritual autobiography. In it, he probes to the depths of his experience, trying to make sense of it in the light of his discovery of God's grace and of how even the most disordered of human loves can be a pointer to the eternal love of the Creator and Redeemer.

For Augustine, erotic attraction was an intoxicating addiction that possessed him. Yet this craving was married to other hungers: for human companionship and love; for beauty, truth and goodness; for God. He longed to be happy, to find rest for his conflicted soul. He longed for a homecoming. It all sounds very contemporary.

> Late have I loved you, beauty so old and so new, late have I loved you. And see, you were within and I was in the external world and sought you there, and in my unlovely state I plunged into those lovely created things which you made. You were with me, and I was not with you. The lovely things kept me far from you, though if they did not have their existence in you, they would have no existence at all. You called and cried out loud and shattered my deafness. You were radiant and resplendent, you put to flight my blindness. You were fragrant, and I drew in my breath and now pant after you. I tasted you, and I feel but hunger and thirst for you. You touched me, and I am set on fire to attain the peace which is yours.
>
> *Saint Augustine,* **Confessions,** *tr. Henry Chadwick (OUP, 1998), p. 201*

Agape and *Eros* married at last.

In the *Confessions,* we touch a human being in the vale of soul-making, like us: a man who is on the way to becoming an individual. That means not only knowing who you are but also how you *came to be* who you are. Kierkegaard said that life has to be lived forward but understood backward. Jung, who often quoted that remark, said that things which lay hidden in shadow in the first half of life, as the sun rises, are lit up from a different perspective as the sun begins to set in the second half of life. This is Augustine reading his early life in the light of what he now knows to be God's loving purposes. For we carry our past within us like geological layers, like the rings in a tree. How we remember and the story we tell of our memories is a necessary part of understanding who we are and who God is and how to love. "And then he thinks he knows / the hills where his life rose and the sea where it goes", wrote Matthew Arnold. To see, to know, to understand, and then to love: these are the only things in life that ultimately matter.

Augustine looks back on the intense experience he and his mother shared as they gazed out of the window that far-off day at Ostia. "At that moment we extended our reach and in a flash of mental energy attained the eternal wisdom which abides beyond all things. If only it could last! . . . Is not this what it means to say 'Enter into the joy of your Lord'?" *If only it could last!* Just what the disciples sighed on the mountain of transfiguration as they looked out of their narrow window on to heaven itself, when, in a flash of glory, eternal wisdom and purpose were disclosed and they looked upon the face of God. And then the window is shut again and the glory fades, and all that is left is its memory—but no, not all, for in remembered glory is a new impetus of hope and joy and love. For Augustine, this ravishing moment was the clue to understanding his chaotic needs and longings. It was the marvellous discovery of gospel simplicity and purity of heart when love finds its true destiny in God alone. "You have made us for yourself, and our hearts are restless till they find their rest in you."

Happiness, homecoming, rest: Lent could be all these things, and God knows we long for them. But maybe they are not far from any of us. The tasks of Lent are love's work: prayer and fasting and acts of charity, a yearly door that is open to us so that we can simplify our lives, turn away from sin, learn once more to be faithful to Christ. For Easter is beckoning, the sunrise when love's redeeming work is done, where with unveiled faces we see the glory of the risen Lord and know it is good to be here.

14 February 2010
2 Corinthians 3:12–4:2; Luke 9:28–36

Mary Magdalen

This colourful, wayward woman who features so prominently in the gospels has always appealed to me. She speaks to my flaws and failings and points to the unconditional way Jesus receives us and transforms our lives. As the first witness of the resurrection, she is also a powerful emblem of the role of women in the church. When I preached this, the Church of England was not yet ordaining women to the episcopate. Now, thankfully, that Rubicon has been crossed. But to achieve true gender equality in the Church will still be a long journey.

Poor Mary Magdalen! Was ever a saint more maligned? Confusion began to surround her very early on. It was clear from the New Testament that she was a woman whom Jesus had delivered from evil spirits and who came to love and follow him. She was present at the crucifixion, and was the first to find the empty tomb and meet the risen Christ on Easter morning. But then came the questions. Was she the notorious prostitute who washed the feet of Jesus with her hair and anointed him for his passion, or Mary the sister of Martha and Lazarus at Bethany? And beyond the New Testament there were further mysteries. Early legends had her in Ephesus with St John, dying in Constantinople; but it was also said that Mary sailed with several others from Palestine across the Mediterranean to France, and landed at the place called Les Saintes Maries de la Mer. She went into holy seclusion in Provence and died there. So where were her relics? This was the subject of one of the most celebrated rows in medieval France. Provence claimed them; but then, miraculously, they popped up in Burgundy several hundred miles to the north, at Vézelay, where they built the wondrous Basilica of the Madeleine in her honour at precisely the same time as this cathedral was going up.

In modern times, her story continues to intrigue and fascinate. In Scorsese's film of Nikos Kazantzakis' book *The Last Temptation of Christ* she is the power of the flesh Jesus must resist if he is to be true to his divinity. That has more to be said for it than the nonsense that has her as the woman with whom Jesus had sex and who carried his bloodline into history, a secret folded into the story of the Holy Grail—*san graal* or *sang réal*—the fantasy millions have fallen for through *The Da Vinci Code*. More thoughtfully, Tim Rice in *Jesus Christ Superstar* artfully portrays her as the conflicted woman perplexed by the passionate feelings Jesus arouses in her: part spiritual, part erotic. "I don't know how to love him," she sings in one of the best songs in the show: "I've had so many men before." When Judas tries to remonstrate with Jesus, "What does a man like you want with a woman like that?" he replies intriguingly, that Mary is giving him what he needs "right here and now". To some interpreters, she is the archetype of the fallen woman at its most threatening to men: libidinous, teasing, seductive, dangerous. To feminists, she is the symbol of the liberated woman who courageously found her own voice and challenged patriarchy. In the spiritual tradition, she is the model penitent and contemplative. She crosses so many boundaries: theology, literature, gender studies, cultural history, social anthropology, psychoanalysis. Of the making of books about her there is no end.

We might ask on her feast day why this is. I think we can point to a number of reasons. For one thing, she stands out in the Gospels as a woman in a world of men, not uniquely, by any means, but more sharply drawn than any of the others, even the Blessed Virgin herself. You imagine her wearing red and purple, like she does in Caravaggio, striding across the gospel story saying "notice me!" For another, her obvious closeness to Jesus raises questions about his emotional life and the part normal human affect played in his psyche. An age absorbed by sex is bound to be obsessed by such matters, and even if we reply that whatever we say is mere speculation, the tide of speculation will still be unstoppable. That may not be a bad thing, because what it tells us is the continuing power of Jesus himself to fascinate and intrigue us even in the twenty-first century. And finally, she is the woman with an altogether unique role in Christian history. She loved Jesus, though not perhaps more than others loved him, especially John. But she was given a privilege denied even to him: to be the first witness of the resurrection and to take the news of Easter to the other disciples. For feminist theologians (and I count myself one of them), her role as "apostle to the apostles" is a powerful argument for the ordination of women as priests and bishops.

So who is she to us? What makes her so memorable is her colourful unconventionality. She doesn't fit the image of the subservient woman in the ancient world. Her relationships were unorthodox, her lifestyle unapproved. She would have struggled to say dutifully, as the other Mary did, "Behold the handmaid of the Lord; be it unto me according to thy word." She seems to subvert all the norms, challenge all the stereotypes. And what is most astonishing, perhaps, is that Jesus seems to affirm her subversive personality. Not once does he criticise Mary as he did others of his inner circle: Peter, James, John, and even his own mother. And she is one of the three women who, in today's reading from St Mark, finds the tomb empty, and to whom the announcement of the resurrection is entrusted—and this when one of the other Easter narratives specifically anticipates how the resurrection message will be ridiculed as just so much idle gossip, exactly the kind of thing women are supposed to be prone to, according to the text. In Mark's spare, understated resurrection story, no one else, and specifically, no man, sees the empty tomb. Why put the story of the resurrection at such risk? Why not suppress the awkward fact of her being the key witness of the resurrection, when the story would have been much more credible had it been Peter or John? Above all, why, of all people, have her sent to tell the others about the resurrection in a role that is nothing short of apostolic?

Maybe because the whole project of redemption is *God's* risk. Will it be believed, received, acted upon? Maybe God himself cannot know the answer; but in faith he sends Jesus because that is all he can do to win the human race. It begins with wayward Mary, the first witness to the resurrection. That word "witness" can sound passive, the onlooker who sees or observes, but is disengaged, doesn't get involved. Yet the Easter story portrays her as the exact opposite of this. She is the passionately committed witness for whom seeing, believing, acclaiming, loving, and following all merge in one great "yes" that transforms her entire life. In Greek, a witness is a "martyr", that is, someone who is so totally at one with the story they tell that they are willing to pay the price of suffering and death. The willingness is all. When Jesus calls her by name in the garden, *Mariam,* she knows that she is alive again, ransomed, healed, restored, forgiven. *Rabbouni!* she cries—and in that moment, a lifetime of passion and pain, search and longing, hunger, fear, and hope is gathered up. It's perhaps the greatest recognition scene in human history, for she recognises him on behalf of the human race, on behalf of *us*.

How shall we in our day bear witness to Christ? I doubt if the reticent, fearful, colourless character of so much organised religion will cut much ice. Why don't we try being passionate for once, as if we believed that the resurrection of Jesus changes everything? This isn't a matter of formulaic answers; rather, it's about giving a reason for the hope that is within us, as the New Testament says. Hope is everything. To say yes to Jesus and yes to life is where hope began for Mary. It is where it can begin again for us.

22 July 2007
John 20:1-2, 11-18

Part 5: Common Grace

In all cathedrals the arts play a big part in mediating spiritual awareness. They are among the gifts of "common grace", reflecting the capacity of the created world to become "sacramental", a window through which ultimate reality is glimpsed. For me, Durham's music has been a wonderful gift, and I have regularly preached on music-related themes. But common grace is everywhere: in every aspect of justice, truth, and beauty, and in the God-givenness of human relationships.

Whitsun and Wisdom

G. K. Chesterton, lost in a book on a train journey and oblivious to the passing of time, found himself more obviously lost when his train reached an unfamiliar and alien destination. So he telegraphed his wife with the message: "Am in Wolverhampton. Where ought I to be?" History doesn't record whether he ever got a reply. But even in Wolverhampton this deeply Christian man could see the hand of providence at work: providence in the strict sense that, in all the changes and chances of life, God moves in a mysterious way. On a better day he wrote,

> You say grace before meals. All right. But I say
> grace before the play and the opera,
> and grace before the concert and the pantomime,
> and grace before I open the book,
> and grace before sketching and painting, swimming,
> fencing, boxing, walking, playing, dancing,
> and grace before I dip pen in the ink.

This kind, generous presence of God in our ordinary days is what theologians call "common grace". It's more than a belief, rather an experience of how the world is, a recognition that the God who created this world as an act of love and placed us in it continues to uphold, sustain, and provide for it. In particular, we see his creative image expressed in human imagination, inventiveness, knowledge, craftsmanship, and skill. And whenever we see it, we should give thanks: "say grace".

A long Old Testament tradition sees in the creation and ordering of the world the hand of wisdom. Our reading today portrays divine wisdom as a noble lady who has been God's handmaid from the beginning. It was by an act of wisdom that creation sprang into being, and through her all-pervasive presence and power the world is constantly nurtured and sustained. And, say the wisdom texts of the Old Testament, if we will befriend this Lady Wisdom and live by her precepts, we will ourselves gain understanding and insight into the complex operations of the world in which we live. Wisdom, in this sense, is *insight, awareness.* Our passage lists "the alterations of the solstices and the changes of the seasons, the cycles of the year and the constellations of the stars, the natures of animals and the thoughts of human beings; both what is secret and what is manifest": science and philosophy, and, in other passages, technology, politics, and art—the only begetter of these things and their teacher is Lady Wisdom, "a breath of the power of God, and a pure emanation of the power of the Almighty".

There is a medieval church on the shore of Lake Chiemsee in Bavaria that has a remarkable capital depicting the Holy Trinity on one of its columns. The Father stands above and behind, presiding; in front of him stands the Son; and nearest to us, held by the arms of both Father and Son, surprise, surprise, a *lady*: not the Blessed Virgin but the Holy Spirit, depicted as *Hagia Sophia,* Lady Wisdom, moving out towards and embracing the world, bringing the creative, redemptive love of God to the heart of creation. It's an extraordinarily bold sculpture; and yet squarely within a theological tradition that sees the Spirit as the feminine aspect of God as both mother and midwife of the world. Perhaps there's an unconscious memory of the creation story of Genesis, where the Spirit of God "hovers" over the face of the deep; the Hebrew word suggests a dove brooding over her eggs so as to hatch the precious life they carry within them.

On Whit Sunday, we traditionally focus on the gift of the Holy Spirit to the disciples as Christ's resurrection gift and presence, empowering them and us to bear witness to him and make known the good news of his kingdom, as Peter is depicted as doing in our New Testament reading from Acts. This divine energy at work in ordinary human lives seemed, to those who experienced it, nothing less than miraculous: they were "cut to the heart", says the text. But the Old Testament paints this on to a much larger canvas. It recalls us to an insight that is easily lost: that the Holy Spirit, Lady Wisdom, is our companion in the ordinary experiences of life as well as the extraordinary. She is the author of this common grace by which, in a thousand ways each day, we subsist and live and grow. She is the giver of those gifts that sustain our daily lives as nations, communities, and individual men and women. By her we live and move and have our being. By her we become wise.

So on this feast of Pentecost, we are invited to celebrate how God is always between, within, and among us. We are invited to reflect that wherever people engage in activity that pushes back the boundaries of knowledge and understanding; that creates sound governance and upholds the common good; that makes for happiness, alleviates suffering, and beautifies our lives—there the Spirit is at work: often unseen, mostly unacknowledged, almost always unthanked. When patients for psychoanalysis came to Carl Jung's practice in Zurich, they would see over the front door a Latin inscription derived from the oracle at Delphi: *Vocatus atque non vocatus deus aderit.* "Called upon or not, God will be present." This is how the Spirit is in the world as an eternal act of love, recognised or not. And if the Spirit is present to us, perhaps the task of religion is to help us become more present to the Spirit, do what Chesterton did by cultivating the habit of recognition, saying grace each time we glimpse some sign, however small, of goodness, truth, or beauty.

"We have", said Chesterton, "at the back of our minds . . . a forgotten blaze or burst of astonishment at our own existence. The object of the artistic and spiritual life is to dig for this submerged sunrise of wonder." Jesus spoke of treasure buried in a field for which you sell everything you have. Only this stone that turns things to gold, this sunrise of wonder, is nearer to us than our own souls. Lady Wisdom, the Spirit of love and truth, will guide us to it if we long for it, if we ask and seek. The Advent cry *O Sapientia* makes the best possible prayer for Whitsun: "O Wisdom, you come forth from the mouth of the Most High; you fill the universe and hold all things together with gentle strength. Come and teach us the way of truth."

The Feast of Pentecost, 8 June 2003
Wisdom 7:15–27; Acts 2:22–38

The Choral Offices of the Church

Dedicated to the Choristers

Adam's thoughts of Hetty did not deafen him to the service; they rather blended with all the other deep feelings for which the church service was a channel to him this afternoon, as a certain consciousness of our entire past and our imagined future blends itself with all our moments of keen sensibility. And to Adam the church service was the best channel he could have found for his mingled regret, yearning and resignation; its interchange of beseeching cries for help, with outbursts of faith and praise—its recurrent responses and the familiar rhythm of its collects, seemed to speak for him as no other form of worship could have done.

George Eliot's Adam Bede was not attending Cathedral choral matins, but he might have been. It is nearly half a century since I attended my first choral service. I had hardly stepped foot inside a church. My parents had little time for religion. But they did love music. To help me develop musically, I was drafted into a church choir that sang to cathedral standard, where things were done properly and well. My first service was evensong. No one took much notice of probationers then. I was left to make what sense of it I could. All of it was utterly new to me. The canticles that autumn evening were *Walmisley in D minor*. I have had a soft spot for that setting ever since.

I remember feeling awed and moved by what I was experiencing, this tapestry of words and music that seemed to be *enveloping* me. It was strange, and yet familiar, as if I had known it all along, but had not known that I knew it. When an author whose books we had admired, but whom we had never met, came and stayed with us, he wrote in our visitors' book: "old friends whom I've met for the first time." That evensong was like that for me: recognising something familiar and reassuring at the same time as it was unknown and new. I realised that, in an important way, I had come home.

These reminiscences are prompted by a little phrase in this morning's first lesson. That text, one of the most ancient in the Old Testament, is introduced as the "last words of David", his final utterance at the end of a long and eventful career as the great king who would forever represent Israel's golden age. "The oracle of David, son of Jesse, the oracle of the man whom God exalted, the anointed of the God of Jacob, the favourite of the Strong One of Israel." That last phrase is the new translation's desperate stab at some admittedly difficult Hebrew. Literally, it is "the sweet one, or favourite, of the chants of Israel". It's a musical reference: David is the one everybody loves to sing about. But the old translation has much to be said for it: David the "sweet psalmist of Israel", if you like, the one through whom God not only *speaks*, as the next line goes on to say, but *sings*.

Many of the Psalms are ascribed to David, or dedicated to him—the text can mean either. It's as if psalmody, the singing of sacred songs, was placed under the patronage of David, just as law was placed under the patronage of Moses and wisdom of Solomon. So what we are about, here in this choral foundation, looks back over a long tradition of more than 3,000 years. At the heart of it lies the daily chanting of the Psalms. I always say to the choristers that the measure of any cathedral choir is not that they can master the motets of Palestrina or the canticle settings of Purcell, but that they can undertake to perfection the hardest part of the choral office, which is also the heart of the service, the singing of the Psalms. It is this discipline, akin to a pianist knowing inside out the forty-eight preludes and fugues of Bach's *Well-Tempered Clavier*, that makes for excellence.

But to come back to the choral services of matins and evensong: what do they mean to us? I mean not only as liturgy or as music, but as a total experience, as a vehicle for God to be present to us and us to him. First, we need to realise that these services are part of our cultural inheritance. They are as much a part of England as the stones and glass and monuments of our cathedrals and churches. Their ancient Benedictine stability, the poignant blend of words and music, the measured rhythm of Anglican chant, the gentle rises and falls of the liturgy: these all create a whole infinitely greater than the parts. It is to me something of a miracle. It is unique to the English-speaking world. We should cherish it.

Second, the choral offices touch us in very deep places. Beauty can remain just an aesthetic experience, or, like Beatrice in Dante's vision, it can be the handmaid who leads us to God. For many people, I suspect the beauty of Prayer Book morning and evening offices resonates with our own experience of being human: of having just risen for the day, of soon going to sleep, of being born, and of dying one day. Each *Te Deum* is a celebration of being alive and having been brought "safely to the beginning of this day". Each *Nunc Dimittis* or "lighten our darkness" is one less till eternity. It haunts you, but heals you as well, for it helps you face your own mortality.

Third, these services offer a gentle, non-threatening approach to God. They entice rather than cajole. You do not have to say or sing very much. You can come in or out at will, find your own level, sit near the back in the half-light where no one will notice you. I don't underestimate the part cathedral offices can play in the mission of a place such as this. The music, liturgy, silence, and architecture work their own alchemy on people. Perhaps this style of evangelism is important when people are suspicious of the hard sell, and respond to a more oblique approach. The nineteenth-century American poet Emily Dickinson famously said: "Tell all the truth but tell it slant."

And fourth, matins and evensong train us to become what we will all one day be in heaven: contemplatives. It is wrong to say that you do not "join in" choral services, that the choir does it all for you. We participate in the most demanding ways: by *listening* in word and in music, by *praying* the liturgy while others perform it on our behalf. When the voice called out to the infant Samuel, he was told to say, not "Hear Lord, for thy servant speaketh", but "Speak, Lord, for thy servant heareth." The choral offices sharpen our God-given faculty for stillness, for paying attention, for contemplation. We learn that we do not need to be busy saying or singing or doing things, but can sit at the feet of Jesus.

I share these thoughts with you on the day the BBC are in Durham to broadcast choral evensong. Through the broadcast, a window will be opened on to the daily rhythm of common prayer in this ancient and beautiful place. Here in this Cathedral, we are never so true to ourselves as when we celebrate the *opus dei* as our Benedictine forebears did. To offer the prayer and praise that is God's due and our joy is the most humanising activity we can ever engage in, for it heals the spirit, exalts the mind, and touches the heart. It's to follow in the steps of King David of old, touchingly remembered as the "sweet psalmist of Israel". As we praise our Maker, what would please God more than that something like this might one day be said of us?

4 May 2008
2 Samuel 23:1–7

Carry On Singing!

Farewells to our choristers and adult musicians come round every summer. I won't pretend it's easy to say goodbye to such consummate artistes, who are also children and grown-ups with whom we have worshipped as fellow members of the Cathedral community and who have become our friends. Emotions can be close to the surface at the little rituals of leave-taking after evensong on the last day of the choir year. But what a debt we owe our choir!

Today we are saying farewell to another cohort of musicians who are leaving us this summer: boy choristers, girl choristers, choral scholars, our Assistant Organist, and our Sub Organist. Goodbyes are bittersweet for those who are leaving and those who are left behind. But our Old Testament reading suggests how to take leave of one another. "You shall go out in joy", exclaims Isaiah, "and be led back in peace; the mountains and the hills before you shall break into song, and all the trees of the field shall clap their hands." They were exiles, older men and women who had not seen their homeland for sixty years, younger people and children who had never seen it. At last, they had the news they longed for: it was time to go back to their own country and rebuild their cities, their temple, their lives. Their release meant a homecoming, freedom, a future, and a new vision of God. "The glory of the Lord shall be revealed and all flesh shall see it together."

For you, this may feel more like going into exile rather than coming home: Durham has been your home and now it is time to leave it behind. Here you have sung the Lord's song, not in a strange land but in one that has been familiar and loved. But it may have felt like exile when you first arrived; it may have taken time to settle here, make friends, be happy. That is how it was for the exiles too. One of the prophets had said to them: make your home in Babylon. Build houses, sow fields, plant vineyards. But there comes a time to leave. And when it comes, we need to know what it will mean for us. Isaiah said: *freedom*, because the next phase of your lives will offer even greater opportunities to make choices, to grow and to flourish, to discover how God's service is perfect freedom. *A future*, because the road ahead is full of new discoveries and God-given possibilities that you cannot even begin to imagine yet. And *a new vision of God's splendour*, for what is life *for*, and what makes it worth living, unless it is to be lived before the God who cares about us, and who wants us to love and enjoy him so that we know true and lasting happiness?

So at this threshold we look back and we look forward. When we look back, we need to celebrate and be thankful. I am not saying that Durham has always been easy. For some of you there have been difficulties and dark times. Perhaps we wish that some things had been different; sometimes endings mean saying sorry as well as thank you. Perhaps being stretched to the limit in your music has felt too much at times. Yet I know that you love what you do, which is why you do it so well. So I hope that the memories you take with you are of a time of gifts for which you will always be thankful: your music, your education, your friendships, your growth, the spirituality of this place, the inestimable privilege of being part of the life of this great Cathedral for a while. I hope that in all this, you have been truly touched by God.

Looking forward brings eagerness; you are among the most privileged of people, with untold opportunities opening up ahead of you. But you wouldn't be human if you didn't feel some trepidation as well. We never know what lies ahead when we stand at a crossroads; what new vistas are going to open up ahead of us? We don't know, for now. To "go out with joy" is not to think that we can map the future, but to believe that the risen Jesus is with us in every step we take, just as he walked with the disciples on the road to Emmaus, as we heard at Peter and Rebecca's wedding yesterday. They did not recognise him at first, and often it is the same for us. When we feel beset by doubt or despondency, we need to believe that he is beside us. Isaiah's exiles found that their journey meant unexpected challenges and hardships; their faith in God was tested at times. If that happens to you, remember the goodness of God while you were here. Remember today's words, "You shall go out with joy", and try and rekindle your sense of gratitude. Remember your friends here who have supported you and will go on praying for you. Remember Christ risen from the dead and the alleluias you sang Easter by Easter. Have faith that everything works together for good for those who love God.

Isaiah might have been speaking to choristers. "The mountains and the hills before you shall burst into song." They are almost his last words; he meant them to be remembered. He is saying that when we make music, the world joins in. When we sing, we make other people sing too. And that makes a difference to those who are needy, lonely, or sad, because the new song of the Lord tells how things can be different. On Tuesday evening, the saxophonist Jan Garbarek and the Hilliard Ensemble gave a marvellous concert of music from their new CD *Officium Novum*. One of their most haunting pieces was based on a native American text, "We are the stars":

> We sing with our light
> For we are birds made of fire.
> We spread our wings over the sky.
> Our light is a voice.
> We cut a road for the soul
> For its journey through death.

We cut roads when we sing because music draws us into worlds unseen. And when those roads lead us through dark places, we go on singing, creating song lines that tell of God's truth and love. "Even at the grave we sing alleluia." Your music-making days here have come to an end for now. But promise me that you won't stop making music in your hearts to the Lord. Make a difference to the world as your lives are changed from glory to glory. Don't lose your hold on the things eternal. Have a joyful leave-taking and a joyful homecoming. Be faithful to Christ and carry on singing. And thank you.

16 July 2011, on the last Sunday of the choir year
Isaiah 55:10–13

Missa Dunelmi

The Cathedral has inspired the composition of outstanding music over the years. James MacMillan is one of the UK's best contemporary composers of religious music. His Durham Mass has become a firm favourite. This sermon was preached at the first performance of this joint commission between the Cathedral and Durham University.

"Is not life more than food and the body more than clothing?" Jesus says in today's gospel. His theme is God's care for us: generous, lasting, tender. Worry has no place when life is pure gift. And soon, his kingdom will be coming. Among life's gifts that we celebrate are those of poetry, music, and art. They matter in a civilised society because they are about more than food and clothing and all the other things we need to survive. It's true that for many people in our world, survival is all they can hope for. In the hierarchy of needs, we do not disparage the most basic. But we are learning that for life to be rich and humane and fulfilling, we cannot live by bread alone. In the civilising and deepening of human experience, we cultivate the life of the spirit, and in this, the pursuit of wisdom, the arts, and the humanities play a vital part.

Today the world hears for the first time another in a long and distinguished line of Durham commissions, James MacMillan's mass setting *Missa Dunelmi*. A premiere from an internationally known composer is always an occasion. Of course, history warns us against judging a work by its first performance; it will take time for us to recognise its qualities, appreciate how it will lend its distinctive accent to our liturgy as it takes its place in the Durham repertoire alongside Byrd and Mozart, Purcell, Langlais, and Britten. It's only with the passing of years that you appreciate how well a great wine drinks. Music is not the written score: it is only truly formed as it is performed and heard and responded to. We are all playing a central part of this process of formation today. What we are doing is welcoming this new setting so that it can begin to be at home in the setting of this Cathedral and its worship. For, like the liturgy, the readings, the sermon, like all the arts of worship, music has to be lived and experienced and embodied. Only then, as Beethoven wrote on the score of his *Missa Solemnis,* will what comes from the heart go to the heart.

James MacMillan has much to say about this chain of musical endeavour that connects composers, performers, and worshippers. He writes about how he has come to his deep commitment to serve the church as a musician. Our mass setting, like much of his best known and appreciated choral music, is high art, and you are perhaps finding it as demanding to listen to as it is to sing. Like prayer, attentive listening is work. But you may be surprised to know that his dedication to sacred music is expressed week by week in a very different setting from a cathedral. He is a committed Catholic who worships in an inner-city parish in Glasgow where he is the musical director. Some years ago, Dominican friars came to St Columba's to care for this run-down, working-class parish. MacMillan says of it that it exuded "an air of brokenness, defeat and alienation . . . this was missionary territory where lives were calling out for healing." One path to renewal turned out to be through music. Forming a parish choir brought people together; as so often, singing released other gifts and fostered new relationships. MacMillan writes regularly for them and for the congregation, with a new responsorial psalm every week. He leads and directs the singing himself, as parish cantor.

MacMillan has thought deeply and intelligently about the place music occupies in the life of the church. He says:

> The God-oriented nature of prayerful liturgy emphasises our true vocation of being the people of God on earth. Through the centuries, in being involved umbilically with liturgy . . . musicians have proved themselves to be the midwives of faith . . . The weekly challenges of assisting the Dominican friars in making liturgy that is beautiful, possible and inclusive has become an aspiration and vocation for me . . . The ultimate goal is to make the kingdom of God palpable in the lives of many, specialist and non-specialist, musician and non-musician, for the poor in spirit as well as those who are more fulfilled in life.

He speaks about the "mysterious power of music" as being central, and yet unnoticed, in the prayer of God's people: central because worship is the most important thing we do; unnoticed because music is to inspire and enrich worship, not get in the way by drawing attention to itself. That is a rich account of music in its human, theological, and spiritual aspects: how it draws out of us our adoration and praise; elicits faith and understanding; creates communities of belief and endeavour; embraces those on the margins of society. By bearing witness to the eternal, music is both missionary and mystical.

And this is true whether it is the immaculately crafted music of the Cathedral liturgy echoing an immaculately crafted architecture, or the rougher-hewn but nevertheless heartfelt praise or lament of an urban parish community. Today, 27 February, is the anniversary of the death of George Herbert in 1633. He was one of England's greatest poets, a priest of the Church of England, and a lover of music. He used to walk each day across the water meadows by the Wiltshire Avon to attend evensong in Salisbury Cathedral. These walks of a contemplative musician find their way into his poetry. In his poem "Church Musick", he celebrates this "sweetest of sweets", who in a time of distress gently brought him into a house of joy and pleasure. There he finds he is taken out of himself, "rising and falling with your wings: / We both together sweetly live and love". He means that in music's ascents and descents, its ecstasies and agonies, life's light and shadow is mirrored and understood in new ways. Like St Paul in our epistle reading, it helps him understand that however dark the day may be, he can glimpse how "the sufferings of this present time are not worth comparing with the glory about to be revealed." For Herbert, church music is nothing less than a journey towards paradise: "But if I travel in your companie, / You know the way to heavens doore".

So he can say, in the poem that we shall sing at the end of this service: "Wherefore with my utmost art I will sing thee, / And the cream of all my heart I will bring thee." This exercise of his utmost art is not for his time only but for all time: "E'en eternity's too short to extol thee." Or to poach the famous lines from a sermon by Hebert's great contemporary John Donne, when we are brought at our last awakening into the house and gate of heaven, and we find ourselves in the habitations of God's majesty and glory, there will be "no noise nor silence but one equal music." So music is a pledge of the world to come, and the ceaseless praise of God that is the joyous work and rest of eternity. Because of this, it is a reconciling, healing, redeeming aspect of our lives now. One of my predecessors, Peter Baelz, has a prayer that we often use before concerts in the Cathedral. "In the making of music you have given us a delight for the mind and a solace for the heart. By the harmonies of your grace resolve the discord of our lives, that we may sound forth your praise in all we do and all we are."

I come back to our gospel. "Is not life more than food, and the body more than clothing?" We acknowledge this every time we gather at the altar and take God's food that is more than food and sit and eat as honoured guests whom God has arrayed in more than clothing. This gift of a new mass setting that we gratefully receive today will help us enter afresh into the church's great thanksgiving that belongs to time and eternity. It will draw us, in a new way, into the everlasting movement of God's love into his broken world, so that we bring a new song to his voiceless and his poor.

27 February 2011, at the first performance of James MacMillan's
Missa Dunelmi
Romans 8:18–25; Matthew 6:25–end

Recognition Scene

Like literature, art, and poetry, great drama has a lot to teach us about how to understand some of the central texts of the Bible. I wish I knew my Shakespeare well enough to have drawn much more on his often dazzling insights into so many aspects of human life. Grasping what Shakespeare is getting at can itself be a startling act of recognition for us.

In English theatre, there is one master of the dramatic climax: Shakespeare. One of his favourite ways of bringing a drama to a climax is the recognition scene where scales fall from the eyes, and suddenly the truth about a person is revealed: the unknown stranger, the disguise that is shed, an enemy turned friend, a friend who has been an enemy all along. It's said that only four of his plays do *not* contain a recognition scene. One of the greatest comes at the end of *Pericles, Prince of Tyre*. A young girl is brought to the silent, grieving Pericles, in the hope that her singing will break through his sadness. As she sings her life story, he realises who the child is. She is Marina, the precious daughter whom as an infant he had given up as lost. He bursts out in ecstatic recognition:

> Put me to present pain,
> Lest this great sea of joys rushing upon me
> O'erbear the shores of my mortality,
> And drown me with their sweetness.

And although no one else is aware of it, he realises that all heaven is rejoicing, for he can hear the music of the spheres. I heard about a performance that had an audience in tears when it reached that scene. Many of them could hardly understand what the words meant, yet they knew about separation and loss and the joyful reversal of fortunes reunion brings. This is the power of drama.

You could say that many of the Easter stories in the gospels are recognition scenes like that: the astonishing reversal of separation and loss in the joyful reunion of followers and friends with the risen Jesus. Think of Mary Magdalen, supposing him to be the gardener, hearing him pronounce her name and recognising him as *Rabbouni*. Think of the eleven behind locked doors and the Visitor who greeted them as only Jesus could, "Peace be with you." Think of Thomas who would not believe, and his radiant confession of faith: "My Lord and my God." Think of Peter and the disciples after the miraculous catch of fish: "It is the Lord!"

But none of the Easter recognition scenes is told with such artistry as St Luke's story of Emmaus that we heard this morning. The two disconsolate disciples schlepping back home, joined by an unknown stranger, their conversation on the road, the supper at which guest turns host, the familiar action of bread blessed and broken, the moment of recognition, the excited return to the city to tell the others—it is exquisitely told. You feel that it is all utterly authentic, St Luke's Easter; there is not a false note anywhere. The story portrays its characters as masterfully as Caravaggio paints his. In its intimacy and naturalness, this recognition scene strikes us as entirely believable. We are there; it is happening before our eyes. Indeed, so vivid is it that we want to go beyond the sense of watching a drama happening to other people and say: *truly this is happening to us.*

This recognition story of broken bread, burning hearts, and opened eyes is full of echoes. The Jesus of St Luke is always on the move; indeed, the Gospel is largely constructed around the theme of Jesus' journey to Jerusalem that culminates in suffering and death. But near the beginning of the Gospel is a story about another journey *from* Jerusalem, like the Emmaus Road: two people once again going home at Passover time. Mary and Joseph think that the child Jesus is with them, but he is not, and when they realise this, they hurry back to the city. The Emmaus two think Jesus is *not* with them, though we know he *is*; and when they recognise him they too hurry back. When his parents find Jesus in the temple, he tells them about what was *necessary*, how he must be about his Father's business; and the risen Christ also speaks about what was *necessary*, how the Messiah had to suffer before entering his glory. Christ incognito, absent yet present, hidden yet disclosed, abased yet glorified, unknown yet well known—these are St Luke's themes. And, says today's story, when the risen Christ comes to us in the word of the scriptures and in the breaking of the bread, as our fellow traveller and as our cherished guest, there is recognition. Our eyes are opened. There is joy.

But take another, more ancient echo in the story. If Luke's Gospel is a travel narrative, it is also a story full of eating and drinking. Much of Jesus' teaching and many of his key encounters take place at the meal table. He famously eats with tax-gatherers and sinners. It's at the last supper that he teaches his disciples about the nature of service and what the giving of his own body and blood will mean. Does this recall how it was through a first supper that the human race was banished from paradise? In Genesis, it was when the man and the woman took the forbidden fruit that "the eyes of them both were opened, and they knew that they were naked". At that primordial meal, two human beings came to a recognition that led to death. At the Emmaus meal, by contrast, two people come to a recognition that leads to life. "Their eyes were opened and they recognised him", says Luke, as if to say: here, at Easter, with the first supper of the first day of the week, here is a new beginning. Humanity's long exile is over. The way back to Eden is open at last, and forever. The human race is remade. There is a new world, a new beginning, a new creation, a new joy, a new hope.

In the Cathedral of Autun in Burgundy, there is a sculpture of Christ on the road to Emmaus. He is dressed as if he were a pilgrim going to Compostela, with a pilgrim staff and scrip decorated with the *coquille* or scallop shell that marked the traveller on his way to Santiago. Jesus wearing the symbol as God's Pilgrim, God's traveller, the bearer of his mystery and love here among us humans. In him, the fellow traveller who is our literal *companion* because he breaks bread with us, the psalmist's prayer is at last fulfilled: "thou art about my path and about my bed; if I climb up into heaven thou art there; if I go down to hell thou art there also. If I take the wings of the morning, and remain in the uttermost parts of the sea, even there also shall thy hand lead me; and thy right hand shall hold me."

In these days of Easter we celebrate with joyful hearts the memory of God's wonderful works. But it is more than a memory. For Luke is saying that the risen Christ walks with us, reveals to us the mystery of his being, crosses the threshold of our lives to make his home there. All of life is Easter. What more do we need to know? Like the disciples on that far-off day, we too are joined by the stranger who walks this earth and speaks to us of peace and hope. "We greet him the days we meet him, and bless

when we understand", when, like this Easter morning, the half-light of
our existence is transformed into the full light of God's new day, and our
eyes are opened, and our hearts burn within us; and, like Pericles, a great
sea of joy rushes upon us and we hear the music of the spheres.

Easter Day 2006
Luke 24:13–35

A Durham Civic Occasion

*To end this section, here are two sermons about human life. The first
was preached at a special service to mark the dissolution of Durham
City Council when the whole county became a unitary authority.
Common grace can—and should—be mediated through our social
and political institutions as they order and add value to our human
life together. My aim in this sermon was not to take a view about a
controversial political change, but to enable those closely involved to
celebrate the past, cross a difficult threshold, and contemplate the future.*

"This was surrender in a grand manner, both abject and comprehensive,
leaving not the smallest loophole through which a lawyer might wriggle at
any time in the future to argue and obtain alteration." That is not a report
on the dissolution of district councils in Durham and Northumberland,
but an historian's comment on a dissolution of earlier times when this
institution we are now sitting in came to the end of an era. It is chronicled
in Geoffrey Moorhouse's book about Durham, *The Last Office: 1539 and
the Dissolution of a Monastery.* The consequences of a royal whim to
reorganise the nation's polity arrived for good in Durham on the last day
of that year. That night, Prior Hugh Whitehead led his monks into this
church for the last time to recite the ancient office of compline. The psalms
finished, they came to a poignant *Nunc Dimittis:* "Now lettest thou thy
servant depart in peace; for mine eyes have seen thy salvation." It is the
canticle of leave-taking and death. And this was a kind of death. When
the sound of plainchant died away on that new year's eve, something died
with it—five centuries of common life and prayer here that this church
would never see again in that form.

This service of leave-taking may be bewildering for some of you,
and poignant for many more. The City Council has not been a feature
of Durham life for as long as the Priory was, but that does not mean
that its dissolution is not deeply felt, at least by those who have given
many years to it as elected members, officers, and employees. Perhaps

the memory that this church has been there before could be important. The re-engineering of institutions is hard because of the memories we carry, but especially when an institution is there for "public benefit". The Cathedral Priory existed to serve God and the community. No doubt it did not always live up to that high Benedictine ideal, but that was not given as a reason for dissolving it. In the same way, Durham City Council has served this city with an energy and distinction that have brought it credit. It comes to an end because government has decreed that things are to be done differently. Whatever our regrets, it is emphatically not a matter of failure or shame. We should celebrate success and give thanks for our achievements, hard though it may be to do today.

Leave-taking is the theme of our reading from the Acts of the Apostles. In it, Paul says farewell to the elders at Ephesus, a place that had impressed itself on his affections, and whose church and leadership he had come to know well. It is not an exact parallel for today: he is speaking about ministry in the church and the proclamation of the gospel, not politics in the city-state. But the spirit in which he says farewell can help us take leave of Durham City Council gracefully. His beautiful speech is one of the most moving in the Bible, comparable to David parting from Jonathan, and Jesus taking leave of his disciples. These are farewells between people who care about one another, between whom love and trust has been fostered. Hence the tears and embraces, especially, says the story, because they knew they would not see one another again.

Paul's words face both ways. They begin by looking back over the time Paul has lived and worked among the people of the city. He does not conceal his achievements beneath a cloak of false modesty (not Paul!). He records how devotedly he served God and the people, taking risks for them, not holding back from hard decisions and courageous truth-telling. And it is right today that we too should celebrate the many ways in which Durham City Council has helped our communities to flourish, how it has upheld the pride in our city's history, its heritage, and its incomparably beautiful environment. Our view of the past cannot afford to be nostalgic or uncritical, but neither must it neglect to honour what has been done for good by many people who, in the spirit of St Paul, have not counted their own lives and fortunes of any value, but who have given themselves so generously and often sacrificially for the service of others and of God.

From the pull of the past, Paul turns to a future that he acknowledges is unknown and untried. So he reminds those who are left behind, the elders with the duty of care for their people, to exercise their continuing responsibility well. No doubt those at the quayside at Miletus would have wished things to carry on as they had known them; we want to preserve familiar landscapes we have learned to find our way around in, especially if they have served us well. But Paul, like his Master setting his face toward Jerusalem when the appointed time had come, knows that this uncertain future must be faced with confidence in God and his providence. He does not speculate on what may happen tomorrow. His emphasis is on the spirit in which the leadership will face it. The clue, he says, is in their personal integrity. It always is in public life. "Keep watch over yourselves and over all the flock of which the Holy Spirit has made you overseers." "Be alert", for in leadership, scrupulous attention to the values of fairness, justice, truthfulness, and transparency are everything. Above all comes the good of those they are to serve: "In all this I have given you an example that by such work we must support the weak, remembering the words of the Lord Jesus, 'it is more blessed to give than to receive.'"

The stakes are not eternal when it comes to local government, but they are still high, not least in the risks attached to large-scale change and how it is managed. We all wish the unitary authority well, and will support its endeavours in every way we can—precisely because the welfare of our county and its city, towns and villages, its industry, its environment, and especially its service to the most needy members of our communities matters to us. They would be uppermost in our minds at any time, but especially at this particular time when the economic threats facing the North East are so severe, and their possible social fallout as yet unknown. Like the Ephesian elders, your successors will need great wisdom as they inherit your responsibilities—the judicious sense of insight and discernment commended in our first reading from Proverbs.

Above all, they will need our prayers. How can we forget the final scene in the story, when words are done and it is time for Paul to commend his beloved hearers to God and his grace, that divine strength and mercy that alone can sustain us in our task. "When he had finished speaking, he knelt down with them all and prayed." The last thing you can do for your successors is to pray for them. The word "goodbye" literally means

"God be with you". This is more than well-wishing. This is a prayer. It's how we should always take leave, whether our farewells are anticipated and prepared for, or whether they come upon us unexpectedly, in the spirit of the *Nunc Dimittis,* like the monks of Durham reciting their last office and then departing "in peace" and in God. "Then they brought him to the ship", says Acts, and I like to think that with the tears, the prayers went on, and there were even smiles and laughter and thankfulness for all God's goodness as they watched it sail away.

11 March 2009
Proverbs 4:20–end; Acts 20:17–24, 32–38

At a Golden Wedding

There is something beautiful about celebrating a long and happy
marriage. Sadly, the couple both died a few years later. I was
privileged to preach at each of their funerals too, and looked
back to what I had said on this happy anniversary. I have
their family's permission to reproduce this sermon here.

I often say that when Jesus attended the wedding at Cana in Galilee, he didn't preach a sermon or give the couple advice. What mattered was to make sure the wine didn't run out and that the party could go on. I dare say he would have done the same at a golden wedding.

So sermons on these occasions should be short. But the central word of marriage and of life is short too: "love". Yet it's the biggest word there is. Where do we find love? In the tiniest hazelnut, says Mother Julian: it exists because God loves it; in the entire sweep of the universe, says Dante, because it is "love that moves the sun and the other stars". And today, love has a human face in Stephen and Joy and the fifty years of marriage they celebrate. Today, we know that love is God's meaning.

A rabbi asked his pupils how they could tell when it was daybreak. "When you see an animal, and there is enough light to tell whether it's a fox or a dog?" one said. "No," said the teacher. "When you look at an orchard, and can tell the difference between an apple and a pear tree?" said another. "No. Day breaks when you look at someone and know that they are your brother or your sister. Until you can do that, no matter what time of day it is, it's always night." So love is a kind of dawn, an illumination. It lights up our lives. We see each other in a new way. And when marriage is not only long-lived, but wholesome and happy and good, we recognise how love lights up not only two lives given to each other in vows and promises and rings, but everyone else who is privileged to be brought into this circle of God-given grace. Marriage is one of the places in human life that demonstrate St Paul's great saying: that love bears all things, believes all things, hopes all things, endures all things. For love never ends.

The gospel reading from St John talks about love in words so simple that a child can understand it. Perhaps we would find it easier to take it in and live it if we were a little more childlike. Jesus says: "As the Father has loved me, so I have loved you. Abide in my love." He is speaking about the new relationships we become part of when we are brought into relationship with God. Divine love has human love as its consequence. The church is a society of friends, says John, a community of truth and love. Our badge is that we love one another. And this is as true of marriage as it is of all the other ways we love. In the Jewish Talmud, it says that the *shekinah*, God's presence, his very glory, dwells between a husband and a wife. *Ubi caritas et amor, Deus ibi est.* Where love is, there you find God. For God is love.

And the model of all loving is Jesus. "As the Father loves, so I have loved you." There is more. Jesus will go on to say, in words familiar from so many war memorials, "Greater love has no one than this, to lay down one's life for one's friends." Anyone who has ever loved knows what the cost of love is, the often little, sometimes big ways we are called to lay down our lives for those we love. Love demands as well as gives. It's tough as well as gentle. It asks everything of us; yet it gives everything in return. Love is not only cross. It's resurrection. When we love as Jesus does, the day breaks, the shadows flee away.

We have already heard from your beloved George Herbert in this service, in Richard Lloyd's exquisite setting of his poem "The Call". But I have another Herbert poem to mark this occasion. The name "Stephen" means "crown". And, happily, the poet brings together your two names, in an echo of St Paul, in a poem called "A True Hymn".

> My joy, my life, my crown!
> My heart was meaning all the day,
> Somewhat it fain would say:
> And still it runneth, muttering up and down
> With only this, My joy, my life, my crown.

He is saying that he wants to sing a true hymn, his best hymn, in praise of God; he has the words, the rhyme, the metre but somehow not quite the spirit. He knows that what life is meant for is to worship God, "my joy, my life, my crown". But how to live the truth of his own song? At the end he finds the way.

> Whereas if the heart be moved
> Although the verse be somewhat scant,
> God doth supply the want.
> And when the heart says, sighing to be approved,
> O could I love! And stops: God writeth, Loved.

The point is: it is being loved that is the secret. To know you are loved and cherished is what liberates the heart to sing and the tongue to praise. This is what moves the heart to recognise and know God. And the love of a long and happy marriage is surely one of the ways in which we love him as "my joy, my life, my crown".

So, Stephen and Joy, "joy" and "crown" with life held between your names: in God's eternal love you had your beginning fifty years ago. In that time you have tasted its length and breadth and height and depth, have glimpsed in each other how the love of Christ passes knowledge, have walked side by side in loving God as your joy, your life, your crown. In his love may you also have your end, and many more golden days to come in the meantime. And as good Tobias prayed, may you both find mercy and grow old together.

1 Corinthians 13; John 15:9–11

Part 6: Seasons of Faith

The Secret Ministry of Frost

In Advent

*I have often preached on the great, portentous themes of Advent:
death, judgment, hell, heaven. But this sermon from the last week
before Christmas comes from an altogether gentler place. It was
the shortest day of the year and this recalled a beautiful poem.
And although the sermon isn't directly about Christian ministry,
the silent, subtle way of frost as it works itself into landscapes and
makes them beautiful could be a thought-provoking metaphor.*

This solstice day calls for a wintry sermon. We may affect not to care for
winter, but painters and poets have always loved it. Here is one of the
great English romantics.

> Therefore all seasons shall be sweet to thee,
> Whether the summer clothe the general earth
> With greenness, or the redbreast sit and sing
> Betwixt the tufts of snow on the bare branch
> Of mossy apple-tree, while the nigh thatch
> Smokes in the sun-thaw; whether the eave-drops fall
> Heard only in the trances of the blast,
> Or if the secret ministry of frost
> Shall hang them up in silent icicles,
> Quietly shining to the quiet Moon.

That is the beautiful last stanza of Samuel Taylor Coleridge's famous
poem "Frost at Midnight", written in 1798. "The secret ministry of frost"
is one of those happy phrases that, once heard, is never forgotten. But
I love that conclusion for its embrace of the entire circle of the seasons.
As the earth turns on its axis and we journey through this shortest day
of the year, our thoughts inevitably turn to the promise of spring's light

and the greening of the earth, the happy warmth of summer we begin to travel towards tomorrow. It focuses our minds on the order of time running its course, the turning of the seasons, the human cycles of birth and death and all that comes in between.

Advent makes us think about first and last things. That can mean the order of time that is marked by equinox and solstice, by feast day and fast, and by the times and seasons that hold memory or significance for us. But at a deeper level, it means what is of first and what is of ultimate meaning for us and for all humanity. And this is the real purpose of Coleridge's poem. He is in a reverie, musing by his fireside on how, outside, "the Frost performs its secret ministry" silently, mysteriously, without the help of wind or weather. Inside all is warmth and peacefulness, a calm, gently fluttering flame inducing a meditation about what it means to be alive. I guess that one of the gifts of Advent, even at this late stage, is to urge on us how important it is to stop, ponder the wonder of things, the sheer gift of being human, and aware, and capable of thought and generosity and love.

Coleridge has a specific focus for his wonder, for he is not alone by his fireside.

> Dear Babe, that sleepest cradled by my side,
> Whose gentle breathings, heard in this deep calm,
> Fill up the intersperséd vacancies
> And momentary pauses of the thought!
> My babe so beautiful! it thrills my heart
> With tender gladness, thus to look at thee,
> And think that thou shalt learn far other lore,
> And in far other scenes!

His infant son prompts thoughts about his own childhood and upbringing— not an unmixed blessing for the poet, sent away from home, deprived of his beloved nature, alienated from his mother. He wants better things for his own child: above all, that he will be at home in a wonderful world, and at one with the God who made it and is present in its majesty and mystery, the Creator who will himself shape this precious human life:

But thou, my babe! shalt wander like a breeze
By lakes and sandy shores, beneath the crags
Of ancient mountain, and beneath the clouds,
Which image in their bulk both lakes and shores
And mountain crags: so shalt thou see and hear
The lovely shapes and sounds intelligible
Of that eternal language, which thy God
Utters, who from eternity doth teach
Himself in all, and all things in himself.
Great universal Teacher! he shall mould
Thy spirit, and by giving make it ask.

His prayer is that "all seasons shall be sweet to thee": in youth and in age, happy or sad, disappointed or fulfilled, walking in darkness or seeing great light. What do we not long and pray for when we think of our own children or grandchildren when they are little and still a source of wonder to us? We gaze on them in awe and tenderness, and ask ourselves and God what will become of them when they grow up. We wouldn't be human if we didn't find ourselves gazing far into the future, hoping that our children will be safe in this precarious world we have brought them into, praying that they will live long and well and happily. What wouldn't we do to protect them from damage or harm? What wouldn't God do? we imagine. For each birth, each infancy, each dawning of awareness is a sunrise for the entire human family, as well as for a child's loving parents and family. It is why the hurt, the abuse children suffer at the hands of trusted adults, is so terrible, so outrageous. All creation cries out against it, this massacre of innocent children, this massacre of innocence itself.

On this last Sunday of Advent, we contemplate Blessed Mary and her vocation to be the mother of the Lord. We acclaim her, as Elizabeth did: *Ave Maria*: "Blessed are you among women, and blessed is the fruit of your womb." It isn't to diminish the force of those words to say that this is the response of every new parent where a birth is waited for with expectancy and joy, like Elizabeth herself looking forward to the birth of her own son. Happy are you, happy is your child, happy your family and community! Mary could not love her Infant more than any other mother loves. She loved, and Joseph loved with her, giving all they had so that their Child would grow strong and flourish. Even when they heard Simeon speak about the shadow that would fall across the holy family one day, the sword that would pierce Mary's heart, it did not change anything. They loved him just the same. Their hopes and longings for the future were just the same. And, like Coleridge, you imagine Mary and Joseph gazing at their firstborn in wonder, filled with thankfulness that God has brought them to this point, offering these tiny hands and feet to God, asking only that he will mould his spirit and shape his life so that he grows "in wisdom and stature and in favour with God and humanity". And that as his feet touch the earth, a new light will dawn upon the world, a light for all nations, a sunrise, a spring.

At each solstice, the Precentor chooses a hymn for the year's turning. *Christ whose glory fills the sky, Christ the true, the only Light.* On this day when the sun scarcely clears the horizon and its warmth is extinct, when darkness is long and spirits low, when nature sleeps, and storm and frost have their way on the earth, it is then that we are roused to pray all the more fervently in the spirit of Advent: *Sun of Righteousness arise, triumph o'er the shades of night; Dayspring from on high, be near; Daystar, in my heart appear!* All of human life is gathered up in this yearly metaphor of the darkness and cold that will one day be banished as the light lengthens and the warmth strengthens. And in four days' time, metaphor will become reality. Like the poet, we shall gaze in wondering love upon the beloved Infant, and see in him all grace and truth, all hopes and longings met; and the secret ministry of frost will be past, and hearts will sing, and all seasons will become sweet for us.

O God, by whose command the order of time runs its course: forgive our impatience, perfect our faith, and help us to have a good hope because of your word; through our Saviour Jesus Christ. Amen.

21 December 2014.
Luke 1:39–55

It Seemed We Had Been Sent

On Christmas Day

*By statute, the Dean is required to preach in the Cathedral on the
days of Easter, Pentecost, and Christmas. It's always a challenge to
find fresh words to speak about the familiar and time-honoured
truths of Christianity. On this occasion, the idea of creating a sermon
about the crib was given to me by poems that had been written
that Advent by two friends and included in their Christmas cards.
Preaching is often shaped by quite little events and experiences in
which, if we are attentive, the Spirit of God is gently prompting us.*

Visitors
We had come our separate ways
Gathering like players on a stage
With voices that were muffled, low,
As though a blanket had been thrown
Our bodies, slow,
For bone and muscle needed testing out
Repositioning
Across this strange new flow.
A birth was quietly transforming roles
Adjusting lives
We caught it in a gesture, chance remark,
Each other's eyes:
I'm glad now that I went
And took my place among them all
Though as I knelt
Such clarity shone through the infant face
Such marked intent—
That glancing round, it seemed we had been sent.

© *Sheila Bryer, 2009*

That poem was written by a friend for this year's family Christmas card. It captures beautifully how it might have been at the crib when news of the birth had spread and the shepherds came to see what had come to pass. Or is it the magi? Or even the angels, converging at the place where heaven touched earth? "Gathering like players on a stage", as if not quite sure what kind of drama this would be and what was required of them—for what performers and what audience can ever know in advance how it will play out in the end? But the low, muffled voices—tentative and unsure, I think, rather than respectful—undergo what turns out to be truly life-changing. "A birth was quietly transforming roles, adjusting lives." Kneeling seems the only possible response to what is in the child's face, "such clarity . . . such marked intent". And that act gives meaning to this scene that is both ordinary yet extraordinary: "it seemed we had been sent."

But could we transfer the scene from Bethlehem into our own age? Could those who have come their "separate ways" be our contemporaries, or ourselves, gathering in front of a twenty-first-century crib in a market square or a living room or a church? Can today's cribs still have the power to create a "strange new flow" in the hearts and lives of human beings? And can that figure of the Bambino, whether in wood or alabaster or papier mâché or even plastic, still touch and move us with its "intent" and "clarity", so that even if we came across it by chance we would have to stay awhile, linger in its presence, find that we are not, after all, kneeling here by accident, for in catching the eyes of others might we realise that we are being caught by the eyes of Jesus?

The Christmas crib goes back to the thirteenth century, when St Francis set up the first *praesepium*, or nativity scene, at a hillside cave at Greccio in northern Italy. His biographer St Bonaventure says:

> To excite the villagers to commemorate the nativity of the Infant Jesus with devotion, Francis prepared a manger, and brought hay, and an ox and an ass to the place appointed. The brethren were summoned, the people ran together, the forest resounded with their voices, and that holy night was made glorious by many bright lights and psalms of praise. The man of God stood before the manger full of devotion, bathed in tears and radiant with joy and chanted the holy gospel. Then he preached to the people of

the nativity of the poor King; and because he could not utter his name for the tenderness of his love, he called him the Babe of Bethlehem. A soldier said that he saw an Infant marvellously beautiful, sleeping in the manger, whom Francis embraced with both his arms as if he would awake him from sleep.

For St Francis, the crib is an *icon* (a word I always use carefully). That is, it is an image in a physical space that embraces the eternal; it draws you into its own life and leads you into a realm beyond, a kind of sacrament of the incarnation where, as we meditate on it, we glimpse the ineffable mystery of God made man. We glimpse it, for its infinite depths are beyond our grasp. Francis intended that the crib should lead people into a new and deeper awareness of how wonderful it is that the divine should enter this world and share our life as Immanuel, God with us. In Germany during Advent, every city and town has its Christmas fair, where you can drink mulled wine and enjoy sweetmeats and buy exquisite gifts and decorations that so often make our English Christmas in public places look shallow and kitschy, as if we cannot give it the effort it needs to be truly beautiful. At the heart of the buying and selling you come to a life-sized crib, lovingly adorned for the festival. They call it *Christkindlmarkt,* the Christ-child market. It's as if the Holy Child himself has come to bless this festive time, be present at our merrymaking, call us back to the true source of our happiness and joy. And who is to say that these iconic images of birth are not each day "quietly transforming roles" with the healing "clarity" of the Infant's face and his "marked intent" of love?

Here in Durham we have our own much-loved Nativity. It was made for the Cathedral by Michael Doyle, a pitman from Houghton-le-Spring. He is shown on the Lambton Lodge miners' banner as an alderman, next to Hugh Gaitskell. Late in life he discovered a flair for woodcarving and created the crib figures in the 1970s. The beauty of his nativity is not only the craftsmanship and the tenderness he has expressed in the faces of his figures, but also the way in which he sensitively incorporates references to Durham's mining traditions into the carvings. By the ox stands a pit pony complete with harness. The Holy Child lies not in a manger but in a "choppie box" such as the pit ponies fed from underground. The innkeeper, who has dropped down on to one knee as he gazes reverently at the Infant, is dressed as a miner with lamp, and water-bottle in his pocket, and his faithful whippet at his feet. It is all quintessentially Durham.

Like St Francis', our crib is an icon, telling not only about what took place *then* but what takes place *now*, as we meet the infant Jesus and his grace and truth gets to work on us like a woodcarver, "adjusting our lives", sculpting their raw material in ways so unexpected that our human roles are truly "transformed". It speaks into our ordinary days, our work, our relationships, our joy, our pain. If these are not touched by Christmas, then it has not yet become real for us. For this pitman's nativity tells how the truth of this day is deeper than we can imagine. Its images mined from the earth's depths seem to say that there is nowhere that is beyond the reach of incarnation. "If I climb up to heaven thou art there; if I go down to hell thou are there also." And to think of miners buried each day beneath the earth and emerging at the end of their shift is an evocative image of the death and resurrection of this Infant who the gospels say must suffer, and die, and be raised on the third day.

I began with one poem harvested from this year's Christmas cards. Here is another, by a friend who had visited Durham and been touched by our miner's crib. The simplicity of her poem moved me: it seems to gather up so much of this season's poignant mix of tenderness and longing and the promise of redemption:

> The rose window gleams
> far off like hope.
> In the pony's choppie box
> a bairn sleeps, carved
> by a man who knew
> each day is a burial
> and perhaps a resurrection.

> *Miners' nativity scene, Durham*
> *Cathedral, © Mary Robinson 2009*

Christmas Day 2009
Matthew 1:18–end

My Child, My Beloved

At Epiphany

One year, there were baptisms on the First Sunday of the Epiphany, the Feast of the Baptism of Christ. There were lots of rich associations to explore. I chose the voice that spoke from heaven and said to the newly baptised Jesus: "You are my child, my beloved." I asked: isn't this what all parents say to their children, not least on the day of their baptism? How beautifully tender those words are; but when we make them our own as parents (or grandparents), how much they demand of us!

I sometimes think that going into the new year, facing the January blues, is a bit like travelling into a strange country. We had got used to 2013. We were at home in it: it felt familiar even if we didn't always like what it brought. January means a doorway. I know it's only turning a page on the calendar. Yet it does feel like crossing a threshold where we have to learn to navigate a landscape that will take time to read and understand.

Throughout life there are thresholds to negotiate. Some, like new years, are common to us all; some—birthdays, marriage, a new job, retirement, bereavement—are personal to each of us. But each time we face one of these threshold experiences, when we cross over and glimpse something different on the other side, there is, to begin with, a kind of exile. It is new, and a bit strange. It's like being away from home, where habits are different and no one quite speaks your language. And when exile is forced upon you against your will and you have to make your own way on alien soil, it is deeply painful. Listen to the displaced of the Central African Republic or Syria, to refugees and asylum seekers anywhere.

Our first reading envisages just such a situation. The Hebrew community had been in exile in Babylon, struggling, as they put it, to "sing the Lord's song in a strange land". For half a century, they'd had no reason to think their exile was coming to an end, or that their desperate longings to see their homeland again would be fulfilled. Prophets like Jeremiah had warned that exile would be long and hard, and the people should learn to accept that this was the will of God, settle down and establish themselves in Babylon, and more even than that, pray for the welfare of this godforsaken place. But then along comes another prophet whose name we do not know, though his writings are found in the book of Isaiah. He is full of hope for the future. He foretells that the time is coming when the people will return home, and glory will fill the land. Indeed, not only Israel but "all flesh" shall see it together. The land will resound to songs of celebration as all the nations inherit the blessing once promised to Abraham, and the world is rebuilt on the foundations of truth, justice, freedom, and love.

And this prophet of homecoming has something specific to say about Israel's vocation as the people of God. What are they to do and be when they return home? "You are my servant, Israel, in whom I will be glorified." Or, as the Greek version has it, "you are my *pais*, my child". It's a lovely phrase, but not a new one to Hebrew ears. Two centuries earlier, in a moving moment of divine self-disclosure, another prophet had declared on God's behalf: "When Israel was a child I loved him, and out of Egypt I brought my son." He went on to record the wayward behaviour of that child. "The more I called them, the more they went from me. Yet it was I who taught Ephraim to walk. I took them up in arms but they did not know that I healed them. I led them with cords of human kindness; I was to them like those who lift infants to their cheeks. I bent down to them and fed them."

What parent or grandparent does not respond to the deep feeling in those words? So now, says Isaiah, the moment has come for the people of the covenant to realise in a new way this vocation to be God's child, to be those through whom God opens his arms wide and embraces the world. "I will give you as a light to the nations," he says, "so that my salvation may reach to the end of the earth."

Our Christian hindsight looks back across the centuries to those words. It looks back and understands that only one person has ever truly embodied that vocation. That truest of Israelites, we Christians say, is Jesus of Nazareth, the one who fulfils the ideal of the Lord's Child, the infant who lay in the manger and whom shepherds and magi recognised as Immanuel; the one who called God *Abba*, Father, who learned to see himself as the child who must be about his Father's business. So we are not surprised that at his baptism, when the sky is torn open and the dove descends, the voice echoes these ancient words of the prophet and cries: "This is my Son the beloved, with whom I am well pleased."

Today, as we baptise Alexander and Lucie, we hear those words again. "This is my child, my beloved." We hear them spoken to Jesus. But we also hear them spoken to the children who come for baptism, and we hear them spoken to each of us. For what is baptism, if not to receive the seal of God's Spirit that affirms that we are indeed children of God? What is it, if it is not the sign that God welcomes us home from exile, receives us back from our strange lands, offers us his generosity, stretches out his arms of love and reaches towards us to embrace us, invites us through Jesus to pray with the words "Our Father"? There is no way of life more dignified, more humanising, more fulfilling than living out this call to be God's beloved child. The voice says "this is my beloved child", and Lucie and Alexander say "yes" to it today, yes to God's invitation to become more truly a human being, find their truest selves, embrace the path of light and love, and life in all its abundance.

All this belongs to Alexander and Lucie today. In baptism, each of us is made "a member of Christ, the child of God, and an inheritor of the kingdom of heaven", as the old catechism puts it. A beloved child of God, the voice from heaven tells us, our names written on his hands: that is what we are when we become members of Christ. Like him, we are in the world to be children, disciples, servants, bearers of light and glory. Where horizons are dark and exile threatening, where so many suffer and peace on earth seems distant, where we quickly lose heart and hope begins to fail, baptism is a sign of the God who keeps faith with us. Because of that voice that spoke from heaven, we can safely entrust this world and ourselves to God's Child who comes to us. With joy we journey on into another year and give a heartfelt welcome to Alexander, Lucie, and all who want to walk this Christian way with us. For if we are God's children, God's beloved, we know there is a future worth living for.

12 January 2014, The Feast of the Baptism of Christ
Isaiah 42:1–9; Matthew 3:13–end

In Praise of Slow

In Lent

The Church is becoming a fast place. More and more, it seems, things have to be done quickly, and against strategic plans and finely-calibrated timelines. This is now the organisational culture of the west, and it is relentlessly demanding on leadership both in the church and in secular environments. No doubt we all aspire to becoming an efficient, well-led, intelligently-managed church that is clear about its direction of travel. At the same time, shouldn't Christian communities be modelling this in ways that are kinder to the human spirit? Lent could be a time to experiment by working at another pace and to a different rhythm.

In 1878, Mark Twain was in Switzerland. He had climbed high up a valley near Zermatt and was looking for a quick way down. Below him was the Gorner Glacier. He wrote:

> I took up as good a position as I could upon the middle of the glacier—because Baedeker said the middle part travels the fastest. As a measure of economy, however, I put some of the heavier baggage on the shoreward parts, to go as slow freight. I waited and waited, but the glacier did not move. Night was coming on, the darkness began to gather—still we did not budge. It occurred to me then that there might be a timetable in Baedeker; it would be well to find out the hours of starting. I soon found a sentence which threw a dazzling light upon the matter. It said, "The Gorner Glacier travels at an average rate of a little less than an inch a day." I have seldom felt so outraged. I have seldom felt my confidence so wantonly betrayed. I made a small calculation: one inch a day, say thirty feet a year; estimated distance to Zermatt, three and one-eighteenth miles. Time required to go by glacier, a little over five hundred years! The passenger part of this glacier—the

central part—the lightning express part, so to speak, was not due
in Zermatt until the summer of 2378, and the baggage, coming
along the slow edge, would not arrive until some generations
later . . . As a means of passenger transportation, I consider the
glacier a failure.

By now, 126 years later, Twain would have travelled about three quarters
of a mile. It's not the slowest form of travel—continental drift takes longer.
But you still get plenty of time to enjoy the view. When my wife and I were
students courting in Bristol, we often walked alongside the Avon Gorge.
We even climbed it once, scaring the life out of ourselves as we gazed
down between our legs at the void below us. It was a thought-provoking
place that spoke to me about the different speeds with which life is lived
and change happens. There were cars rushing along the main road and, at
a more sedate pace, local trains, diesel multiple units rumbling along the
line to Avonmouth and Severn Beach. There was the river itself, muddy,
languid, and slow. And then there were the geological strata you could
see running along the cliffs: ancient memories preserved in rock, patterns
that were there millions of years before human beings came along and
that will still be there long after we have gone.

God has plenty of time: this is how the world now strikes us if we have
eyes to see it. A friend of mine said that it was like walking a toddler in the
park and forever waiting for him to catch you up—the toddler being an
image of a God who is never in a hurry. The Japanese theologian Kosuke
Koyama called him, in a wonderful phrase, "Three Mile an Hour God". He
points to the forty years it took God even to begin to teach the Israelites
the single lesson that man does not live by bread alone. God uses his time
in a carefully calculated way. In today's gospel, Jesus says: "Listen. Today
and tomorrow I am casting out demons and performing healings; and on
the third day I finish my work." This is in answer to those who told him to
abandon what he was doing and run away because of a threat to his life.
But Jesus says no. Like Sir Francis Drake playing bowls on Plymouth Hoe
as the Spanish Armada bore down on England, Jesus knows that there is
a time for everything under the sun, a more spiritual way of being that
does not live merely by efficiency or achievement or outputs, but that

cherishes and cultivates integrity, carefulness, and truth. It's an aspect of what one spiritual writer called "the sacrament of the present moment".

I am trying to learn, late in life, that the race is not always to the swift nor the battle to the strong. Ours is an age where speed is everything. Wherever you turn, in business, in industry, in education, even in the church, success is measured by this: that you make changes *fast*. When I was in Sheffield and steering a big development project for the Cathedral, I asked a wealthy businessman for funding. As he wrote out the cheque, he said to me: "Michael, it's really important that the church models something different from the hectic pace at which we in the public and private sectors expect to see results. The Cathedral has been here for centuries. It can help us take the long view. It can help us learn the meaning of patience." Perhaps this is what St Benedict meant by *stability* in his rule for monks: not running feverishly from place to place, either physically or metaphorically, but being committed to the present where God has placed us, living according to the long view. It was a necessary message as the Roman Empire fell apart, and landmarks familiar to generations crumbled into dust.

And help is at hand. If you go to www.notbusy.co.uk you will find resources put together by Canon Stephen Cherry and Sacristy Press based on his book *Beyond Busyness*. The idea is to give up busyness during Lent and regain control of our lives by living more at God's pace than our own. You can even get a wristband telling the world that you're not busy. For me, the first sign of success will be to disagree with anyone who says to me, "You must be so busy". Indeed, authentic Christian ministry means the very opposite: having time for other people and for God. I see this as the work of love: ours for God and for others, but most of all, God's love for us. If Lent means anything, it should be that we become more aware of Love's work in us and all around us, and learn to live it for ourselves. As everyone who has loved knows, love has its own speed. It is "slow", yet it is lord over all other speeds. It goes on in the depth of our being, whether we notice it or not, whether we have mountains to scale or torrents to span or are crossing the quieter welcome prairies of our existence. If you ask me about the speed God walks, I would say: *adagio, lento,* sometimes *andante,* but not often *presto* or *vivace*; the still small voice, not the earthquake, wind, and fire.

Sometimes, it is true, God can seem in a hurry, when events happen at a bewildering pace and we are left breathless. But that's rare in my experience. Mostly, he is so slow his movement is undetectable except to those who remain still for long enough. Perhaps the spiritual task in such a fast world is to learn how to become contemplatives: men and women with time, so to speak, to sit on the glacier and travel at God's speed; to be open to the gift of love, celebrate the sacrament of the present moment. The world needs such people who can see into the life of things and bring to its relentless flow and flux the gifts of stability and peace. Love works slowly, but God has plenty of time. We can afford to wait for the Lord. For soon it will be spring, and the earth will blossom, and our lives with it; and, most of all, our hope will grow during Lent as we prepare to celebrate the resurrection of our most glorious Lord of life.

Hunwick Church, 24 February 2013
Luke 13:31–end

A Dark and Dreadful Death

In Holy Week

In 2015, the Chapter agreed to preach through St Mark's passion
narrative on each Sunday of Lent. For me at least, it was a revelation
to immerse myself in that extraordinary story and to preach two
sermons in the series. There is no substitute for taking the biblical
text with the utmost seriousness and listening to the resonances it has
with contemporary human living. This concluding sermon turned
out to be tougher than I had expected: for the preacher certainly,
and possibly for those who heard it. There is no way we can make
Jesus' last sabachthani word from the cross easy or comfortable.

Throughout Lent we have walked the *via dolorosa* with Jesus. Today we
have arrived at its awful destination: Golgotha, crucifixion, darkness,
desolation, and pain. It is a world away from Palm Sunday with its hosanna
acclamations and royal expectations. If ever you needed a reason not to
trust a crowd, it is Palm Sunday. For look what has become of this king!
The mob has bellowed for his crucifixion. He cannot, will not, save himself
from this destiny, St Mark's three fateful "musts" that have pointed to this
journey's end. Today, on this Sunday of the Passion, we contemplate him
as the man of sorrows, acquainted with grief.

If we are honest, part of us does not know what to make of him hanging
there. The trouble is, we know this story too well. We know, or think we
know, what lies beyond the end of it, which is next Sunday's theme. We also
know how the other three evangelists tell it, and they colour our reading
of St Mark. If we only had this first among the Gospels, it would both
appal and baffle us. We would be baffled because Mark does not explain
why the innocent Son of Man should undergo such suffering. We would
be appalled because Mark does not spare us the agony: the darkness that
falls on the scene, the desperation of this man's last cry, the hopelessness
of this death. And, worst of all perhaps, he endures all this alone, taunted

and mocked on every side, deserted by his friends, abandoned by God. This is a narrative of *dread*. We should tremble to read it.

Let me explore some of the themes in this part of the story. The first is the *darkness*. Forget about eclipses, even though they are a recent memory this year. Mark's darkness is altogether deeper than a mere shadow. It's the darkness of judgment in our lesson from Amos, which Mark quotes earlier in the Gospel in a famous apocalyptic passage: "In those days after that suffering, the sun will be darkened and the moon will not give its light, and the stars will be falling from the sky, and the powers in the heavens will be shaken" (13:24–5). Jesus is speaking just before the passion narrative begins. He says that the kingdom of God cannot come until there is an utter collapse of the present world order: the great stones of the temple will be toppled, human communities and relationships will disintegrate, the entire cosmos will fall in an instant like a house of cards. Mark expects us to remember that saying, so that when we hear of the sun's light failing in the middle of the day, we recognise what it represents. It is the end of the world, and it is the end of Jesus' world. He must be extinguished like the sun. He must collapse and die as everything dies round him.

That is dreadful enough. But my second theme is darker still: Jesus' *last word from the cross*. Was ever a cry more desperate and more desolate than this awful cry with which he dies? *Eloi, Eloi, lema sabachthani?* We must tread carefully here, for we are on holy ground. Our "Lama Sabachthani" crucifix in the north quire aisle captures something of it: the figure of Jesus whittled down to its bare essentials like the skeleton of a dead tree, his back arched in agonising pain. "Was ever grief like mine?" he seems to say to us. But this is more than physical suffering. There is a godforsakenness of the soul as the world ends for him and his existence is snuffed out. "My God, my God, why have you abandoned me?" The quotation is of course from Psalm 22, one of the psalms like 69 that so profoundly influenced the way in which the evangelists shaped their passion stories. These psalms end on a note of hope that God does not forget his suffering children and will bring them to a place of deliverance and thankfulness. Does Jesus anticipate the rest of the psalm when he cries out in its opening words, as if he can envisage his own resurrection? I doubt it. I believe that as the abyss opens up beneath him, he takes to his lips the words no doubt learned from childhood that so aptly echo his despair. God has handed him over, betrayed him. He has turned his face away. He may cry, but there is no answer. Elijah will not come to save him.

At the instant of his death, an extraordinary event takes place not far away from Golgotha. This is my third theme: "the *curtain of the temple* was torn in two, from top to bottom." For the evangelists, this was remembered as deeply significant on that terrible Friday afternoon. But what did it represent to them? The "veil" hid the holiest part of the temple, where only the high priest was allowed to go, once a year on the Day of Atonement. Does this violent tearing symbolise the passing of the old religion, with its worn-out dependence on rituals and ceremonies? For now a new and living way to God is opened up through the blood of Jesus. And Mark sees this as another scene in the apocalyptic drama acted out on the cross. Like the darkness at noon, like Jesus' wrecking of the money-changers' tables in the temple precinct, the rent veil stands for judgment on Jerusalem and its religious institutions. The old must be swept away before the new comes. By the time Mark wrote, the temple had already been destroyed by the Romans. Was this not a sign of the end of days? When Mark speaks of the tearing of the temple veil, he uses a word he has already used in his Gospel. At Jesus' baptism, he says that the sky is "torn open" as the dove descends and the voice from heaven speaks, and Jesus begins to announce that the kingdom of God is at hand. Golgotha heralds that new world order we call the kingdom. The cup he must drink, that will not pass from him, requires that he drink the dregs from the pressed red grapes of the vine-press of the wrath of God. If he is to save the world, he must be utterly crushed.

What strange work is set before us in Holy Week at Golgotha! But what do we need to do as we watch these events unfold? Mark answers his own question. Forget the crowds shouting *hosanna* one day and *crucify* the next; forget the disciples who forsook Jesus and fled; forget the cynics who hail him as king, or the thieves and soldiers who mock him. There is an individual who stands out from the crowd and sees differently: the centurion. Maybe he is in charge of the soldiers who have crucified Jesus. Watching, this gentile Roman, this Jew-hater, this military man whose trade is power and cruelty, has an epiphany. "Surely, this man was the Son of God." Not just innocent, not just a good man, but the Son of

God. The centurion isn't a bystander now. He has become a participant, whose words form the climax of the entire Gospel in one of the Bible's great recognition scenes. Mark sees this not just as one man's confession of faith but as speaking for all humanity, for *us* as we acknowledge the majesty of this crucified Messiah. Bach took it this way when he gave these immortal words to the full chorus in his *St Matthew Passion*, the two greatest bars of music ever written. The only reason Mark is writing his Gospel is to make believers out of us, to draw us from being bystanders to participants as we become subjects of God's kingdom and follow the crucified Lord. In last week's preacher's words, God renounces all power but the power of love, yet faith is possible in the teeth of suffering and ridicule. In the darkness, we can still believe.

This means that we cannot simply watch him hanging there, but must summon up an act of faith that acclaims him as our Lord and puts right our perspective on the world as God's, with ourselves as loyal followers and subjects. To mould the church's faith and our own in this cross-shaped way is the only reason we observe Holy Week with such care and devotion. It is so that we place at the very centre of our lives this saving death, this life that is poured out for us in what today's collect calls God's tender love.

Palm Sunday 2015
Amos 8:9–12; Mark 15:33–41

White Easter

*It may already be evident from this book that I often find that
my preaching is coloured by times and seasons of the natural
world: solstices and equinoxes, phases of the moon, warm
and cold, light and dark. Here is an Easter sermon from a
year when the weather made it feel more like Christmas.*

It is a wintry Easter that we are celebrating this year, for all of us cold
and, for some, very white. It's no comfort to be told that a March Easter
is more likely to be white than Christmas Day. The psychological and
emotional effect of this equinoctial cold is all the more potent because
we do not expect it and were not prepared for it when the days became
longer than the nights. Fierce has this unseasonal winter's grip been in
upland Britain, which begins not twenty miles west of here. Ask the
elderly. Ask the farmers.

Lent is an old English word for spring. We have ached for spring, for
its luminous duck-egg skies, its birdsong, its fresh colours and flowers.
We would love to see cumulus bubble up again, borne on a southerly
zephyr, letting loose sharp showers to wash the landscape. We would love
to feel the gentle warmth of the strengthening sun as it climbs towards
the zenith. When spring comes, it will never have been more welcomed.

Of course, whether it is white or green, Easter is always a bursting
forth of light and colour and life. In this Cathedral, and in every church
in the land, and in the hearts of all who feel the slightest pull of spiritual
reality, it is springtime today. *Rise heart, thy Lord is risen. Sing his praise
without delays.*

> I got me flowers to straw thy way;
> I got me boughs off many a tree:
> But thou wast up by break of day,
> And brought'st thy sweets along with thee.

But perhaps this prolonged winter brings a gift with it: to help us to enter into an aspect of the Easter story that we might not have felt in quite this way before. I mean the complex emotions of those who loved Jesus, and who on Good Friday experienced the most terrible sense of bafflement, confusion, and loss. For them, the aftermath of Golgotha would have been nothing less than a winter of the soul when, as R. S. Thomas says, there is a "black frost" encrusting the heart.

In her cycle of radio plays about the gospel story, *The Man Born to Be King*, Dorothy L. Sayers has John discover a pair of old sandals that Jesus had worn. He hides them from Peter because of what memories charged with sight and feel and smell would do to him, "like a sick animal that has crawled home to die. He can't eat. He can't sleep." One of the normal symptoms of bereavement is aching for the presence of the loved one, with an instinct to search that will not go away. Who is to say what brought the women to the garden at dawn on Easter morning? They went to anoint a body with spices, but what else drove them there? Surely, the need to see him again, feel the tender skin, remember his voice, his touch, his scent. Perhaps this year we have glimpsed this in an attenuated way by our sense of the cold, our own wintry longing for Easter, for springtime, for warmth.

Easter answers our longings and desires. It does this by both changing how things were, and transforming our view of them. We would not be here if we didn't believe that something infinitely life-changing took place on Easter morning when the women went to the tomb and found the stone rolled away and the grave space empty. There is no getting away from this singularity in history. "Why do you look for the living among the dead? He is not here," say the two men in the garden. A real absence, indeed, but a vacuum that gives the women what they most need: permission to dare to entertain the possibility that all was not as it seemed, that they were in the presence of the most profound of mysteries that nevertheless had the capacity to turn round despair. "He is risen. Remember how he told you." Here is where fantasy meets reality, where longing is transmuted into hope. The women begin to see reality differently. We begin to. The world is a different place. The garden has flowers. There is blue sky above our heads. The earth begins to warm. At last it is spring. Everything changes.

Of course, all this is to collapse a long disclosure and its realisation into a few moments. Luke himself keeps us in suspense here: the disciples did not believe the women at first. The two who walked the Emmaus Road with the unknown stranger did not recognise him; there was a journey to make, not simply along a dusty, cratered, Near Eastern cart track, but an inward journey of the soul to bring springtime to their bleakness, coax their frozen spirits back into life. The important thing is: there is disclosure. There is a new world. Winter has fled, and with it, its gloomy shadows and oppressive captivity. He is risen.

St Augustine has a beautiful passage in a commentary on the feeding of the crowd where he speaks about our human longings and hungers. "Give me a lover: a lover will feel what I am speaking of; give me one who longs, who hungers, who is a thirsty pilgrim in this wilderness, sighing for the springs of his eternal homeland; give me such a person, for they will know what I mean." He might have added: give me one who is longing for spring, yearning to be rid of burdens, tired of this endless Narnian winter, weary in themselves, weary for our globe that strives to find some hope as it struggles under the weight of unhealed conflict, sorrow and pain.

If this echoes your experience, then come to the risen Lord today. Sit down at his Easter feast. Eat bread and drink wine. Find your healing and refreshment in him; be glad that he is among us as our beloved brother, who was lost in his death but found in his resurrection, who opens up the way home for all people and welcomes us to celebrate here in his Father's house. For here, at least, "the winter is past, the flowers appear on the earth, and the time of singing has come. Arise my love, my fair one, and come away."

Easter Day, 2013
Luke 24:1–12

Three Degrees

At Rogation

This sermon could have been included in the earlier Part, "Singing the Lord's Song in a Strange Land". Climate change is perhaps the biggest and most intractable challenge the human race has ever had to face. The season of Rogation, when we pray for God's blessing upon our soils and our harvests, seemed an appropriate time of year to speak about it.

"Three degrees of latitude is enough to overthrow the whole of jurisprudence . . . Strange justice that is bounded by a river or mountain! The truth on this side of the Pyrenees, error on the other." Pascal's point is that you don't have to travel very far for the climate of law and custom to look utterly different, and possibly very threatening.

That saying of one of Europe's greatest thinkers haunted me as I was reading a book I had recently bought. It was purely a word association at first, triggered by its title, *Six Degrees: Our Future on a Hotter Planet*. It's by Mark Lynas, an environmental commentator who has devoted himself to highlighting the urgency of the threats posed by climate change. His book has six chapters chronicling what would happen to the world were climate change to result in global warming of one degree, two degrees, three, four, five, or six degrees Celsius. His thesis is that the world's ecosystems can sustain a rise of at most two degrees. Beyond that, a tipping point is reached, resulting in irreversible change to our planet's climate. The consequences are perhaps unimaginable, but they must not be; for unless we imagine them, we shall be their victims. The book is all the more alarming for being written in a cool-headed, matter-of-fact way that marshals evidence from palaeontologists, climatologists, biologists, and social historians, and invites readers to draw their own conclusions. There is a growing consensus that unless worldwide carbon emissions peak and begin to decline in the next few years, global temperatures will inevitably rise by more than two degrees by the middle of this century.

Pascal's three degrees take us into territory where we do not want to go. Here is part of the scenario. At three degrees, the glaciers of the entire Himalaya would recede over the coming century, and finally vanish. Among them are the three and a half thousand glaciers that feed the River Indus, the mighty river at whose banks, famously, Alexander the Great stopped and wept because there were no more worlds for him to conquer. If water flows in the Indus were to drop by 80 per cent, the effect on the country whose agriculture is almost wholly dependent on it would be catastrophic. A south Asian breadbasket would revert to desert, and famine would result. Tens of millions of refugees would flee to the cities in search of livelihood, water, and food. This would be a human disaster anywhere. When the nation is already dangerously unstable and has nuclear weapons, we are foolish not to worry. That country is one about which we are hearing a good deal at present, most of it unsettling. I mean Pakistan. It is one scenario among many others that persuades me that the greatest threat now facing us as a human race is not global terrorism, not the financial crisis, not worldwide pandemics, not population growth, not nuclear weapons. It is climate change. And, like a vortex, it will suck in these other threats we face. We are foolish to ignore it.

This week we mark Rogation, when the church traditionally prays for kind weather, good harvests, and an abundance of crops to feed the human race. But it has also become a time to reflect on what is happening to the world's climate and its effects on the world's harvests, especially in the developing nations. Once, Rogation processions in the fields to bless the newly-sown crops were joyful celebrations. Now, this season has a decidedly edgy feel, for it draws attention to the responsibility we in the developed countries bear for climate change, and what we must do to reverse it. Our second lesson today captures the note of urgency. The letter to the Laodiceans is addressed to a complacent, affluent society whose very success has made it deaf to talk of crisis. "You say, 'I am rich, I have prospered and I need nothing.' You do not realise that you are wretched, pitiable, poor, blind, and naked." Of course, it is not responsibility for climate change of which the writer accuses Laodicea, though we could say that there has been a sentient moral and spiritual climate change that can be laid at their door. And this is the attitude that colours the way the church is: easy-going, living for the day, untroubled by any nagging self-doubt, those uncomfortable night thoughts that there might, just might, all be something in this talk of coming nemesis after all.

The letter uses a striking metaphor to depict the condition of the Laodiceans. "I know your works: you are neither hot nor cold. I wish that you were either cold or hot. So because you are lukewarm, and neither cold nor hot, I am about to spit you out of my mouth." That Goldilocks image of being not too hot and not too cold seems perversely to be a rather desirable state of affairs for the world's climate; but not as an image of our attitude to it. For when God challenges us to wake up to reality, lukewarmness is not only sickly: it is fatal. What is needed is to respond decisively. To do this out of the belief that God cares about our world and has entrusted it to humanity for its safe keeping is to take the first steps towards change. We know this is true in our personal lives: repentance and conversion of life is the first step towards transformation and renewal. Perhaps we are beginning to recognise how it is also true for societies and nations, how our own survival and wellbeing and that of our descendants depend on the decisions we make in our generation.

In this the churches are giving a lead. The General Synod has debated climate change on a number of occasions. Local churches are being urged to "shrink the footprint", undertake carbon audits, promote energy efficiency, and stimulate public thinking about how we can all minimise our impact on the planet. The Cathedral has been examining its own part in this, and has an environmental policy and a committee to advise the Chapter on a range of measures: lower lighting levels, better insulation, lessening our dependence on gas and oil, exploring renewable energy sources. They are small things, and the temptation would be to think that they could make a difference. They won't, by themselves; what is needed is a sense of common purpose and the political will to effect change. Yet we should not despise the day of small things. Many littles amount to more, and raise awareness daily, hourly, that our planet is burning away. It is denial that is the enemy of repentance, because it's the enemy of truth. To recognise that we face threats that are real and far-reaching is the first step towards doing something that will make a difference.

Three degrees does not sound much. But they would overthrow the whole of civilisation. Lynas' book ends with a chapter entitled "Choosing our Future". He quotes Dante: "the portals of the future close." His point is that they have not closed—yet. There is still time, a few years, perhaps a decade, in which to make the decisions that will save us. In these Rogation Days, we should remember those who lead the nations, and pray that God will help us all avert the disasters that will otherwise come upon our world. This Christian Aid Week we have had on our hearts the poor and desperate of the developing world, who will be, already are, the first victims of climate change. We should listen to the prophetic voices of the good science we must heed if we are to save ourselves. This act of collective repentance will need resources of courage, collaboration, and determination that we have never yet called upon as a race. But we also need to hear the promise with which our reading ends, and which we need to sustain us in these difficult tasks we face: "Listen! I am standing at the door, knocking; if you hear my voice and open the door I will come in to you and eat with you, and you with me." The knock on the door could mean our nemesis. But if we have an ear to listen, it could save us from ourselves.

17 May 2009
Revelation 3:14–end

A Humble Ascent

On Ascension Day

*This short homily was given on the day of an important
announcement for Durham. We did not know then that our new
Bishop would in a short while become Archbishop of Canterbury
and that his time with us would be brief. It challenges our received
ideas that height is always the same as dignity or power. The true
power and dignity of love lies in humbling ourselves and taking
the form of a servant, as our Master did in the upper room.*

Today we have learned who our next Bishop will be. After many months'
waiting, it is good to know at last, and we look forward to making Justin
Welby and his family welcome when he begins his ministry among us.
The significance of this announcement on Ascension Day has not been
lost on us. To many people, preferment is a kind of ascension; and in the
Bishop of Durham's case, his enthronement will literally involve ascending
Bishop Hatfield's great *cathedra*, which was built to be the highest throne
in Christendom. No doubt, in the popular piety of Durham in the Middle
Ages, when the Count Palatine mounted many steps to sit on high in his
throne of glory, it was as if the ascension of Jesus was being acted out, the
glory of a human throne an image of the heavenly one.

However, the truth is a little different. In St Luke's story that we heard as
the epistle reading, the ascension is not a magnificent spectacle heralded
by fanfares, even if painters and musicians have often depicted it that
way. He tells of a more modest, intimate event, witnessed by a handful
of people who were left with the memory not of Elijah's fiery whirlwind,
horsemen, and chariots, but of a lonely cloud and a vast and empty sky.
The angels, when they do appear, are simply two men dressed in white
who engage in ordinary conversation. Perhaps this is what we would
expect of Luke's story of the one who came into the world in a manger,

was crucified between two thieves, and who revealed the resurrection incognito in the breaking of bread.

Luke's Jesus says before his passion, "I am among you as one who serves." So Jesus' exaltation is splendid not for its outward demonstration of power and authority but for the inner character of kingship that it reveals. His throne of glory is always the seat from which compassion and love flow out to the world, from where he continues to minister to us and serve us as he did when he was among us in this world. "Yet he loves the world he leaves", as Wesley's hymn puts it: for whatever makes love *love* does not change when it passes beyond physical sight and touch. We need to understand the Ascension as of a piece with the gospel narrative of which it is part: not a void created by the departure of a magnificent but absent monarch, but the promise of a new fullness by which the risen Jesus will be present to us and among us through his Spirit.

On Maundy Thursday at the eucharist of the last supper, we wash feet at the foot of this mighty bishop's throne. The message is: whoever would be the greatest among you must be the servant of all. This is how Jesus was and always is. And this is how all leaders must be, and most of all, those called to leadership in the church of God. So on the day when our new bishop is announced, we pray that he will emulate the ascension of Jesus when he is enthroned here in a few months' time. How he climbs these steps and sits down on his mighty *cathedra* will set the tone of his episcopate: not to be over us so much as among us as one who serves; one to wash feet and break bread as well as stir hearts, as he leads us in sharing the mission of the risen and ascended Lord to his world. Michael Ramsey used to say when he was Bishop of Durham that on his throne, he was the only person in the Cathedral who could see the world outside. It put him in his place, reminded him of what lay at the heart of ministry: not losing touch with the good earth, bearing humanity in his heart, connected to the world in its complexity and need. That is how Christ is in his humiliation and in his exaltation. That is why we give thanks on this great day.

Ascension Day 2011
Acts 1:1–11

The Fiftieth Day

On the Feast of Pentecost

This is more St Bede's sermon than mine, but it was new to me and perhaps it was new to those who heard me speak. In the long line of biblical scholars, few have been better interpreters of the sacred text than our own beloved Bede. I often stand at his shrine in the Galilee Chapel and am moved to be in the presence of a man of such extraordinary learning. Biblical commentaries, poetry, astronomy, mathematics, history, rhetoric, classics—Bede was a master of them all.

Today's readings are not quite what you would expect on Whit Sunday: Moses and God on Mount Sinai in the Old Testament, and St Paul's commentary on that story in the New. The connections seem arcane, to say the least. But help is at hand in the shape of the man we commemorated on Friday, our own St Bede, the greatest biblical scholar of his day. He has a sermon for Pentecost that I am tempted to pass off as my own (it's rather good). Here is part of it.

> The Jewish feast of the Law is a foreshadowing of our feast today. When the children of Israel had been freed from slavery in Egypt by the offering of the paschal lamb, they journeyed through the desert toward the Promised Land, and they reached Mount Sinai. On the fiftieth day after the Passover, the Lord descended upon the mountain in fire, and with the sound of a trumpet and with thunder and lightning, he gave them the ten commandments of the Law. As a memorial . . . he decreed an annual feast on that day, an offering of the first-fruits, in the form of two loaves of bread, made from the first grain of the new harvest, which were to be brought to the altar . . . Just as the Law was given on the 50th day after the slaying of the lamb, when the Lord descended upon the mountain in fire; likewise on the fiftieth day after the resurrection

> of our Redeemer ... the grace of the Holy Spirit, descending in
> the outward appearance of fire, was given to the disciples as they
> were assembled in the upper room.

So the point is that today is *Pente*cost: the fiftieth day of redemption. Let's take the three points Bede makes and see how they help us understand some of the many layers of meaning in Whit Sunday.

First, the law of Moses given at Pentecost. Bede quaintly links Moses "going up" a mountain to receive the law with the disciples being in an upper room when the Spirit is given:

> The height of the mountain and of the upper room show the
> sublimity of both the commands and the gifts. At the sealing of the
> first covenant, the people remained at the base of the mountain,
> a handful of elders went partway up, and only Moses ascended
> to the summit. At the sealing of the second covenant, the whole
> community of God's people was gathered at the summit, in the
> upper room.

Moreover, the gift of the law was given to only one nation, the Hebrews; whereas the gift of the Spirit is for the proclaiming of the gospel to every living person on the face of the earth. And this is St Paul's argument in our second reading. There was a glory disclosed to Moses, he says, and we heard in Exodus how Moses prayed, "Show me your glory." But in the new covenant, there is an even greater splendour, for the gift of the Spirit is to remove forever the veil that obscures the glory of God, so that we are transformed into his image "from one degree of glory to another". And this is one of the aspects of Whit Sunday for which we give thanks today, that in Jesus, it is given to us to know and to love God face to face, as Moses says, "as one speaks to a friend". So the high mountain on which the law is given becomes an image of how, in this era of the Spirit, our covenant relationship with God is filled with the most precious intimacy. The covenant means, quite simply, to know God, to love God, to obey God. So Bede's first insight is about *discipleship*.

Bede's *second* point is how the Hebrew feast of Pentecost originated in the offering of the first-fruits of the harvest of the land. In a beautiful passage elsewhere in the Torah, a worshipper is required to bring a basket of first-fruits and set it before the Lord, and celebrate how God has made of wandering semi-nomads a people settled in their land, filled with gratitude for all the goodness he has bestowed on them. For Bede, this is a picture of how, in the era of the Spirit, the gospel is preached with a new power: people of every nation both hear and believe. These new believers, he says, are the first-fruits of the new covenant. "So every year on the feast of Pentecost, the Church baptises, and so offers to the Lord an offering of the first-fruits of the redeemed from the face of the earth, an offering of both Jews and gentiles." The Acts of the Apostles tells how Pentecost was a truly defining event, both in the transformation of lives and in the energy with which the gospel is proclaimed in every place. Those first Christian converts demonstrated the truly international, universal character of the gospel—how it was not a sectarian message for the few, but a summons of good news addressed to the whole of humanity. Acts tells how these first-fruits of the response to the gospel were harvested. This harvest continues today: mission is part of our lifeblood. And if we want to live out the meaning of Pentecost, then like the first Christians in their explosion of confidence and joy, we will gladly share our faith with others in order to "make God believable", as Rowan Williams puts it. So Bede's second insight is about *mission*.

Finally, Bede comments on how the Law was given to the Hebrews on the fiftieth day of their journey to the promised land. "The grace of the Spirit", he says "was given to the people of the new covenant on the fiftieth day, so that we might know how our journey is directed toward that heavenly country that is our eternal rest, our place of deep and abiding satisfaction." He links this with the law's command to keep a jubilee every fiftieth year as a memory of God's redemption and an incentive to celebrate his praises. In that year, debts were cancelled, slaves set free, and even beasts of burden eased from their yokes.

> This number indicates the tranquillity of that greatest peace when, at the sound of the trumpet, the dead shall be raised imperishable, and we shall all be changed into glory. Then, when we are freed from every yoke of sin, and our debts . . . have all been forgiven and cancelled, the whole people of God will give themselves to

the heavenly vision, and the Lord's command will be fulfilled: Be still, and know that I am God.

Which is to say: Pentecost is a promise of something greater than we can ever see or know. It's the first-fruits not only of the human family's "yes" to God, but of the gift of his own glory and the transformation of all things, the new heaven and the new earth. There is work to do here and now, and we shall spend and be spent in the tasks of discipleship and mission to which we pledged ourselves in baptism, and for which the Holy Spirit empowers us. But a greater and more enduring glory awaits, when all things are God's, and we know him as we are known and see him face to face.

This is Bede's final insight about *hope*. Hope is perhaps the greatest gift of the Easter season. It keeps us alive, sustains us day by day, makes our alleluias possible, gives purpose to our discipleship and mission. I can't add to Bede's magnificent and moving words immortalised on the wall of the Galilee Chapel by his shrine where we stood last Friday and rekindled our hope in the God who was his and is ours today: "Christ is the Morning Star who when the night of this world is past brings to his saints the promise of the light of life and opens everlasting day." For him alone we live; to him alone be praise and honour on this festival day and all our days.

Whit Sunday 2007
Exodus 33:7–20; 2 Corinthians 3:7–end

Part 7: Heritage Seeks Holiness: North East People and Places

This concluding section is also the longest. It consists of sermons I have preached in various parts of North East England that have drawn out some meanings inherent in its long Christian history. Some of these have been occasioned by particular places such as Lindisfarne, the Farne Islands, Sunderland, Hexham, and of course living and working in Durham. The others are about some of the great souls who have populated this rich part of England and whose legacy continues to inspire us today. It's a story that's yet to be completed; I have been privileged to meet some great souls of the twenty-first century: who knows whether future preachers will be inspired by the quality of their Christian discipleship in our own day?

Part 7: Heritage Seeks Holiness: North East People and Places

A Living Foundation

Durham Cathedral Then and Now

On 11 August 1093, a momentous event took place here on this peninsula. On that day the foundation stone of this Cathedral was laid amid much pomp and ceremony and in the presence of royalty. We are celebrating it at services today, the Sunday nearest.

It was a watershed spiritually, historically, politically, and architecturally. As we know, we have the Norman bishop William of Saint-Calais to thank for it. It was he who embarked on the enormous project of replacing the Saxon "white" church with a great new cathedral in the Romanesque style that by the late eleventh century had become familiar across France and, after the Norman Conquest, England too. No doubt he was motivated by many aspirations. We can take it that he wished to build to the glory of God. But he also wanted to honour St Cuthbert, whom the Normans adopted as the North's patron saint, not least to win the Saxons' allegiance. Then he intended to express visibly the ideal of the great monastic church of a religious community, following the introduction of Benedictine monks to Durham a decade earlier. Finally, and perhaps not least, because human motivation always comes into things, he wanted to build big and grand to demonstrate that the Normans now held power in the land and to signal to Saxons and Scots alike that this peninsula was the seat not only of spiritual but of secular authority.

William of Saint-Calais did not live to see his cathedral finished, nor even the placing (or "translation") of Cuthbert's body into its final resting place behind the high altar when the shrine had been completed in 1104. But I always tread lightly near his grave in the Chapter House; the monks had wanted to bury him near Cuthbert, but he insisted that he was not worthy of it. (When my wife and I went to Saint-Calais, a little town in the Loire region of France, we found an elderly woman cleaning the church and asked about the great Norman bishop of Durham who was baptised there. She had never heard of him, and realising that we were *anglais,* told us that we must have confused Saint-Calais with the better known ferryport on the English Channel.)

You do not need me to tell you what we owe to him. This Cathedral is consistently regarded Britain's best-loved building and praised as a masterpiece the world over. That is a tribute to his vision and his eye for architecture. If you wanted to imagine a church that would be an embodiment of the Benedictine virtues of stability, balance, and the beauty of good order, you would not do better than Durham. Here is a building to lift the spirits, point you to the skies, drive you to your knees, enlarge the imagination, guide you to contemplate the vision of God and dream about a world in which his will is done on earth as in heaven. But it is also a building that affirms our humanity, holds us in a safe place, protects us from threat; a church that doesn't crush us with its awesomeness but upholds our human dignity, makes us feel honoured and valued. The laying of the foundation stone in 1093 inaugurated an era that, despite the changes and chances of centuries, still goes on in our day, drawing admirers, guests, and pilgrims in their millions. We who worship here, live here, volunteer here, work here are privileged to be a part of this history of a place of awesome majesty and beauty.

But the word "foundation" is perhaps misleading. For what took place in 1093 was not of course the founding of the Cathedral itself. That had existed on this site since the Saxon community of St Cuthbert, with their bishop, the relics of their saints, and the Lindisfarne Gospel Book, arrived here at the end of their long journey round the North a century earlier, and recognised that this was where the body of their saint would lie. Their cathedral had been lovingly built around Cuthbert's shrine. No doubt those who had known it shed tears when they saw it being torn down, just as some of the Jews returning from exile wept at the dedication of the new temple because they had not forgotten the old. So when we speak the language of "foundation", we should not forget an earlier history so deeply embedded in the founding story of this place: how (according to legend) the community was first guided on to this peninsula by a lost dun cow and the milkmaids looking for her. This "foundation" of 995 is important too, for it marked the point at which a wandering community of Lindisfarne exiles established itself as settled in one place, like the Hebrews entering into the promised land. It was another threshold that needed to be crossed, with awareness of the untested demands of a new, unknown environment.

But even this is not all we need to say today. If you look at the list of Bishops of Durham in *Crockford's Clerical Directory*, you will see that it begins not with the Saxon bishops who arrived here in the tenth century, or the Normans who succeeded them, but with the See of Lindisfarne founded by St Aidan himself at the instigation of King Oswald in 635. St Oswald's head is interred in the shrine along with Cuthbert, and we celebrated his feast last Tuesday with a procession to the feretory in which we remembered how he was the founder of the mission to Christianise Northumbria. So the true foundation of the See of Durham and its Cathedral lies not here at all, but eighty miles to the north, on the Holy Island where Aidan first gathered around him as bishop a community of prayer, study, evangelisation, and the service of the poor. This is where the story of our Cathedral begins. This is where the word "foundation" ultimately points.

This is important. It matters that we are accurate about our history. The monks of Durham were always clear that, as the shrine of St Cuthbert, this Cathedral looked back across an honoured era of Christian life and witness that preceded the Durham years by centuries. It also matters that we recognise that this Cathedral has been through many different incarnations and they are all part of the story of our "foundation". You could say that the Lindisfarne era was our apostolic age, when saints like Aidan and Cuthbert, Hild and Bede, Wilfred, Chad, and Cedd walked the landscapes of Northumbria and bore witness to the gospel of Jesus Christ with such power. You could also say that what followed it was just as significant: the century of exile after the Vikings had driven us from our Holy Island and forced us to travel around the North, ending up at Chester-le-Street, where the Cathedral was resident for more than a century. We learned through that experience to be a roving cathedral: a community that was discovering how to travel light, to adjust to ever-changing circumstances, realising that there is something deeply ingrained in Christian faith about being readily responsive to God's call. There is something attractive to me about being a Cathedral on the move. In a metaphorical and spiritual sense, this is how we must always be as we are led by God into futures that glow with possibility and promise. "To live is to change; to live long is to have changed much," said John Henry Newman.

So "foundation" is not finally about great stones and magnificent buildings. The fabric of a sacred space is there to demonstrate the deeper truth of our New Testament lesson. St Peter refers to "living stones", people like us from St Oswald and St Aidan to the present day, whose life in this community is founded upon Christ the Living Stone. And, he says, while we are aliens and exiles like our Hebrew forebears, nevertheless we carry the mark of Jesus' cross and resurrection, and are always ready to give a reason for the hope that is within us. That is why Durham Cathedral is here. And that is why it is good to celebrate its foundation today.

10 August 2014
1 Peter 2:1–12

An Island Where Faith Was Forged

The Inner Farne

There are few places I know that are as "thin", spiritually, as the Inner Farne, though Iona and Lindisfarne would be among them. To understand the spirit of the Saxon saints, a pilgrimage to the Farne is essential. You may have to try more than once: the sea is often rough and even the hardened sailors who ferry countless day-trippers across from Seahouses will not take risks around the treacherous basalt rocks. It makes you appreciate all the more the rugged fortitude of Aidan, Cuthbert, and their like.

Yesterday I went with the choristers to the Farne Islands and then to Holy Island. If you love Cuthbert as Durham people do, then you want to discover the places he loved too. If you had asked him where especially, he would have said: go to the Farne. Imbibe the spirit of that remote place where the North Sea's cold, slatey waters beat against the Whin Sill rocks, where guillemots, puffins, and terns have their island home under the wide Northumberland sky. Who knows where the name comes from? An old British word *farran* meaning "land", or *faran* meaning a traveller, or that the island group was thought to resemble a *fern* in shape?

Bede says that the Farne "is an island far out to sea"; that it was a "remote battlefield", haunted by demons, and that Cuthbert was the first person brave enough to live there alone; that he built himself a "city", which is how hermits talked about their cells, consisting of a circular wall cut out of the rock, a shelter to live in, and an oratory to pray in. He prayed hard, dug a pit, and lo, God turned the solid rock into a standing water whose supply never failed. He built a lodge for guests and cultivated the meagre soil whose first harvest was a good barley crop. When the birds set about devouring it, he told them off. "Why are you eating crops you did not yourselves grow? If God has said you can, so be it. If not, be off with you and stop damaging other people's property." Here Cuthbert spent the last part of his life, dying there on 20 March 687. The islands passed to Durham Cathedral Priory, which kept a cell of two monks there. Prior Castell built a pele tower; the earlier chapel is probably on the site of Cuthbert's oratory. You may not realise that the Farnes remained the Cathedral's property until as late as the nineteenth century.

I have preached often on our northern saints. They are among our prized gospel texts here in North East England. I put it that way because when the gospel is written on the hearts and lives of men, women, and children, it comes alive in a unique way. "They being dead yet speak", says our miners' banner in the south transept, a quotation from the letter to the Hebrews. The writer wants to inspire his readers to courage in following Jesus, so he lists some of the great heroes of faith in the Hebrew Bible and says: live like them; believe like them, hope like them. We read the passage in that chapel: "seeing we are surrounded by a great crowd of witnesses, let us run with perseverance the race that is set before us, looking to Jesus the pioneer and perfector of our faith."

But as I put it in my book *Landscapes of Faith*, holy people are inseparable from the places they populated. The places where they lived and walked and preached and prayed have become sacred sites, where pilgrims travel to remember how the saints did the work of God and bequeathed their spirit of faith and hope to those who came after them. So places become gospel texts too. Where the Spirit touches the earth, a sacred geography is established, a way of reading "place" in terms of its influence on human beings and their influence on it; how people of faith have responded to God's presence in particular places. We are sitting now within a sacred geography: this Cathedral and the city that grew around it, what the monks called an English Zion, all because of the monks who brought St Cuthbert's body here a thousand years ago and created a spiritual legacy that has shaped lives ever since.

The Farne is another of these places. So let me ask: what is the gospel written into the old eternal rocks and the deep salt sea that swirls round them? Among many words I hear there is one about *creaturehood*. I mean that these remarkable islands tell me something important about the natural world and how I must try to find my place within God's creation. I doubt that this has much to do with the conventional response of saying how beautiful they are. That would not have impressed Cuthbert. When the sea is stirred and the wind is up and the sky is like gunmetal, their gaunt isolation seems to seize hold of you, and the sense of exposure can be threatening. The thousands of birds wheeling round a vast sky and nesting precariously on the basalt are one of the awesome sights of England; yet, as Cuthbert knew, they too are not always comfortable bedfellows.

Yet it is this numinous quality of nature, ravishing or grim, that grasps you. It puts you in your place, reminds you of your own smallness in the face of what can't be tamed. We learn that we are mortals and not gods. The Farne is one of those places where our vision is brought back into focus, where we see what we always were and are, fashioned by our Creator and an integral part of the same chain of being as the islands, the rocks, the birds, and the sea. How important that corrective is for our whole existence as a human race capable of destroying the planet given to us as our home. It keeps us humble to recognise that we must act with courtesy towards all living things, as Mother Julian says, not out of enlightened self-interest, but because reverencing God's world is part of reverencing him for himself. To honour his handiwork in sky and earth and sea ought to teach us to honour one another, made as his image, charged with the care and stewardship of what he has made.

Reverence for God and courtesy for his fellow beings lay at the heart of Cuthbert's life on the Farne. He went there, as Bede says, to find solitude and devote himself to prayer. Bede is clear that this was not an act of withdrawal for the sake of gazing out on beautiful sunsets and thinking beautiful thoughts. The hermit saints looked for fierce landscapes where they would not be distracted from doing God's work of prayer. Cuthbert knew he must focus on this daunting spiritual ordeal, just as Jesus did in the desert. The sea journey our monks frequently made across the sound from Holy Island to the Farne were often difficult under the fierce blasts of wind that rush down from the Cheviot. The voyage was its own metaphor of arduous spiritual endeavour. When you step on to the Farne, you are reminded of how demanding it is to take up your cross to follow Christ.

Yet we find this tough spirituality sits well with reverence for nature. The solitaries have always been strangely companionable. It is not that they are reclusive; rather, their friends—humans or birds, animals, plants, or rocks—are those they perceive as also belonging to a world that is charged with the grandeur of God. For where our inner noise begins to be stilled, we become open to God in new ways, more responsive to our fellow travellers and the environments we share with them. So while this Cuthbert vocation is not for most of us all of the time, it could be for all of us some of the time. I'm thinking of how good it is for our minds and bodies as well as our souls to find regular times and spaces to be still and alone and prayerful. Whether it is for minutes or hours or days, we can embark on journeys large or small for the sake of travelling more deeply into God and into our own selves.

As people of faith, it's natural to want to imitate Cuthbert in seeking places that would nourish the spirit, as Jesus himself often did when he went up the mountain or into the desert to wrestle and pray. In the words of a desert father, "Go into your cell, and your cell will teach you everything." So go wherever your soul finds it can drink deep of the Spirit of the living God, whose risen Son shows us the Father, and as our way, our truth, and our life, looks for human hearts in which to make a home.

18 May 2014
John 14:1–14

Two Mothers

Lindisfarne and Durham

This was a Mothering Sunday sermon, though not the usual kind. It was preached in the little thirteenth-century church on Lindisfarne by the ruined priory that stands on or near the site of the monastery St Aidan founded in the seventh century. It was one of those luminous spring mornings. Holy Island could not have looked more ravishing.

A year ago yesterday, St Cuthbert's Day, I was installed as Dean of Durham. There was shadow over that service, for it was the day that war broke out in Iraq. But as I knelt at the shrine of St Cuthbert while the sound of Northumbrian pipes wafted across the Cathedral, I knew I was back in the North East, in "Cuthbertsland". I used to be an incumbent in Northumberland, and though I am not a native northerner, I came to love this rough, rugged county and its people, and its spiritual heart, Lindisfarne. When I visited Durham, I would get a pitying look from Northumberland people who would tell me that while Durham had the body of Cuthbert, his soul was still here on Holy Island. Well, of course Lindisfarne is the mother of Durham and the mother of us all in the North, for it was from here that so much of England was evangelised by those great men and women of the Northumbrian church such as Aidan and Hild and Chad and Aebba and Cuthbert. And because it was from here that the Saxon community set out with the relics of St Cuthbert and the precious Lindisfarne Gospels on that journey of more than a century that ended in Durham, our Cathedral is indeed the daughter of Lindisfarne.

But if we are your daughter, then we are also your mother. For in the violent years after the Norman Conquest, the Saxon community of St Cuthbert at Durham was displaced by Benedictine monks. And it was these who came back to Lindisfarne from Durham to found a priory here, one of many across the North of England. For the Christian presence had disappeared here and needed to be re-established. As you stand in the

Priory ruins here on Lindisfarne, and admire the patterned piers and the rainbow arch, you might think you were in the ruins of a smaller version in red sandstone of the mother house, Durham Cathedral. I remember having to remind my pilgrimage groups that the ruins we love so much here are those of the Benedictine daughter house of Durham, not the Saxon church where Aidan and Cuthbert had prayed.

On Mothering Sunday, we think about the relationship between mother and child. Good enough mothering is essential for human life to exist at all. A wholesome, loving relationship between a child and her mother is one of the most beautiful gifts we can ever know and celebrate. Each belongs to the other, gives to the other, enriches the other, even from before the moment of childbirth. And nothing so damages a human being as a mother who is distant or cruel or who walks away from her child. Our gospel reading today, the story of the prodigal, is all about sons and fathers: where is the mother of those two sons in this most moving of all the parables? Yet we can see in Jesus' image of fatherhood the same tenderness, the same compassion, the same longing that the Old Testament prophet Hosea pictured when he spoke of God as the mother of her people, bending down to feed Israel her beloved child.

So on Mothering Sunday, we think of Lindisfarne, the older mother of Durham, and of Durham, the younger mother of Lindisfarne. What gifts do they bring to each other and to us today? For they are rather different, these two mothers: they come out of different worlds, different cultures, they walked different spiritual paths. Could Cuthbert the Northumbrian shepherd, brought up in the Irish Christian traditions of Iona, ever have conceived being buried beneath an elaborate shrine behind the high altar of a Cathedral that was so visible a statement of ruthless Norman power? And would these sophisticated, efficient Normans ever have felt at home in the strange simplicity of Cuthbert's Holy Island? And, recognising that all human traditions are flawed and imperfect, how do we ask this question in a way that brings out the best of both, rather than romanticising the older and lamenting the younger?

Lindisfarne, our Saxon mother with so much Irish blood in her, gave us Cuthbert himself: the holy man, the prior, the missionary, the hermit, and the bishop. It gave us the unforgettable memory of a man who offered himself to God without holding anything back, who burned out of love for God and out of a desire to see all creation brought into unity with its maker. It gave us a saint who was fearless in battle, which is why he chose the solitary life on Inner Farne—not to escape the challenges of this world, but to engage more passionately in combating evil through prayer. And he did this on an island in the direct line of sight of Bamburgh Castle, where the kings of Northumbria had their seat, as if to say that even politics, our life in society with all its ambiguities and confusions, must become holy, must be lived before God to whom we must all give account. In him, we see a picture of Jesus' obedient emptying of himself before his father for the sake of the world; we see what we could become if only we took God at his word and gave ourselves up to him in prayer and in pursuit of the vision of God.

And Durham our Benedictine mother gave us a way of Christian discipleship that has also been hugely influential in the life of our church. Of course, Durham, wealthy and powerful as it became, was only one of many great Benedictine houses across Europe. These monasteries were different from Saxon communities, though Cuthbert knew and valued the Rule of St Benedict, one of the great Christian texts of all time. The rule committed monks to "stability" in their life together. Its foundation was prayer, the *opus Dei,* the work of God, seven times a day. Flowing from prayer was the ordinary daily work of the monastery—in field and hospitality, in kitchen and cellar; and the study of scripture and the fathers, for the monasteries and cathedrals were the great centres of education and learning in the early Middle Ages. And this, too, gives a picture of the Christian church that is deeply attractive in its balanced focus on spirituality, relationships, work, and growing in our faith.

Both these ways have been an inspiration for generations of ordinary people. And if Lindisfarne and Durham are mothers of two ways of being Christian in our part of England, they are not in competition. For Cuthbert is the common bond: the beloved Northumbrian saint as he was in his lifetime; and as he became after his death in a shrine, installed 900 years ago this year in the great Cathedral Priory of Durham. It moves me to think that Britain's best-loved building, which I now have the privilege to care for, should have been built as home to its best-loved saint. So whether it is on this bleak and beautiful windswept Holy Island, washed by the surf of the North Sea under the wide Northumberland sky, or the simple stark black slab of his burial place beneath the rib vaults and Romanesque arcades of Durham Cathedral, we find ourselves drawn back to his story in ways that continue to inspire us, and put to us the great questions, God's questions, about who and what we are, what it means to be the church of God, how to turn away from sin and be faithful to Christ in the times in which we live.

St Mary's, Lindisfarne, 21 March 2004

Welcome Back to Cuthbert

I say in this sermon that to understand Durham properly, you
need to think of it not as a Cathedral that contains a shrine, but
as a shrine around which a Cathedral was created. The shrine
of St Cuthbert was and is the emotional and spiritual heart of
the building that has drawn pilgrims here for a thousand years.
"Pilgrimage", that is, a journey with a spiritual purpose, has lain
at the heart of this Cathedral's purpose since the beginning.

I once preached on the Mississippi Gulf Coast and visited that most characterful of all American cities, New Orleans, enjoying the legendary breakfast at Brennans, the French Quarter, and street jazz. I stayed with an elderly Christian couple in their lovely home on the sea front between Gulfport and Biloxi. It is, or was, a beautiful coastline. They showed me, not without some pride, a line high up on their living room wall that marked the height the waters had reached when Hurricane Andrew struck that coast in 1992. They had lost everything in their old age, had had to rebuild their home and their lives from scratch. If you live on the Gulf Coast, you run the risk, they said. And now, after Katrina, you would think an atomic bomb had exploded somewhere over the Mississippi. Our thoughts and prayers are with our friends in the southern states at this desperate time.

The awesome power of the storm is embedded deep in the imagery of the Bible. The psalm speaks of Yahweh the God of Israel thundering over the mighty waters, his voice shaking the wilderness and stripping the forest bare. There is a terrible glory in this that puts us in our place, brings us to our knees. In the stories Bede tells of Cuthbert, there are at least three where storm and sea are at God's command. For instance, the boy Cuthbert sees monks in their rafts being blown out to sea at the mouth of the Tyne. As peasants shout and jeer from the shore, gloating over this judgment on the monks' suppression of pagan practices, Cuthbert tells them it would be better to pray for their safety. As he intercedes, the

wind changes direction and brings the rafts safely to land. It would take a
Cuthbert to divert Hurricane Katrina. But Cuthbert and his like scarcely
walk this earth these days.

And yet . . . For us in Durham, and for our friends on Lindisfarne
where he was first Prior and then Bishop, Cuthbert is not only a figure
from the past who stilled storms, taught the faith, and fed the poor. He is
our contemporary. Here, as this cathedral was being built 901 years ago,
his cherished remains were placed in the feretory behind the high altar, to
be honoured for all time by worshippers and pilgrims and people in need
of a saint's prayers and touch. Today is the feast of the Translation of the
Relics of St Cuthbert. He had already been brought here over a century
before by that loyal band of fellow travellers known as the Community
of St Cuthbert, his *Haliwervolc,* who, after their exile from Lindisfarne
by Viking raids, carried his coffin, together with the Lindisfarne Gospels,
around the North of England for so many decades. It is one of the most
moving stories of English Christianity. And while Cuthbert would hardly
have welcomed being interred at the heart of a building that speaks so
forcefully of human conquest and power, nevertheless, he has made this
his home now; indeed, the stories tell of how he specifically *chose* this
place and gave this rocky peninsula its marvellous destiny.

Durham Cathedral is not a church in which a shrine has been installed,
but a shrine around which a church was built. And to say this is not to
attribute magical qualities to a saint's relics, but to recognise both his
central part in the history of this place, and the drawing power of the
humility, the holiness, the zeal for the gospel, the care for ordinary people,
and the sheer devotion to God this extraordinary man stood for. Helen
Julian, in her thoughtful little book *The Lindisfarne Icon: St Cuthbert and
the Twenty-First Century Christian,* tells how she was in this Cathedral
one day and felt an irresistible pull towards the shrine. She ran up the
church, dodging the visitors, and clambered breathlessly up the steps to
the shrine. She fell on her knees and exclaimed "I'm here!" For her it was,
she says, a kind of falling in love. (If you see people running towards the
east end, please don't try and stop them.)

There are storms and storms. And in the history of this place, one
period stands out as tempestuous almost to the point of swamping the
great ship Durham Cathedral. In 1537, the King's Commissioners stripped

Cuthbert's shrine of its jewels and precious metals, and attempted to smash the relics to dust, an action thwarted by the awkward fact that the skeleton was still intact and defied destruction. How typical of Cuthbert to make life difficult for authority. So he was reburied and left alone. Two years later, on the last day of 1539, the monks of the Benedictine Cathedral Priory sung their last office of compline, and next day, Prior Whitehead surrendered the monastery. The Prior and his senior monks had cooperated, so they were allowed to stay on as the first Dean and Chapter. But the tide of reform was unstoppable. In May 1541, Henry VIII enacted new statutes for the refounded secular Cathedral. These suppressed the name of Cuthbert from the Cathedral's title: shrines and pilgrimages and a saint's bones had no part in the new order. From then on, we were known as "Christ and Blessed Mary the Virgin".

Now we have put Cuthbert back into the title of the Cathedral which is now dedicated to "Christ, Blessed Mary the Virgin and St Cuthbert". We did this by altering the Cathedral's constitution and statutes, a legal process provided for under the legislation governing cathedrals. The canon lawyers agreed with our view that a church dedication is given in perpetuity; not even a Tudor monarch has the power to change what has been effected forever at the consecration of a church. I confess I take some satisfaction in subverting, even in a small way, the arrogant divine right of kings; only one King has divine right: the one Cuthbert followed and whom we worship today. I should like to think that what we have done is to recognise who and what we are as the church of God in England: not the creature of a human king, still less of his divorce, but a living part of the church catholic, that worldwide society of God's people for whom Cuthbert and Blessed Mary the Virgin are among the saints in whom we honour Christ's living image, and in whose company we are inspired to travel on towards the celestial city.

What we do today can be understood at many levels. We honour the North East's best-loved saint whose shrine this Cathedral is. We celebrate what Durham Cathedral means to this region called Cuthbertsland (how good it would be to see signs on the A1(M) as you cross over the Tees welcoming you to the land of St Cuthbert). We are reconnected in a symbolic way with our Saxon and Benedictine past. But at its heart, we are reminded of what matters most for Christian believing, whether in the Middle Ages or our own era. To be true to Cuthbert means that we should seek first God's kingdom and his righteousness, as Jesus urges us in our gospel reading: the kingdom for which he says we must strive, and which it is our Father's good pleasure to give us.

4 September 2005
Luke 12:29–34

This is the text of the declaration I read publicly at the service:

> In the name of the Father, and of the Son, and of the Holy Spirit. Amen.
>
> At its foundation as a Benedictine cathedral priory, this church was dedicated to the Blessed Virgin Mary and St Cuthbert the Bishop. Following the dissolution of the monastery by King Henry VIII, the dedication to St Cuthbert was suppressed and the church re-founded on 12 May 1541 as The Cathedral Church of Christ and Blessed Mary the Virgin. This is the title by which it has been known since that date. Following the promulgation of the revised Constitution and Statutes for Durham Cathedral dated 2 July 2005, and with the consent of the Chairman of the Cathedral Council and the Lord Bishop of Durham, I now declare that this church shall henceforth be known as The Cathedral Church of Christ, Blessed Mary the Virgin and St Cuthbert of Durham.
>
> *Proclaimed in Durham Cathedral on the Feast of the Translation of the Relics of St Cuthbert, 4 September 2005.*

The King Who Shared His Bread

St Oswald

When I preached this sermon, I did not know, of course, that the author whose book I quote towards the end would become a household name in connection with the difficulties his former bank got into. But his words still stand. It is up to all of us, but especially our leaders in church and society, to live up to them. As Oswald did: a great Northumbrian king.

In today's gospel, the crowd does what crowds always do: follow the leader who promises bread. Jesus has just fed them with the five barley loaves and two fish. Now they follow him across the lake, still hungry and expectant. The appetite of crowds is never satiated. "Amen I tell you, you are looking for me, not because you saw signs but because you ate your fill of the loaves." In the unfolding of Jesus' awareness of his vocation, this is a milestone. Last week's gospel reading told us how, after the distribution of the loaves, Jesus realised that they were about to come and take him by force to make him king, so "he withdrew again to the mountain by himself". Later, when Jesus has taught how he is the living bread from heaven, John says: "many of his disciples turned back and no longer went about with him." Crowds are fickle barometers of favour. From popular acclaim to the loneliness of ridicule and contempt is a short journey, as the passion narrative shows. Never trust a crowd. When the thousands have vanished and only the disciples are left, Jesus faces them and himself with an awful truth. "Did not I choose you the twelve? Yet one of you is a devil." The shadow of betrayal is felt. This king has come to die.

The king who gives bread and dies for his people is celebrated in one of the saints of this place, whose feast falls on Wednesday. The king who feeds the poor is how Bede lovingly depicts St Oswald. One Easter Day, he and Bishop Aidan sat down to feast.

A silver dish was placed on the table before him, full of rich foods. They had just raised their hands to ask a blessing on the bread when there came in an officer of the king, whose duty it was to relieve the needy, telling him that a very great multitude of poor people from every district were sitting in the precincts and asking alms of the king. He at once ordered the dainties which had been set up in front of him to be carried to the poor, the dish to be broken up, and the pieces divided amongst them. The bishop, who was sitting by . . . grasped him by the right hand and said: "May this hand never decay".

In a thirteenth-century missal there is a charming image of Oswald's charity. Under the table where he and Aidan are sitting are two poor men crouching like dogs, pathetically lifting up their hands to catch the crumbs falling from their masters' table. Oswald holds the precious vessel he is about to break up, a symbol, perhaps, of how he will give up his own life. On the table are bowls with loaves and fishes. The meaning is plain: Oswald is like Jesus. He gives bread to the hungry. He gives himself to his own.

Maybe Oswald is Durham's neglected saint. His head had been interred with the relics of St Cuthbert and carried here with the Lindisfarne Gospels by Cuthbert's community, finally to be laid to rest in the shrine behind the high altar. There in the feretory there is a thirteenth-century statue of Cuthbert. He has lost his own head in some violent act of the Reformation or Civil War. But he has kept Oswald's head, which he holds in his left hand, which is how Cuthbert is often portrayed in medieval iconography. Once there would have been a statue of Oswald, like Cuthbert, flanking Blessed Mary in the central, most prominent niches of the Neville Screen above the high altar. You can see him in stained glass, in Thetis Blacker's striking banner in the feretory, and, it is said, in a wall painting in the Galilee Chapel. Of all our saints, Oswald is the one whose relics appear all over central Europe as a true catholic martyr. Given his vital role in the unification and Christianisation of Northumbria, and therefore the Christianisation of England, he deserves our recognition.

What do we know about him? He was not the first Christian king of Northumbria: that honour belongs to Edwin. But it was he who decisively led his nation into embracing the gospel. He had been exiled on Iona as a young man and had been baptised there. After Edwin's death, he inherited a weak and divided kingdom threatened by native British rulers. Famously, Oswald set up a cross at the place we now call Heavenfield, above the Tyne near Hexham, and ordered his soldiers to pray for victory against the British king Cadwallon. This established both Oswald's kingship and his faith. From Iona he summoned Irish missionaries to preach the gospel in his kingdom; Aidan came and founded his monastery on Lindisfarne as the base for the Northumbrian mission. Oswald often travelled with Aidan on his journeys, translating the message into English, caring for the poor, and building up the church. He was both parent and midwife of a project that changed the face of England. He died in battle in 642 at the hand of the pagan king Penda of Mercia, "slain by the heathen fighting for his fatherland", says Bede, not just for Northumbria but for a kingdom not of this world.

Oswald is a potent model of the Christian statesman. Bede portrays him as the ideal king, a new David who unites his kingdom against the threats it faces, establishes a secure capital, promotes religion, dispenses justice, cares for the least of his people as well as the greatest, and finally gives himself up for their sake. The synergy between the two cities, sacred and profane, church and state, is symbolised by the geography of the sites associated with the Northumbrian royal court. Oswald's capital at Bamburgh and Aidan's monastery on Holy Island were within sight of each other. It was a reminder to this world's ruler of his divine call and accountability: "knowing whose minister he is and whose authority he hath", as the Prayer Book puts it. For Bede, the politics of God and of mortals serve the same end: that justice, truth, and peace should be established in the nation. He is saying something that we may not always welcome: that God works through institutions as well as individuals. This is why we have organised religion embedded in the structures of society, part of the glue that holds it together.

If Aidan is a model of mission, Cuthbert of sanctity, and Bede of wisdom, Oswald is an inspiring image of leadership. No doubt public life today is infinitely more complex than in the seventh century, but that does not mean it is more exacting or difficult. Yesterday, I led a pilgrimage of Cathedral Friends to the wondrous Saxon cross at Bewcastle, deep in the Cumbrian fells. The church is dedicated to Cuthbert, so perhaps Cuthbert's body and Oswald's head rested there on their long journey. The cross dates from Cuthbert's time, the generation after Oswald. You can see a replica of it in the Cathedral dormitory. As I gazed at the intricate knotwork chequers and vine scrolls on the shaft, I thought about complexity and order. It's as if the artist is saying: this world is puzzling and chaotic. How do we chart our voyage across it? And how, in particular, does any leader negotiate the hazards of public life in the face of difficulty and threat? The answer is: by going to the source of pattern and order, God the Creator and Saviour of the world, and by emulating this ordered life in how we live out our humanity. And given that this is a churchyard cross, it is also saying to us: the clue is self-giving, service, sacrifice.

I have been reading a book called *Good Value: Reflections on Money, Morality and an Uncertain World*. Its author, Stephen Green, is Chairman of HSBC. He is writing about globalisation and the question the economic crisis is putting to us. We can assume that in his role, to negotiate the economic, political, and societal challenges of today is a daunting assignment. But he is not only an economist but an ordained Anglican priest. He is not afraid to speak about what is demanded of us in these difficult times, how we need to live according to wise, ethical, and humane values that are not simply based on the impersonal market forces of price and profit. He is keen on altruism and on doing something for posterity, instead of falling for the Faustian bargain of selling our soul for the pursuit of gain. He calls for a style of leadership that is less about dominance and more about serving the common good; for while dominance ends up by diminishing not only the led but also the leader, true self-giving service nourishes both, and turns out to be vastly more effective in its fruits. He might have been writing of Oswald sharing bread, giving himself for the people. Bede would certainly have approved. Our leaders should be paying attention. So should we all.

2 August 2009
John 6:24–35

In Gentleness and Joy

St Aidan

When Bede wrote about the Saxon church, he went out of his way to praise St Aidan. It was generous of him, because he could so easily have dismissed him for his Irish ways, by Bede's day long superseded by Roman usage. But, as Bede saw, Aidan's life was illuminated by Christian faith and hope and love, and this was what he communicated so effectively to the kingdom of Northumbria when he came as an evangelist at Oswald's invitation. He says to us: our words matter, but it is the lived sermon we embody as human beings and Christians that is remembered.

The Rolling Stones famously got their "kicks" on Route 66. Well, I head straight for the A68, the royal route into Scotland over the Cheviots at Carter Bar and my favourite road in the land, swinging and plunging magnificently over the ridges and furrows etched into the landscapes of County Durham and Northumberland. The Roman legions once trod the military road known as Dere Street as they headed through the windswept North Pennines for Hadrian's Wall, up Redesdale and over Carter Fell to gain the Antonine Wall on the Firth of Forth. Later, the Scots marched south along it to engage the English in battle, and the Border Reivers wrought havoc along its flanks. In peaceful times, the drovers used it to usher cattle to the town markets. This undeviating line across the marches of England encapsulates an entire political and social history. But it is not a road to be driven in a hurry: not only would you miss the views, but you risk shipwreck on the exhilarating but dangerous sudden crests and hidden dips the signs warn about.

Earlier this month, my wife and I drove along it up into Scotland to re-visit the Border Abbeys that cluster round it at Melrose, Jedburgh, and Dryburgh. To Durham people, this countryside is honoured as the birthplace of Cuthbert, in the days when Saxon Northumbria stretched right up to Edwin's Burg on the Forth. It was at Melrose, at the behest of

King Oswald, that Eata and probably Aidan himself founded a community in the seventh century where Cuthbert would come to learn monastic life. So Melrose, like Lindisfarne, is a link between this Cathedral and the mission of the monks from Iona to convert the English. Two centuries later, Cuthbert's body returned to Melrose on its long journey towards the Durham peninsula. The A68 is a pilgrim's way in Cuthbertsland.

The gaunt red ruins of the Cistercian Abbey in the town of Melrose don't mark the site of Aidan's monastery: that is at Old Melrose, to the east in a loop of the River Tweed. It reminds you of the Durham peninsula; you see it best from across the river at the famous vantage point known as Scott's View (after Sir Walter Scott). The interpretation boards have a lot to say about romantic novels and border ballads, but nothing about Aidan or Cuthbert. It's true that there is not much to see, only a beautiful view of skies and trees and river, with the Eildon Hills as a reredos, and a patch of grass by the brown waters where the community lived. You have to use your imagination. Yet it's poignant to think of the holiness and devotion of Aidan and the monks who settled there all those centuries ago, whose Christian vision changed for ever the history of our island.

We honour Aidan for many things: his pioneering missionary vision; his gentleness and patience; his native kindness, humility, and care for the poor; his courage, love of truth, and holy perseverance. If Christianity is caught rather than taught, then Aidan was one of those rare people with the gift to make faith attractive to others. Among the "others" was Cuthbert, whom he never knew, whose vision of Aidan's soul being taken up by angels into heaven brought his own vocation to birth, first as a monk and later as prior and bishop. And that suggests how important it is for all of us to cultivate *naturalness* in our Christian witness. I mean the gift to be what we are, say what we say, and do what we do, not out of some falsely conceived heroic effort to become what we *ought* to be, but out of the God-shaped character that is being formed in us over time by the work of God's Spirit within us. This is always where authentic mission begins.

But Old Melrose, like Iona and Lindisfarne, tells us something else about Aidan and those who worked and prayed with him for the conversion of Saxon England. These places, inspired by Irish monasticism, embodied two principles of mission. One was the need to settle a community in a well-protected place where prayer could be nurtured in a sustained, disciplined way, and where an intense focus on God's purposes could be maintained, not dissipated by exposure to extraneous demands or distractions. The Irish knew that offshore islands and rocky peninsulae were good for these things; in such places they found wilderness, and they had learned from the desert fathers of Egypt that wilderness mattered for spiritual growth.

The other principle of mission was the need to be able to travel in order to bring Christianity to as many as possible. In this, Aidan looked back to portrayals of Jesus in the gospels as the itinerant evangelist proclaiming the kingdom of God, feeding the hungry and healing those who were damaged and hurt. "Foxes have holes and birds of the air have nests, but the Son of Man has nowhere to lay his head"; this memory powerfully influenced the Irish missions and the Saxon communities that followed where they had led. So the fact that Lindisfarne is so close to the Great North Road, and Old Melrose to Dere Street, is no accident. These land arteries were as vital to mission as the seas and rivers. And those who today walk St Cuthbert's Way from Melrose to Lindisfarne, or who motor up and down the A68 or the A1, are following ancient paths that, like the ways to Canterbury or Jerusalem or Compostela, are the prayer-lines and mission-lines of Christendom. Mission means to pray and to travel: to be centred in your community of faith yet to face the risky new horizons each journey opens up.

Our gospel reading captures the spirit of those first missioners who came out of the north into England not brandishing a sword but proffering good news. In the risky venture of prayer (because we never know what God intends) and in the hazardous adventure of travel (because we never know what lies over the horizon), the gospel says: "Do not worry. Your heavenly Father knows what you need. Trust him. Seek first his kingdom." This is so evidently how Aidan lived. Not for him the futile, febrile activity of trying to build or grow the kingdom of God himself. Rather, we see him taking the time it takes to discern God's purposes and aligning himself to them through the disciplines of the spiritual life: stillness, study, reflection, prayer. And then with courage and devotion to make long journeys and undergo many hardships to win hearts and minds for Jesus Christ in every place, knowing whose work it ultimately was.

I don't pretend that it is easy to be a faith-sharer. But there is a delicate and beautiful interlacing of what *we* do and what *God* does through us, always more than we could ever ask or think. What matters is that we are open to God's opportunity, and have the imagination and courage to grasp it. Baptism commits us to nothing less than this. And who knows how many lives have been touched by our prayers, our acts of service, and our willingness to speak, however falteringly, about the hope that is within us? We should learn not to worry; rather, face the fear and do it anyway, for Christ's sake. For as today's epistle reading warns, woe to us if we do not preach the gospel!

St Aidan's Day, 31 August 2008
1 Corinthians 9:16–19; Matthew 6:31–34

Finding a Voice

St Hild and Caedmon

One of Bede's best stories is of how St Hild taught Caedmon to sing.
His song is said to be England's earliest poem. I see public ministry
as finding our voice and discovering how to speak about the gospel.
We owe so much to those who helped us on this vital journey of self-
discovery and who gave us the confidence to share what we have been
given with others. Here in Durham we call her by her Saxon name,
rather than its Latin version Hilda, but what matters are the beautiful
qualities she exemplified as a Christian leader in turbulent times.

What's your recurring nightmare? Falling off a cliff? Taking that exam? Having a tooth out? One of mine is a dream quite common among clergy, apparently: being strangled by my own priestly vestments as I try to get out of them after a service. Today's gospel reading reminds me of another of my nightmares. When I hear Jesus' parables about great feasts, I imagine myself at a party finding that I'm expected to do a "turn". There are two kinds of people: those who seize the main chance, glimpsing celebrity just minutes away; and those who shrink from the awful certainty of public failure, embarrassment, and shame. They know how to take the lowest place. We all know which class we belong to. And even if there is some chance of faking it, you still feel in your heart of hearts that everyone is seeing right through you.

The Venerable Bede wrote about just such a shrinking violet in his *History of the English Church and People*. The year was AD 680. He says that when the guests at a feast were asked to entertain the gathering, a lay brother saw the harp coming his way and got out as fast as he could, fleeing outside to a stable to sleep. And his worst dream came back to haunt him: someone standing beside him, telling him to sing something. "I can't sing," he replied, "that's why I left the party and came out here." "But you shall sing," persisted his visitant. "What about?" asked Caedmon.

"Sing about the creation of all things." And this untutored man, who had never written or sung a verse in his life, broke into the purest song of praise. Next morning, he was brought to the abbess of the double monastery where there were both women and men. She saw at once that divine inspiration had taken hold of him. She had him admitted as a monk and taught him the scriptures which he turned into verse and, says Bede, through his gift, inspired his hearers "to love and do good" and prepare for the joys of heaven.

Caedmon was the earliest English Christian poet. I am telling you about him because of that abbess who recognised his gift: Hild, as the Saxons called her; Hilda in Bede's Latin. She was one of the great leaders of the Saxon church in the seventh century, a princess called back to Northumbria by St Aidan, admitted to the religious life and associated since then with three places in the North East commemorated on the kneelers executed by our broderers at the Hild altar in this Cathedral. The first is South Shields, where the parish church in the town centre plausibly stands on an ancient Saxon place of worship. Next comes Hartlepool, where one of the North East's great churches, the grand, gothic pile of St Hilda, stands on the numinous windy headland near the medieval sea wall where a plaque tells you that you are not far from the monastery where she was abbess.

Finally comes Whitby, which is properly Yorkshire, but, for today, an honorary part of North East England and definitely Northumbria. The marvellous abbey ruins on the cliffs above the town stand on the original Saxon site. Here too, Hild was abbess, and hosted the Synod of 664 at which the Northumbrian church made the difficult choice to follow continental Roman customs for calculating the date of Easter rather than the Irish traditions of Lindisfarne in which she herself had been schooled. I see her trying to find reconciliation between those two ways of being Christian, for, unlike others, she did not abandon England when the decision went against Lindisfarne.

I love the story of Hild taking in the unknown Caedmon as the midwife of his gift so as to bring it out into the open. There is always a risk in this, discerning and nurturing what perplexes other people, recognising the work of God in the life of another human being. In the gospel reading, Jesus speaks of the importance of invitation: it is the poor, the crippled, the lame, and the blind who should be welcomed to the banquet. And this is what Hild did for Caedmon, recognising his gift of poetry and song, a gift not only of *versification* but of *interpretation*: understanding the ways and works of the Creator and speaking about them. It's a lovely picture of how human beings grow and flourish when they are, so to speak, brought inside and their gifts and talents are celebrated.

Some of you will know the film *Little Voice*. Jane Horrocks plays an ultra-timid daughter who is so dominated by her overbearing mother that she can't speak above a stage whisper. She spends her days in her bedroom listening to LPs of songs from the shows: Judy Garland, Marilyn Monroe, and Shirley Bassey. And she sings along with them, sings *as* them, for she *can* sing—not just hum or whistle but *really* sing. One evening Little Voice is overheard by a seedy, dead-end talent scout, Michael Caine, who recognises her gift and realises this is his last big chance for a big prize. So he puts her on the stage. It's not a straightforward rags to riches story. But it is a picture of finding one's voice, and through it, finding oneself. Through Hild, Caedmon, a seventh-century Little Voice, found his gift, found his voice, found his God, and found himself.

I see in this a metaphor of Christian ministry. I don't mean what the clergy do, but what we all do for one another as the people of God, our companions in the church. Isn't the task of ministry to try to recognise what God is doing in the world and in those around us, and help make it conscious, articulate, so that they find their God, their voice, and their gifts? That is much harder than baldly stating the truths of Christianity or pressing home moral certainties. As I read the gospels, I find Jesus going about his work in a way that brings out the possibilities inherent in ordinary men and women, enticing them into responding more fully to the love and grace of God; piping so that people not only listen but dance. It's suggestive rather than insistent. It offers people the freedom to say yes, or no, or maybe, or it's hard, or I wish I could; but this is how to draw out of them the song they alone can sing. Oscar Wilde said that what makes Jesus a poet is that he makes poets of us all. Precisely this gift of opening the lips of others to proclaim the words and works of God is how I read Hild's act in bringing another person to life.

There are few things more important than to do this for one another. We can never know how much a little word of encouragement can mean to someone else: "thank you", "that touched me", "God spoke to me through what you did for me." Words and gestures like these are so often how God gives us the gifts and the strength to carry on serving him as followers of Jesus. It means being open to other people, responsive to them in their tentativeness and lack of confidence, glimpsing what God is doing and could do through them, as Hild discerned with Caedmon. There are those who have done this for us. We must do it for others. This is how the church is built up as we respond together the to "one hope of our calling". Who knows whether there is a Caedmon somewhere waiting for us to encourage them to find their voice, their God, and their truest selves?

St Hild's Day, 17 November 2013
Luke 14:7–14

A Saint for Sunderland

St Benedict Biscop

I have "form" when it comes to Sunderland, as I explain at the beginning of this sermon. To some citizens of this ancient place, Durham is a latecomer, a south-western suburb at the far end of the A690, for Sunderland's origins go back at least three centuries earlier, when Benedict Biscop founded part of his double monastery at the mouth of the River Wear.

My association with this city goes back to 1973, Sunderland's *annus mirabilis*. My wife's parents were childhood sweethearts at the Bede School here and were married at St Gabriel's Church in 1937: an apt year for a couple who were lifelong supporters of Sunderland AFC, for before 1973, that was the only occasion on which the club had won the FA Cup. (The nearest they had got to it previously had been in 1913, the year my in-laws were born, when the Rokerites were runners-up.) I met my wife in 1972, and the following year we became engaged. We chose a certain Saturday in May to do this, speculating that should Sunderland win the Cup it would be an auspicious day on which to ask favours of her father, and if they didn't, it might take his mind off things. They did, and the rest is history.

My memories from that time include visiting the extended family in those single-storey terraced houses that are such a feature of this city, and which I'm glad to say the planners have not yet allowed to be swept away in the name of progress; an evening in The Wavendon, heaving with working men drinking Newcastle Brown, where not one woman was to be seen on the punters' side of the bar; walking the seafront at Roker in the bitterest of east winds and a sky like steel; and, I recall, attending a deanery evensong when, one Sunday evening, I stumbled into a service at St Peter's being conducted by Bishop Kenneth Skelton, one of the great Christians of the twentieth century, whom I subsequently came to know and admire in Sheffield and whose memory I am sure will always be green in Sunderland.

Perhaps it was then, sitting in a place so resonant with the memories of Saxon Christianity here in the North East, that I first heard the name Benedict Biscop. I can't remember. But as we gather here on the eve of his feast day tomorrow, and on the sixth anniversary of the inauguration of this church as a minster, I find myself asking why this man, indelibly associated with the North East, is not better known and honoured even in his native land. He was, as you know, a seventh-century Northumbrian of noble birth who spent his youth in the royal court of King Oswiu. He was a great traveller across Europe who came under the influence of the Benedictines and took religious vows in France. It was he who brought the Greek Archbishop of Canterbury Theodore of Tarsus to England and introduced him to our English ways. In 674, he founded the monastery of St Peter here at Wearmouth, and, in 682, the linked community of St Paul at Jarrow. He was one of the great scholars of the Saxon era, bringing huge quantities of books and manuscripts to furnish the monastic libraries here. He was a devotee of the arts who adorned his churches with paintings, relics, and the first stained glass in England. He played a significant part in helping the Northumbrian church, with its Irish traditions, conform to the customs of the majority of western European Christendom. And one of his most important actions for the future of literature, history, and theology in this country was to accept into his monastery and care for a seven-year-old child called Bede, who became a lifelong member of the community and whose influence on the English-speaking peoples is incalculable.

Well: Lindisfarne has the memory of Aidan, and Jarrow has Bede, and Hartlepool has Hild, and Chester-le-Street and Durham, posthumously, have Cuthbert. What about a saint for Sunderland: something to put on the road signs with rather more content than "Land of the Prince Bishops" or "Catherine Cookson Country"? I know many of you believe Benedict Biscop to be the best possible candidate. How might we make the case for him? I believe there are three reasons for putting him forward with confidence as a patron saint for Sunderland, three reasons why his historic connection with Wearmouth can speak to us about the life of this city today and tomorrow.

In the first place, he was one of the most travelled men of his day. His journeys across Europe familiarised him with the wider world of church, court, and cloister. He was a citizen not only of his nation but of his world. And this breadth of vision seems to me to be vital for an ancient town and a young city like this. With its tradition of shipbuilding, Sunderland has always looked across the sea to bigger horizons; and this is precisely what will make this city successful, by developing partnerships, encouraging inward investment, and being a vibrant economic and cultural factor in the life of our region, our nation, and in the new Europe. An old Bantu proverb says that "he who never travels thinks mother is the only cook." In the spirit of Benedict Biscop, Sunderland needs, as we all need, to look beyond ourselves, embrace the world with all its possibility and potential. It should be one of the UK's core cities, which through their programmes of urban renewal and regeneration are a true sign of hope to this nation.

Second, Benedict Biscop's deep commitment to learning, culture, and art speak directly to the way in which this city, any city worth the name, deepens the hinterland of its citizens and helps them to become not simply observers but *participants* in our common life. A city is more than a marketplace. It is also an academy, a gymnasium, a forum where ideas and energies can be brought together, where individuals contribute to something larger and life-changing. I had the privilege recently of delivering a lecture in the University of Sunderland, and was impressed by what is being achieved there and by the cultural industries of this city. Glass is only one way in which the memory of Benedict Biscop is being brought alive again on the banks of the Wear. At a time when arts and education are being massively and disgracefully undermined by lack of public funding, I hope Sunderland will be a beacon of light in sponsoring a vigorous intellectual and cultural activity here. Recall how Benedict Biscop brought leadership from overseas back to England, how he recognised the gifts of the child Bede and nurtured them. Who are the leaders of tomorrow whose gifts need to be recognised and developed here today?

Third, Benedict Biscop's religious devotion says something about what ultimately gives life meaning and depth. A city is indeed home to marketplace, academy, and gymnasium, but historically all the great institutions of a city gathered round the sacred space of shrine and temple. At the heart of ancient cities was the symbol of divine presence, for every city belonged ultimately to the gods. The cathedrals of Christendom testify to this belief that the entire life and activity of cities derived its ultimate significance from the God who had entered human life in the person of Jesus Christ. And this is why, when Sunderland became a city, an imaginative leadership asked that this new status should be marked by the designation of a minster church in the city centre. And we are here tonight to celebrate six years of minster ministry that has provided a place where the issues of public faith and civic life can be transacted, where a spirituality of city life has begun to be explored, where social justice and the care of the needy have been honoured as they must be in a civilised society. Above all, it is becoming a place where God's continuing commitment to this world and this city is being recognised and celebrated.

For in this Epiphany season, we recall how, in the birth of Jesus, a light has come among us that is illuminating the whole world. The people who walked in darkness have seen a great light, says the prophet. In tonight's first reading, there is an invitation to seek the Lord while he may be found, to call upon him while he is near. To this invitation the magi responded, making their great journey across the known world in order to find Jesus and lay their gifts at his feet. Benedict Biscop wanted Wearmouth to be another Bethlehem, to which people would be drawn by the light and goodness of God. His vision calls across thirteen centuries of flux and change; yet should it not also be our own vision, our own hope for this city today in the infinitely more complex realities of our contemporary life, in all the brokenness and pain that so many experience, in the doors of hope and possibility that are opening before us here? We have a saint for Sunderland. Where he has led, we can follow; and if we do this with the capacity to listen to what is required of us here in our own day, we can be sure that God will be with us.

11 January 2004, at the sixth anniversary of the inauguration of
Sunderland Minster.
Isaiah 55

Faith Seeking Understanding

St Bede

*Bede has already featured in this book, so here is a sermon in honour
of him. I see him as the patron saint of religious literacy, a quality that
is sorely needed in our world where, increasingly, faiths are colliding
once again, often dangerously; yet our leaders seem increasingly puzzled
by what religion represents to people and communities. We need
more Bedes today, who, by drawing on their sense of history, culture,
and spirituality, will help us understand rightly and act wisely.*

Six years in Durham, and I have not yet preached on Bede. It is time to
put that right, for tomorrow is his feast day. Happily, it falls once again
in the season of the Ascension. For he died on the eve of Ascension Day
in the year 735. He had sung the antiphon on which the collect for today
is based: "O King of Glory, who triumphing this day ascended above the
heavens: leave us not orphans, but send to us the promise of the Father,
even the Spirit of Truth!" Abbot Cuthbert tells us that, on his death bed,
Bede was as he had been throughout his life. He was still instructing his
brothers. He was still translating the scriptures. He was still radiating
thankfulness and joy. He was still praying with the simplicity and humility
for which he was loved. Then he sang the *Gloria* and died. It is a wonderful
thing when a good man or woman dies as they have lived, when the act
of dying shows how their hard-won holiness and devotion to God are
intact. Such deaths are never forgotten.

What is it about Bede that we admire so much? Not the scale of his
intellectual achievements alone, despite his being the only native English
doctor of the church. It is more how sanctity and Christian character shine
through all his writings, be they poetry, astronomy, biblical commentary,
theology, or history, in a rare alchemy of temperament and talent. There
is something reliable and consistent about his scholarship that echoes
his personality. Not given to fantasy or conjecture, he lived close to

his sources, observed the evidence closely. Such devoted attentiveness feels contemplative, as if it was an act of love. Such a man could, as he himself said, "live without shame and die without fear." It is an oddity of history that in 1022, a monk from here engaged in a bold act of what medieval people called "sacred theft" and stole his relics from Jarrow. We in Durham have found ourselves the guardian of these borrowed bones for a thousand years. And we discharge our stewardship with a sense of privilege and honour.

Bede would not wish me to dwell on him but to apply myself to the New Testament text given to us today, for one of his legacies is a great commentary on St Luke's Gospel. Somewhat at a venture, let me see if I can draw out of the second lesson some insights that reflect Bede's life of learning, discipleship, and prayer. You recall that Jesus has emerged from the desert and returned to his Galilee, where he begins to teach in the synagogues. Much is made in this passage about his Galilean roots: "he came to Nazareth where he had been brought up," says Luke; and later the crowd demands that he do in his home town the things he has done elsewhere. "A prophet is not without honour except in his own country," he says. The strong sense of place that runs through this episode is a feature we immediately recognise in Bede, especially in his last and greatest work *The History of the English Church and People*. It is a book every English Christian should read often. We call Bede "the father of English history", but the book is much more than simply a chronicle. What he achieved was to give meaning to Englishness by telling how God's providence had dealt graciously with this land through the goodness and sanctity of its holy women and men. In Bede, we see a distinctively English embodiment of faith that lies at the heart of the identity and tradition of this land. Christianity, he believes, will civilise and unite the nation and be a life-changing power that will redeem it and make it whole. Sense of place is one of the gifts of an embodied, incarnational faith.

But it is more than a matter of Christian identity. It is also about vocation. Jesus' first synagogue sermon is the declaration that he embraces his vocation with joy. "The Spirit of the Lord is upon me, because he has anointed me to bring good news to the poor." Jesus is taking up the oracle we read as the Old Testament lesson, in which a prophet looks forward to the rebuilding of Israel's shattered homeland after the exile. So here is the anointed one announcing his call to bring life and salvation to a people who long for hope. For Bede, living close to the relics of ancient empire and civilisation associated with Hadrian's Wall, there must have been a sense of departed glory, for all that his native Northumbria was a civilisation famed throughout Europe for its dazzling cultural and intellectual achievements. But, for Bede, these are not where the glory of a nation lies. It lies in a people's obedience to God. Bede attaches special importance to the vocation of people in public life: think, for example, of how he dwells on the conversion of Edwin, the first Christian king of Northumbria, and on King Oswald's role in fostering the mission of Aidan in Northumbria. Their obedience led to the transformation of a people: that is his story. But, he says, vocation belongs not only to the greatest but also, and especially, to the least. Bede himself exemplified it in his lifelong obedience to the religious life from the day he was given to the monastery as a boy. His *History* will only have achieved its purpose if it succeeds in getting each of us to consider our own obedience to God's call today. For in baptism, every Christian not only can but must say with Jesus: "the Spirit of the Lord is upon me"; for like him, it's the vocation of us all to bring hope to a broken world.

And here is a final observation from our lesson. Jesus "stood up to read". Reading matters to Luke, the most literary of the gospel writers; for it was Luke more than any other New Testament author who elevated Christian narrative writing into an art form. So when he tells of Jesus taking the scroll, reading from it, and commenting on it, he is honouring the hermeneutical activity of encountering a text and eliciting meanings. But this is not simply any reading. Jesus was in the synagogue, the place of prayer. So it is holy reading, *lectio divina*. From Jesus the Reader, Bede took his cue. Immersing himself in the library Benedict Biscop had created at Wearmouth–Jarrow, Bede became the first Englishman who, by reading, began to bring knowledge human and divine into a coherent whole, and so begin to be at home in the three worlds he inhabited: human history, creation, and the life of faith. By reading the classics, he saw how his nation could inherit the civilised order of the Roman world and the Latin church. By reading the natural philosophers of antiquity, he understood the patterns inherent in an ordered universe. By reading the scriptures and the fathers, he recognised order as being theological in character, originating in the God who shapes all things and governs the destinies of human beings. To gain insight in this way was more than a personal aspiration. It was a programme for an entire people called, as he saw it, to spiritual, moral, and scientific *intelligence*. I do not need to tell you how important it is to cultivate a deep, informed religious literacy. It matters in every age, but perhaps never more than ours; and not simply for professional theologians and clergy: it is too important to be left to them.

Another word for this would be *wisdom*. Recalling how the scriptures closely associate the Lady Wisdom with *Hagia Sophia,* the Holy Spirit, we come back to today's text, with Jesus opening a book and announcing that "the Spirit of the Lord is upon me." It's the vocation to be wise and to lead others into wisdom. This is "wisdom and ministry" for a few; it is wisdom in thinking, speaking, praying, and living for us all.

A beautiful prayer of Bede makes this its focus, and I end with it:

> We entreat you, O Lord, that as in your mercy you have given us grace to drink in with joy the word that gives knowledge of you, so in your goodness, grant us to come at length to yourself, the source of all wisdom, and to stand before you for ever; through Jesus Christ our Lord.

The Eve of St Bede's Day, 24 May 2009
Isaiah 61; Luke 4:14–21

At a College Day

St Chad

*Opposite the east end of the Cathedral on the North Bailey stands
St Chad's College. Its Principal, the late and much lamented Joe
Cassidy, invited me to be first its Visitor and then its Rector. It is
an independent or "recognised" college within Durham University
that is an Anglican foundation that once trained ordinands for
Christian ministry. I have loved the roles I have played there. St Chad
was one of Aidan's "boys", educated in his school on Lindisfarne.
Although life took him away from Northumbria, he always
emulated the qualities he so admired in his teacher. This sermon
was preached at the annual College Day service in the Cathedral.*

Our College has one of those Saxon names we're familiar with from
Durham colleges: Aidan, Hild, Bede, Cuthbert. Like them, St Chad lived
in the seventh century. We know a little about him, but not much. Yet
what we do know tells us everything that matters. We heard some of it in
our reading from Bede's *History*. Here is how he sums it up: "in addition
to all his merits of temperance, humility, zeal in teaching, prayers and
voluntary poverty . . . he was greatly filled with the fear of the Lord and
mindful of his last end in all he did." Like Cuthbert, he strikes us as one
of those completely authentic people who knew what he was put on this
earth for. There isn't a false note anywhere. His motto might have been
non vestra sed vos: it's not what we have, or what we achieve, or even how
we are remembered that matters in the end. It's what we are.

We are proud to call ourselves Chadsians. So perhaps it's worth asking
what it is in St Chad that is worth remembering, and even being inspired
by, thirteen centuries later? I'm thinking here both of our college and of
each of us as its members, whether we are students or staff, governors,
members of the SCR, or college fellows old and new. So let me focus on
one of the qualities that made him so memorable to those who knew him.

I want to call it *simplicity*. This was an aspect of Chad that Bede especially admired when he wrote about him. Theologians say that God is infinitely simple: not made up of a many parts but pure being, pure love, justice, goodness, truth, and beauty. To be simple in this good sense is to try to focus on being what God has made us, for we are made in his image. Knowing our place in the universe keeps us focused on simplicity: our place before God, before other people, before a great and mysterious cosmos. It's a deeply attractive virtue to have: Chad had it, and people loved him for it. But how difficult this is in a complex, sophisticated world: it goes against a culture of having and craving and giving in to our needs. Those things destroy us if we devote their lives to them. But to cultivate simplicity will make us better, happier, more generous people. It will make our world a better, more sustainable place, with a future we could be assured about. Can Chad's, with its strong social conscience, find new ways of modelling simplicity in our time? *Non vestra sed vos:* not what you have but what you are. So be simple.

Put this another way: let's call it *singleness of heart*. Buddhists speak about being "single-pointed", meaning that life is most useful and fulfilled when we try to reduce it to its essentials and focus on what really matters. When Jesus said "happy are the pure in heart", this is what he meant: not being distracted by so many cares and concerns that we fail to achieve anything worthwhile. For Chad, this focus was the kingdom of God. It called him out of the comforts of his youth and into a lifelong journey of service to God and his fellow human beings. We are not all called to be evangelists or social campaigners. But we are called to be what God made us to be. Our education should involve this kind of discernment because it is the formation of the whole of us as mature people. So the questions, "Who am I?", "What could I become?", and "What is my destiny?" are the most important we can ever face. And what's true of each of us is true of all of us as a college. How could our community become more "single-pointed" in its aims, more true to its founding vision? *Non vestra sed vos*: not what you have but what you are. So stay focused.

This comes down to something very straightforward: what do we really love? What gets us up each morning, gives direction to the day? What we love defines us, for good or ill; it always comes down to that. It's clear from Bede that Chad's whole life was given away, with nothing held back. And the secret was clear: it came from the fact that he *loved*. He loved the world of living things. He loved his fellow human beings and befriended them because he saw in them the image of God, however marred and disfigured. Above all, he loved God. And this was where the generosity of his life came from: he loved God because he knew that God had loved him first. So my question to us this morning is: what will we love in life? What does our College set itself to honour and cherish? What do we truly value? We so easily find ourselves loving the wrong thing, devoting ourselves to the fruitless or the trivial or the destructive when there is so much more in life that demands our attention and invites our devotion. Chad knew what his life's task was, because he knew where his devotion lay. *Non vestra sed vos*: not what you have but what you are. So be clear about what you love.

In the biblical reading, a host is turned down by the people he invites to his party, so he goes out to look for guests who want to be there: the poor, the needy, the outcasts, anyone who longs to be welcomed into the circle of love and warmth and conviviality. Those guests perhaps were Chad's inspiration: their simplicity (because they had nothing and knew it), their single-mindedness (because they longed to be included), and their devotion (because they loved the one who invited them in). So different from the others who stiffly excused themselves because they were so encumbered. Here is a spiritual, social, and moral vision we can embrace; here are values to live by; here is a vision that could truly inspire us today, and make us proud to bear the name of Chad.

In St Chad's Time, 3 March 2012
Luke 14:12–24

The Centenarian Voyager-Hermit

St Godric

*This colourful, eccentric, long-lived man is one of Durham's own.
He was so taken with the example of Cuthbert that after travelling
the extent of the known world he decided to become a hermit. If
that were not enough, he embarked in mid life on an education at
the hands of the monks of Durham Cathedral Priory who taught
him to read and write. The beautiful remains of Finchale Priory,
enclosed in a bend in the River Wear a few miles downstream
from the Cathedral, mark the site where he lived and prayed.*

"He was broad-shouldered and deep-chested with a long face, his grey
eyes clear and penetrating. His beard was bushy, his lips of moderate
thickness. His neck was short and thick, knotted with veins and sinews.
His legs were slender, his instep high, his knees hardened and horny
from much kneeling. His skin was rough beyond the ordinary until all
this roughness was softened by old age." It's an extraordinarily detailed
description of a saint by someone who knew him well. Here's more. "In
winter, barefoot, this holy man would walk through snow and ice to
find some poor frozen animal which he could bring back and warm in
his bosom. Winter and summer, he would seek out the sick ones and
administer medicine to make them well. Seeing stags as they were being
pursued by hunters, he would bring them to his cell and hide them until
the danger was past. Animals would come running to him for protection
sensing his great sanctity."

I'm talking about a man who was born just before the Norman Conquest
and who lived for more than a century. He was one of the most travelled
men of his age, a merchant seafarer who made pilgrimages to Jerusalem,
Rome, and Compostela. Once, he visited the island of the Inner Farne,
where St Cuthbert had lived and died. He was so impressed by Cuthbert's
memory that he decided to follow his way of life. He settled for a time

with a hermit in Weardale and visited the monks in the Judean desert. Back in Durham, he resolved in middle age to learn to read and write, so he went to school with the Cathedral choristers at St Mary-le-Bow. Then he settled on land downstream from Durham in a loop of the Wear, where he built a church dedicated to the desert prophet John the Baptist. Here he led the austere hermit's life of penitence, prayer, and simplicity. He was the first recorded poet who wrote in Middle English: hymns to our Lady and St Nicholas have come down to us, together with the music he composed for them. Among those who asked for his prayers were Archbishop Thomas Becket and Pope Alexander III. He died in 1170, undoubtedly the oldest saint in the calendar. His life spanned the entire time it took to build this Cathedral. His biographer and friend was the famous monk Reginald of Durham.

The man himself was Godric. Yesterday, 21 May, was his feast day. In my time here, I am trying to preach about all the saints of the North, and I have not yet tackled Godric. It's true that his cult was largely confined to medieval Durham, so he only features in the Book of Durham Festivals, not in the calendar of the national church. But so revered was Godric's memory here that the Benedictines of Durham built a daughter house at Finchale where he had lived and died; it is these ruins in their beautiful riverside landscape that we enjoy today. The twentieth-century American writer Frederick Buechner wrote a novel about him called, simply, *Godric*. It is written in a rough, rugged prose that avoids words of French and Latin origin, so as to reflect both Godric's Saxon roots and the austere craggy character of the man himself. It was that book that first introduced me to him.

I could speak about many aspects of his life: his closeness to nature, his pilgrimages, his poetry, his Cuthbert-like love of animals, his devotion to music and song. But I want to focus on what lay at the centre of it all, his vocation to be a hermit. The word is derived from the Greek for "desert", and recalls the men who first went into the Egyptian desert in the early Christian centuries to devote themselves to the life of *askesis* or disciplined holiness. It was Cuthbert's life that inspired him to take up this severe calling. But in one way, Cuthbert and Godric were different. Godric did not withdraw to the desert or to a remote offshore island. He settled near the city, near Cuthbert's shrine: perhaps he wanted physical closeness to

Cuthbert. But he also knew that holy solitude can be cultivated anywhere, peopled or remote; what mattered was to give himself utterly to God and to Jesus, live more simply and closer to God's world, and deepen the life of the spirit. Finchale was Godric's desert. It symbolised the submission of the self to God, the gift of undistracted simplicity, the call to be holy.

In 1975, a Roman Catholic writer, Catherine Doherty, wrote an influential book called *Poustinia: Christian Spirituality of the East for Western Man*. "Poustinia" in the Orthodox Church is literally a room or a cabin in the forest where you go alone and shut the door to meditate, fast, and pray. Her book describes *poustinia* as wilderness, a deserted place for penitence, intercession, self-emptying, thankfulness, and discovery of God. It can be anywhere we choose to find it or create it. The point is that this should be a normal part of Christian spirituality. It is not about heroic sanctity, but a willingness to go with God attentively into silence, solitude and prayer. *Poustinia* can happen at home, or at work, or out of doors, or in church, so long as it is a place where we know God is near; a thin place, as they say on Lindisfarne. We may find such places, or they us, or, like Cuthbert and Godric, create places that can carry significant meaning for us. But ultimately, *poustinia* means the desert of our own heart where God alone sees who we are and what we are living for. It is what Jesus taught us in the Sermon on the Mount when he said, "when you pray, go into your room and shut the door; and pray to your Father who is in secret; and your Father who sees in secret will reward you." Alfred Whitehead said that religion was "what a man does with his own solitude." It's not altogether an adequate definition, but it carries the important insight that what we do when we are alone defines who and what we are to ourselves and to God. If God is to be real to us, he must be real to us when we are alone, real in the depths of our own soul.

It can sound escapist and privatised, afraid of grasping hold of being alive with all its risks and opportunities. Safer to hide away, perhaps. But this old ancient eremitic tradition is the opposite of that. When Cuthbert went to the Farne, Bede says it was not to find an oasis of calm but to wrestle with the demons he saw in the world, the church, and himself. The constant traffic to and from the Farne or Godric's Finchale shows how alert these hermit saints were to the complex affairs of the world. Catherine Docherty was herself a social activist, not a contemplative by nature. So *Poustinia* is not about finding refuge so much as equipping ourselves spiritually for the task of living well in a complex world that needs the grace of God. We nurture our contemplative side so that we can live out our ordinary days in ways that make a difference as we touch the lives of others. Today's collect, so Augustinian in spirit with its unspoken emphasis on the divine grace that goes before us, sums up this calling: "Grant unto thy people that they may love the thing that thou commandest and desire that which thou dost promise; that so among the sundry and manifold changes of the world, our hearts may surely there be fixed where true joys are to be found." In our journey towards that great end, our native Durham saint Godric is our fellow traveller.

In St Godric's Time, 22 May 2011

Irascible but Faithful

St Wilfrid

*In the North, people who admire their native saints often have not a
good word to say about Wilfrid. Unlike his teacher St Aidan and so
many who came after him, he was pugnacious and quarrelsome. Yet his
achievements speak for themselves, visible in the surviving crypts of his
great churches at Hexham and Ripon. His fervour as an evangelist was
second to none. His concern for the integrity of catholic Christendom
could not be faulted. He travelled far and was not afraid of taking
risks in the service of the gospel. I was specifically asked to preach this
sermon in his defence. It was not as hard to do as I had imagined.*

Tomorrow is the feast of St Wilfrid, the 1,300th anniversary of his death
in 709. Hexham would not be here if it weren't for him. Wilfrid built
the first church here in the seventh century on such a grand scale, says
his biographer Eddius, that no other church north of the Alps could
compare with it. Your marvellous crypt, all that is left of Wilfrid's church,
is one of the holy places of the North, for it links us directly to the saints
of Northumbria's golden age, like his other crypt at Ripon, and like
Wearmouth, Jarrow, and Escomb, whose stones still stand as a record
of the Saxon church. And even where those layers of primitive faith
have been overlaid with the centuries, as at Bamburgh and Whitby,
Lastingham and Hartlepool, Coldingham, the island of the Inner Farne,
and Lindisfarne itself, the fountainhead of them all, the memory of the
saints is still powerful. These numinous places have a power to move us
that is all their own. Their testimony is undimmed with the passing of
time, for you feel, as perhaps nowhere else, the fervour of holy men and
women who prayed here. Coming from Durham, I include in that list
the shrines of Cuthbert and Bede in our Cathedral, for, though buried
beneath the grandest of Romanesque canopies, it is the simplicity of their
faith that touches and inspires us today.

Nowhere else in England has such a concentration of ancient Christian sites, and nowhere has such a constellation of saints whose lives have so affected the course of English history. Of these, Wilfrid was without doubt one of the most able and most influential. He was one of Aidan's boys like Chad and Cedd, a native Northumbrian who was sent to Holy Island to be educated at the monastery there. From there his studies took him to Canterbury, Gaul, and Rome, an experience that gave him an understanding of the wider continental church few others of his generation had, and which gives us the clue to his life. Here, of all places, I do not need to rehearse his colourful career as ecclesiastical statesman and politician *par excellence,* striding out across Europe like some new Joshua to conquer lands for God. From the beginning, as Abbot of Ripon and Bishop of York, and as apologist for the Roman way at the Synod of Whitby, he courted controversy. Combative and pugnacious, he fell out with practically every Saxon king and prelate in the land, first imprisoned and then exiled, and making not one but two long journeys to Rome to appeal to the Pope. Finally, and not without controversy, he returned to Northumbria, where his church at Hexham became a centre of his see.

Of all the saints of his era, Wilfrid is usually presented as an unattractive image of worldly ambition and self-interest, corrupted by the power he craved. He was said to be carried to his consecration on a throne supported by nine bishops: not exactly an icon of servant leadership. While his teacher Aidan had preferred to walk rather than ride, Wilfrid never had a conscience about his fine horses and retinue of servants and warriors. His reforms of Irish customs at Ripon led to the rough expulsion of Cuthbert, who was guest master there; an event Durham finds it hard to forgive. And so it goes on. He looks like the antithesis of the gospel simplicity we associate with Lindisfarne which Jesus speaks of in tonight's reading: "I thank you, Lord of heaven and earth, because you have hidden these things from the wise and intelligent and have revealed them to infants." This is how we like our saints to be: childlike, humble, innocent. Wilfrid, worldly-wise, power-hungry, clever, and not a little ruthless, puzzles us.

So, at your Rector's specific prompting, let me attempt the difficult but important task of defending Wilfrid. I am not going to paint over his faults, though he is not the only saint to have them. But it seems to me that we can make the case for his being one of the Saxon church's most far-sighted, dedicated, and courageous leaders. Let me try.

First, let me say something about the collision of Irish and Roman customs at the Synod of Whitby in 664. By then, the date of Easter was already celebrated on the same date both across continental Europe, and also in much of Ireland as well. The Columban communities of Iona and Lindisfarne were a tiny minority. Wilfrid understood where the future lay: not because it was "Roman" rather than Irish, but because he was committed to the unity of the church, and believed that the bishop was the visible focus of her teaching and her sacramental life. His passion was for a church that was one, holy, catholic, and apostolic, extending across the known world. This explains much in him that otherwise seems like a puzzling denial of his own Northumbrian traditions. If we love the church because we love God, then a larger vision of the church, and in particular the pursuit of unity among Christians, is given in the gospel. The church exists as an institution with a catholic shape and structure, in order that it may have continuity in time as well as place through the preservation of what is handed on across the generations. Wilfrid understood how the tides of history as well as theology were flowing, which is why he threw his weight behind Europe and Rome. It is a fantasy to think that the outcome could have been different, even if "Celtic Christians" with more romance than historical sense continue to argue that it should have been.

Secondly, we should celebrate in Wilfrid one of the most energetic of evangelists and founders of monasteries of his day. To establish religious communities, build churches, nurture their faithful, establish schools for the education of the young, and proclaim the gospel all belonged together as "mission". This is precisely what Aidan had done at Lindisfarne. In this, Wilfrid was the loyal imitator of his teacher, planting Christianity as far afield as Sussex and the Isle of Wight, as well as in Mercia and possibly in Frisia, another instance of the extraordinary confidence and flair of the Lindisfarne mission. And the evidence is that Wilfrid was conscientious in the pastoral care of his people as missioner, teacher, and bishop. We do him a disservice if we somehow imagine that he was interested only in the institution of the church and its power relations with the state, rather than in its community of disciples. His great church here at Hexham testified, no doubt, to human power as much as to the glory of God. Yet the crypt that remains, its layout designed to give the faithful access to the relics of the saints, seems to speak more of the power of holiness, the spiritual quest to reconnect with what truly belongs to the foundation of a life lived before God.

Finally, we should honour Wilfrid as one of the two men who first introduced into England the Rule of St Benedict. (We don't know whether he or Benedict Biscop was the pioneer, but we can honour them both for it.) This is more important than it sounds. As a matter of history, it paved the way for the upsurge of Benedictine monasticism in the late Saxon period, itself the soil in which the great monasteries of the high Middle Ages were planted. The influence of the Benedictine life in English history is incalculable, not only in the great libraries that flourished in monasteries such as Durham, or in the economic impact of the religious houses that controlled estates in every corner of the land, but in the spiritual legacy it bequeathed to the English church. It can be argued that the liturgy and spirituality we love the Church of England for, particularly in the *Book of Common Prayer,* is a direct legacy of its Benedictine past, with its instinct for order, balance and seriousness, pattern and rhythm, for the reticence that prefers to listen before speaking, for its profound care for human beings individually and in community. We owe Wilfrid more than we know for his commitment to this wise and humane rule. It took a well-travelled man to grasp why it mattered.

Jesus says in our reading tonight: "Come to me, all you that are weary and are carrying heavy burdens, and I will give you rest. Take my yoke upon you, and learn from me; for I am gentle and humble in heart, and you will find rest for your souls." Benedict's rule makes humility its principal virtue. He likens it to Jacob's ladder, each of the twelve degrees of humility bringing us nearer to heaven; only the steps lead downwards rather than up, for the lower we go, the closer we are to God. In Wilfrid's quieter final years, the years of peace as Bede calls them, could it be that politics and power lost their appeal, and instead it was the call to be gentle and humble in heart like his Master that he heard again, as in his boyhood he had heard it on Lindisfarne, where sky and sand and sea spoke of simple things, and the Lord called as once he had called disciples by the lakeside and had said, "follow me"?

Hexham Abbey, 11 October 2009, on the eve of the 1,300th
anniversary of the death of St Wilfrid
Matthew 11:20–end

A Journey to Scotland

St Margaret

*In the grand eastern transept of the Cathedral, two altars are dedicated
to women who were saints: Hild and Margaret. Four centuries separate
their careers, but both exemplified Christian character at its toughest,
yet also at its gentlest. Queen Margaret of Scotland was said to have
attended the laying of the foundation stone of Durham Cathedral in
1093, the year she died. She is buried at Dunfermline Abbey and is
especially remembered in the little Romanesque chapel of St Margaret at
the highest point of Edinburgh Castle. I knew little of her until I came to
Durham; I have since become an ardent admirer, as this sermon shows.*

You have to be ready for anything in this job. Last Tuesday, I was invited
to visit Dunfermline Abbey. Unknown to me, that very day was the 700th
anniversary of the death of William Wallace, that legendary Scottish
warlord and harrier of the English. As a guest of the Abbey, I was led out
by bagpipes along with the great and the good of Fife to a ceremony by a
hawthorn tree in churchyard. There we stood under an awning in the rain
while a large crowd of ordinary people got very wet. The Lord Lieutenant,
the Lord Provost, the Cardinal, and the local aristocracy all spoke. Then
without warning came the dread invitation: would I also like to say a few
words? So I found myself in front of TV cameras improvising on the theme
of William Wallace and his significance for Scotland, a special subject I
had not exactly worked up for the day, and about which any Englishman
speaks at his peril. Too late to regret not having seen *Braveheart,* I told
the assembled company how Durham Cathedral is famously "half church
of God, half castle against the Scot", where Norman kings had installed
prince bishops to guard the northern frontier of England against just such
men as Wallace. I ended by saying that despite a bloody history, I came
in friendship, and that seemed to go down well.

What took me to Scotland, however, was to honour someone of a very different stamp, whose name has linked Durham and Dunfermline since the eleventh century: St Margaret, Queen of Scots. She was married to King Malcolm III, who was present when the foundation stone of this cathedral was laid in August 1093. Her confessor, friend, and first biographer was Durham's Prior Turgot. Malcolm and one of her sons were to die later that year at the Battle of Alnwick, another place I have some connection with; out of grief as well as illness and the rigours of fasting, Margaret herself died a few days later. To honour her memory, her son David, a great builder of monasteries, had Dunfermline Abbey built, its great incised drum piers so reminiscent of Durham; indeed, he probably used Durham masons for its construction. When she was canonised, her body was reinterred in a shrine which is there to this day.

Here in Durham, we have our own project to celebrate this remarkable woman. The St Margaret Altar, with its new hangings and kneelers, will be dedicated on her feast day in November this year. But the painting by Paula Rego commissioned by the Cathedral is already in place in the Chapel of the Nine Altars. Paula Rego is without doubt one of our greatest contemporary artists. Her painting shows Margaret near the end of her life, perhaps having heard about her double bereavement. She is gazing into the far distance, as if her sights are already set on the next world, like Jesus in our gospel reading, setting his face to his imminent passion and death. Her face is lined with the marks of suffering. Her hand rests upon her cherished gospel book. At her feet sits David, her son and king-to-be, wise beyond his years, perhaps caught between the lure of the weapons lying like a child's toys around him, and the summons of his mother's gospel book to fight different, spiritual, battles. Son and dying mother: a kind of *pietà* in reverse that echoes Fenwick Lawson's sculpture nearby of the Virgin holding the body of her son. And in a way, the themes are the same: a kingship not of this world, a vocation where royalty means walking a *via dolorosa,* the path of suffering servanthood lived out and died out by the one who "entered not into glory but first he suffered pain".

It is not a comfortable painting, but then Margaret was not one to reign in easy state while others suffered. Her story strikes a very contemporary note. A Saxon-in-exile, she was brought up in Hungary, and having come to England, was once again exiled as a result of William the Conqueror's ruthless policies towards the Saxons, this time to Scotland. Malcolm took her in as an asylum seeker and married her. She and David were perhaps the great architects of medieval Scotland. Her devotion to the Holy Trinity and to the cross, her wisdom, her care for the poor and needy were legendary even in her lifetime. These are symbolised by the gospel book in her hands. But the resolution, courage, and resignation written in her face to me says something about how hard-won are the civilising Christian influences of learning, charity, justice, spirituality, that she sought to instil in the people of Scotland—the values of the transformed life spelled out by St Paul in today's epistle. They were constantly at risk in a cruel age when poverty, disease, and war meant that for most people life was nasty, brutish, and short.

It's no accident that St Margaret's symbol is her holy rood or black cross that, after being captured from the Scots at the Battle of Neville's Cross, was brought here and hung in the south aisle of this Cathedral until the Reformation, when a reforming Dean's wife probably burned it for firewood. The cross is the theme of today's gospel, where Jesus speaks about the cost of discipleship. He says that we can only count ourselves as his followers if we are willing to walk in his way and take up the cross. He tells us that he himself is called to suffer, and the only way of discipleship is this cruciform way where our existence, the values we live by, are radically redefined, reconfigured, by the cross: "those who want to save their life will lose it, and those who lose their life for my sake will find it." This, says Jesus, is to be transfigured, as he himself is about to be. It is to have our sights lifted above what is transitory and illusory to what endures forever, to have our restless hearts quieted as they find their rest in God, as St Augustine, whose feast day it is, put it. This is not palliative care that takes away the pain of living, a safe haven from life's storm and stress. It is the promise of the gospel to give us the courage, the faith, the inward stability, and the joy with which to sail life's seas with equanimity.

This is the challenge of Paula Rego's painting. It says to me, and I try to listen because I hear the gospel saying it too, that the great mistake of our age is to think, when the thorns begin to press into our flesh, that somehow this is *unfair*. There is always a cost of discipleship; I cannot make Christianity mean anything else. But the painting, and the gospel, holds out the possibility of something more: that we can become wounded healers, our pain transformative so that we are sensitised in heart and imagination and can begin to offer a new kind of compassion to those in pain. And most of all, it speaks of the hope and promise that we can know peace of mind and tranquillity of spirit even in the worst of times. As another great Christian woman was to write 300 years later, "He said not: *thou shalt not be tempested, thou shalt not be travailed, thou shalt not be afflicted*; but he said: *thou shalt not be overcome.* God willeth that we take heed to these words, and that we be ever strong in sure trust, in weal and woe. For he loveth and enjoyeth us, and so willeth he that we love and enjoy him and mightily trust in him; for so *all shall be well.*"

28 August 2005
Matthew 16:21–end

The Beauty of Holiness with a Social Conscience

Bishop John Cosin

*The long line of distinguished men and women associated with
the Cathedral did not come to an end in Norman times. Among
the most distinguished post-Reformation Bishops of Durham was
the celebrated John Cosin, who took it upon himself, following the
depredations of the Civil War, to restore dignity and beauty to the
Cathedral's interior. He played a prominent part in the development
of the 1662 Book of Common Prayer, and is also remembered
as the author of the fine Pentecost hymn "Come Holy Ghost, our
souls inspire", the only hymn to be included in the Prayer Book.*

"O worship the Lord in the beauty of holiness": we sang it earlier in one
of the classic Epiphany hymns; or, as the verse in the psalms puts it, sing
praise "in holy array". I link it with that enigmatic saying of Jesus in this
morning's gospel: "you will see heaven opened and the angels of God
ascending and descending upon the Son of Man." It is an allusion to the
story in the book of Genesis where Jacob dreams of the ladder to heaven
and sees angels ascending and descending, "in holy array", we might say.
When he awakes, he exclaims: "How awesome is this place! This is none
other than the house of God, and this is the gate of heaven." So he names
it *Beth-El*, "house of God". In St John, Jesus is saying that he is that ladder,
that way to God, the one in whom heaven comes down to earth and earth
is raised to heaven: not in a dream, this time, but in God's presence and
his very self, and essence all divine. He is the way, because he has come
as the truth and as the life. In epiphany, we behold his glory and celebrate
it, full of grace and truth.

How do we do this? We encounter him in many ways that we do not
always recognise at the time. For he takes us by surprise, as he did Jacob, as

he did Nathanael. It is often not at the time but afterwards that we ponder that unexpected epiphany, that strange meeting, and say to ourselves, "Surely the Lord was in this place and I did not know it!" Here on earth, we see through a glass darkly, and do not yet know him face to face. So human instinct has always been to build temples that will memorialise some sacred encounter or holy man or woman, symbolise our yearning for what is beyond us, guard the possibility of glimpsing the holy and transcendent in our midst. And in the long history of constructing earthly temples, there has always been the belief that something of heavenly glory can be contained within a humanly-created shrine, there can be a ladder to heaven with angelic presences and a holy array.

Here in Durham we have one man who embodied this vision *par excellence* and gave it substance. I am referring to John Cosin, Canon Residentiary and then Bishop of Durham, the anniversary of whose death in 1672 falls today, 15 January. All over North East England, but especially around Durham, you can see how he brought splendour and richness into parish churches such as Brancepeth (before the fire consumed it all), Sedgefield, and Haughton-le-Skerne, his own chapel at Auckland Castle, and especially into this Cathedral. The Civil War and Commonwealth had left this building a forlorn, empty shell after the Scottish prisoners Cromwell held here were said to have stripped out everything combustible to keep themselves warm during the terrible winter of 1650–51. On St Andrew's Day we dedicated a plaque by the St Margaret Altar to commemorate the many who died here. The Restoration of 1660 was nowhere welcomed more warmly than here in Durham, when Cosin returned as Bishop and determined to put right the wrongs this bleak chapter of history had inflicted on the Cathedral. His achievements are all around you: the mighty font cover, the organ screen at the west end, the stalls in the quire that echo the great fourteenth-century Neville screen behind the high altar. The message was: seventeenth-century Anglicanism stood in direct continuity with the medieval church in pursuing the beauty of holiness. This sumptuous woodwork, for which only the best craftsmen would do, tells us that Cosin's vision of the church was as a place of beauty and glory where all that human creativity and craftsmanship could achieve would be pressed into the service of God. He believed that the church building should bring you to your knees. In his *Private Devotions* he prays that we, "evermore endeavouring to set forth the beauty of thy church militant here on earth may at last be transported to the glory of thy church triumphant in the heavens".

After being Canon of Durham, Cosin went to Peterhouse, Cambridge, as Master of the College. Its chapel had been built by his predecessor, but it fell to Cosin to furnish it. In the chancel, there was an inscription in Latin, Jacob's saying: "This is none other than the house of God, and this is the gate of heaven." It expressed Cosin's belief that the worship on earth and in heaven were one activity. Above the altar was the dove of the Holy Spirit with carved cherubim all around. The altar was covered with bright silk, and, in front of it, incense burned as the offering of prayer to the Most High. This was a chapel that made you pray. Rich choral music filled the incense-laden air, for Cosin believed that music should serve "for the dignity and glory of God's high and holy service, and be also a means to inflame men's affections, to stir up their attentions, and to edify their understandings". Alas, like Cosin himself, like this Cathedral, his noble chapel suffered at the hands of puritan iconoclasts. Much of the glory departed, though enough was put back at the Restoration (thanks to the generosity of Bishop Cosin, as he became) to recall what it had been like.

In Durham, of all places, we should celebrate the importance of Cosin's legacy to the Christian life of our nation; he deserves to be better known and honoured than he is. His investment in the liturgy and spirituality of the Church of England was profound. His version of the Latin hymn *Veni Creator Spiritus* is familiar and loved the world over as an essential introduction to the ordination prayer in the Anglican rite. In Cosin's Library on Palace Green, they have a most precious book, his own copy of the *Book of Common Prayer* known as the *Durham Book*. It has his painstaking handwritten comments, elaborations, and suggestions for revision, some of which would find their way into the 1662 Prayer Book we have inherited today. But it is not only as an architect of that book that we remember him, nor simply for his classically constructed (and very long) sermons, nor his contribution to architecture, liturgy, and the arts. He used his wealth to found almshouses for the poor (including Cosin's Almshouses on Palace Green), build schools, endow libraries, provide for the needy in many places, and even give money to liberate a party of Christian captives in North Africa. This illustrates Cosin's belief that the beauty of worship and the service of humanity must always walk hand in hand. Liturgy must always have a social conscience: we do not leave the pain of the world outside at the church door, but bring it with us into the presence of God, because it is his and our special care. Cosin would have said that to invest in sacred space, and in the worship offered there, is to sensitise us who pray to the imperatives of our world: to care for those who need our help, to look for reconciliation and wholeness in society, to reflect our love of God by loving our neighbour as ourselves.

In the new Jerusalem, there is no need of shrines and temples, says the Apocalypse. But in this life, meanwhile, we still need sacred spaces whose beauty will enchant us to reimagine the world as God designed it and as he purposes in Christ to remake it: a world premised on justice and mercy, goodness, truth, and love. In our worship, this is the world we recreate for a while: we play-act the life of the world to come, live for a while as a people for whom there are "no ends nor beginnings but one equal eternity". "Come to church and be in heaven" would not be a bad marketing tag for any parish or cathedral. And we carry heaven out with us as we cross the threshold and return to our ordinary days; we take it into the world and become the sources of renewal, like little ladders between earth and heaven where angels congregate in holy array, and epiphanies happen, and the doors of paradise are flung open, and humanity is welcomed home.

15 January 2012
John 1:43–end

Lightning Source UK Ltd.
Milton Keynes UK
UKHW05f1303170618
324324UK00016B/735/P

9 781910 519103